T0113217

Tony Barnstone and Chou Ping

The Anchor Book of Chinese Poetry

Tony Barnstone is an associate professor of creative writing and American literature at Whittier College. His first book of poetry, *Impure*, was a finalist for several national literary awards, among them the Academy of American Poets Walt Whitman Prize, the National Poetry Series Prize, and the White Pine Prize. His other books include *Out of the Howling Storm: The New Chinese Poetry*, *Laughing Lost in the Mountains: Selected Poems of Wang Wei* (with Willis Barnstone and Xu Haixin), *The Art of Writing: Teachings of the Chinese Masters* (with Chou Ping), and several textbooks about world literature. His poetry, translations, essays, and fiction have appeared in dozens of literary journals, from *The American Poetry Review* to *Agni*. He lives in California.

Chou Ping writes poetry in both Chinese and English. His poems and translations have appeared in such journals as *The Literary Review* and *Nimrod*. Born in Changsha City, Hunan province, in 1957, he holds degrees from Beijing Foreign Language University, Indiana University, and Stanford University. He is the translator, with Tony Barnstone, of *The Art of Writing: Teachings of the Chinese Masters*, and he has taught at Stanford, Washington University, Oberlin College, The College of Wooster, and Reed College. He lives in Oregon.

Please visit *The Anchor Book of Chinese Poetry* Web Companion: http://web.whittier.edu/barnstone/poetry

The Anchor Book of

CHINESE POETRY

The Anchor Book of

CHINESE POETRY

Edited by

TONY BARNSTONE

and

CHOU PING

Anchor Books

A DIVISION OF RANDOM HOUSE, INC.

NEW YORK

AN ANCHOR BOOKS ORIGINAL, FEBRUARY 2005

Copyright © 2005 by Tony Barnstone and Chou Ping

All rights reserved under International and Pan-American Copyright Conventions. Published in the United States by Anchor Books, a division of Random House, Inc., New York, and simultaneously in Canada by Random House of Canada Limited, Toronto.

Anchor Books and colophon are registered trademarks of Random House, Inc.

Permissions acknowledgments can be found at the end of the book.

Library of Congress Cataloging-in-Publication Data
The Anchor book of Chinese poetry /
edited by Tony Barnstone and Chou Ping.
p. cm.
Includes index.
ISBN 978-0-385-72198-1
1. Chinese poetry—Translations into English.
I. Barnstone, Tony. II. Chou, Ping, 1957–
PL2658.E3A496   2004
895.1′1008—dc22   2004051824

Book design by Rebecca Aidlin

www.anchorbooks.com

146122990

This book is dedicated to

Caroline Heldman
and
Joey

Contents

A Note on the Selections
and Some Words of Thanks

*Unless otherwise noted, the selections in this anthology
have been cotranslated by Tony Barnstone and Chou Ping.*

IN THIS ANTHOLOGY WE HAVE ATTEMPTED TO BRING TOGETHER
into one volume the essence of Chinese poetry. The selection begins
with the *Book of Songs* (the ancient anthology of folk songs sup-
posedly collected by Confucius himself) and culminates in the polit-
ical and experimental poetry of contemporary Chinese poets, many
of whom are in political exile in the diaspora that followed the
Tiananmen Square massacre of 1989. We have sought to represent
in fine translation the well-established canon of great Chinese
poems, and to deviate from that canon in ways we found interest-
ing. Here you will find many of the familiar classical gems, popular
favorites, and anthology pieces, and yet we have chosen to cut out
old touchstones that don't fare well in translation in favor of
including poems that read in English as poems in and of themselves.

We have also attempted to adjust the canon, here and there, to
shine a spotlight on fine poets whose work is often overlooked, and
especially to make room for the poems of Chinese women. In the
classical Chinese anthologies, the voices of women were largely
ignored. Relegated to a few pages at the end of the volumes, they
have survived the ravages of the centuries at significantly lower
rates than those of men. The work of many of the finest Chinese
women poets has been lost entirely. Those we know are represented
by only a few poems or a few dozen poems, if we are lucky (while
for many male poets, hundreds or even thousands of poems sur-
vive). Perhaps one could argue that we are skewing the canon by
including a fifth of the fifty extant poems of the great woman poet

Li Qingzhao, while including only one thousandth of the poems of Lu You, who wrote more than ten thousand poems. However, our goal is not to be merely representative in this anthology. We have chosen to swell the selections of poets whose work we particularly admire (Tao Qian, Wang Wei, Li Bai, Du Fu, Bai Juyi, Han Shan, Su Shi, Mao Zedong, Bei Dao, and others) so that the reader can truly come to know their work. We consider such larger selections to be "pillars" that support the book, little books or chapbooks within the larger book that show the range and development and depth of the finest poets of this extraordinary tradition.

To aid the general reader (as well as students and scholars of Chinese) in navigating such a large selection of work by so many poets, we have provided an author index with both Pinyin and Wade-Giles transliterations of the authors' Chinese names. To help give readers the context necessary to ground their reading of this selection from three millennia of Chinese poetry, we have outfitted the book with an essay on the key issues that confront the English-language translator of classical and contemporary Chinese poetry, a short history of the development of Chinese literary forms, and introductions to each major historical period.

I would like to thank the poet and novelist Ha Jin for generously putting us in touch with Anchor Books and helping this project find a home. I would also like to thank our editor, LuAnn Walther, and John Siciliano at Anchor Books, for their patience with the book's slow development and for making the project possible. Although the majority of the selections in the volume have been team-translated by Chou Ping and myself, I supplemented our translations with exceptional examples by my father, Willis Barnstone, and by other poet-scholar-translators of Chinese, among them Arthur Waley, Sam Hamill, Kenneth Rexroth, David Hinton, Xu Haixin, Eliot Weinberger, Newton Liu, Ko Ching-p'o, Burton Watson, Michelle Yeh, Arthur Sze, Gregory B. Lee, John Cayley, A. C. Graham, J. P. Seaton, John Rosenwald, Mabel Lee, Sun Chu-chin, Bonnie S. McDougall, Chen Maiping, James A. Wilson, and Ho Yung. They have played an extraordinary role in carrying Chinese poetic genius across oceans and centuries and transplanting it in American soil, and I would like to thank them for allowing me to reprint their translations here. Finally, I would like to thank my coeditor and primary cotranslator for his good humor and insight, which have made it a pleasure to work with him on this and other projects since we first met in my small apartment in Beijing in the winter of 1984.

— TONY BARNSTONE

Preface

The Poem Behind the Poem:
Literary Translation as English-Language Poetry

I ORIGINALLY CAME TO CHINESE POETRY AS AN AMERICAN poet learning how to make the image. Like many other American poets, I was led to China by my interest in Ezra Pound, William Carlos Williams, and other modernist poets who developed and modified their craft in conversation with the Chinese tradition. I came to China, in other words, to learn how to write poetry in English. This is also how I came to translation: as a way of extending the possibilities of poetry written in English. I wanted to learn from the Chinese how to write better poems in English, and to learn from the English-language tradition how to translate better from the Chinese. A translation, after all, is the child of parent authors from different cultures, and however assiduously the translator attempts to remove his or her name from the family tree, the genetic traces will be found in the offspring. What the translator brings to the equation can never be reduced to zero. Translators bring their linguistic patterns, cultural predispositions, and aesthetic biases to the creative act. They don't merely hold up a mirror to something old but give the original text new life in a strange environment. Even a perfectly translated poem—one in which every word is turned magically into its doppelgänger and in which form, sound, and rhetoric are retained—is still a product of misprision, and the translator does not so much create a text in the new language *equal* to the old one as a text that strives to be *equivalent* to the original.

This is particularly true of translators of Chinese poetry. From a set of monosyllabic, largely pictographic characters calligraphed perhaps on a Chinese painting, fan, or scroll, the poem proceeds through a hall of mirrors, reappearing on the other side of time, culture, and speech as a few bytes of memory laser-etched on a white page in the polysyllabic, phonetic language of the English-language translator. The effect is that of moving from the iconic, graphics-based Macintosh operating system to the text-based DOS system. It is very difficult to make the systems compatible because the conceptual paradigms that underlie them are so radically different. We can create a neutral language that will transfer information between the two systems, but small things will change: the formatting will go awry, certain special characters will disappear if their correspondents are not found, and attached files—such as graphics and footnotes, which modify our sense of the text—may become separated or lost. Raw information will be preserved, but the aesthetic unity, the gestalt of the poem, will be lost in the translation. Literary translation is more than anything an attempt to translate that gestalt, which a machine is not sensitive enough to detect, much less reconstruct.

Those who discount the creative element in translation believe that translations should consist of word-for-word cribs in which syntax, grammar, and form are all maintained, and in which the translator is merely a facilitator who allows the original poem to speak for itself in a new language. Poetry, however, can't be made to sing through a mathematics that doesn't factor in the creativity of the translator. The literary translator is like the musician who catalyzes the otherwise inert score that embodies Mozart's genius. In that act, musician and composer become a creative team. However, it won't necessarily be good music just because the musician can keep time and scratch out the correct notes in the correct order. Musical skill inevitably enters into the equation. Fidelity comes from a musician's deeper understanding of the music. As John Frederick Nims says, "The worst infidelity is to pass off a bad poem in one language as a good poem in another."

From the early metrical and end-rhymed translations of Herbert Giles to the so-called free-verse translations of Ezra Pound, Arthur Waley, and Kenneth Rexroth, Chinese poems have been reinvented in English. The Chinese poem in English is like a stolen car sent to a chop shop to be stripped, disassembled, fitted with other parts, and presented to the consumer public with a new coat of paint. But despite its glossy exterior, it's a Chinese engine that makes it run, and fragments of the poem's old identity can be glimpsed in its lines, the purr of its engine, the serial number, which we may still be able to read. In these thoughts on translation, I wish to discuss ways I've found of negotiating between Chinese and English-language poetic paradigms, and to touch on the aspects of English that have proved compatible with the Chinese poem, which has been a part of Western poetic traffic since the early years of modernism.

Daoist philosopher Zhuangzi says, "The fish trap exists because of the fish; once you've gotten the fish you can forget the trap. . . . Words exist because of meaning; once you've gotten the meaning, you can forget the words. Where can I find a man who has forgotten words so I can have a word with him?" Words are the net we cast upon the waters in search of knowledge, meaning, enlightenment. Ultimately, though, the fish has to come to us of its own volition (Native American hunters believe that when the hunter is in harmony with nature, the animal comes to him and sacrifices itself). In his poem "The Placid Style," Sikong Tu, a famous ninth-century poet whose "The Twenty-four Styles of Poetry" is a Daoist treatise on how to write poems, speaks of the need to find poetic inspiration through *lack of effort*: "You meet this style by not trying deeply; / it thins to nothing if you approach." There is always something ephemeral about the knowledge behind a poem, about the inspiration that creates it—or that creates a translation. To find a poem in translation we need to discover what I call "the poem behind the poem." Sometimes we can't find it just by looking; we also have to see. Sometimes we can't find it by trying; it comes to us while we're doing something else.

Let's take as an example the following poem, "River Snow" by Liu Zongyuan—translated by Chou Ping and me. But before discussing it, let's take a moment to read it out loud, slowly. Empty our minds. Visualize each word.

> A thousand mountains. Flying birds vanish.
> Ten thousand paths. Human traces erased.
> One boat, bamboo hat, bark cape—an old man
> alone, angling in the cold river. Snow.

"River Snow" is considered a prime example of minimum words/ maximum message and has been the subject of numerous landscape paintings. It is terrifically imagistic: the twenty Chinese characters of the poem create a whole landscape, sketch an intimate scene, and suggest a chill, ineffable solitude. To get this poem across in translation, we strove to reproduce the sequential way the characters unfold in the reader's mind. The syntax is particularly important because it is perfectly constructed. We walk into this poem as if walking into a building, and the spaces that open up around us and the forms that revise themselves at each step unfold according to the architect's master plan.

The first two lines create a fine parallelism: birds passing through the sky leave no trace, just as human traces are effaced in the mountain paths. It makes me think of the Old English kenning for the sea: "whale path." Here the sky is a bird path. In the second line, it's clear that the snow is the active agent in erasing humanity from the natural scene, yet snow is never mentioned. After the last trace of humanity disappears with the word "erased," a human presence is rebuilt in this landscape, character by character, trace by trace: "One boat, bamboo hat, bark cape" and—the sum of these clues— "an old man." These first two lines sketch a painterly scene: the vast emptiness of the sky above and the snowy solitude of the landscape below have the same effect on the reader as a glance at a Chinese landscape painting. And then the tiny strokes that create a man in the third line direct our imagination deeper into the poem, as if we had discovered a tiny fisherman's figure on the scroll. The next line tells us what the old man is doing. He is alone and fishing in the cold river. The Chinese word for fishing is "hooking," so we used "angling" for its specific meaning of "fishing with a hook." We see the man fishing the river, almost fishing *for* the river. Silence. We take in the last character, which sums up the entire poem: "Snow."

Snow is the white page on which the old man is marked, through which an ink river flows. Snow is the mind of the reader, on which these pristine signs are registered, only to be covered with more snow and erased. The old man fishing is the reader meditating on this quiet scene like a saint searching himself for some sign of a soul. The birds that are absent, the human world that is erased, suggest the incredible solitude of a meditating mind, and the clean, cold, quiet landscape in which the man plies his hook is a mindscape as well. Thus, there is a Buddhist aspect to the poem, and Liu Zongyuan's old man is like Wallace Stevens's "Snow Man," whose mind of winter is washed clean by the snowy expanse. He is "the listener, who listens in the snow, / And, nothing himself, beholds / Nothing that is not there and the nothing that is."

"River Snow" is a perfectly balanced poem, a tour de force that quietly, cleanly, easily creates its complexly simple scene. To merely paraphrase it in translation is to ignore the poem behind the poem. The translator must discover the poem visually, conceptually, culturally, and emotionally, and create a poem in English with the same mood, simplicity, silence, and depth. Each word must be necessary. Each line should drop into a meditative silence, should be a new line of vision, a new revelation. The poem must be empty, pure perception; the words of the poem should be like flowers, opening one by one, then silently falling. As William Carlos Williams was fond of saying, a poem is made up of words and the spaces between them.

If this technique is taken to extremes, it can create a poem that sounds too choppy. The magical economy of "River Snow" lies in the unfolding of visual clues in a meditative sequence of discrete images, but with too many dashes, colons, or periods, the poem can seem fragmented. Alternatively, a translation that fills in the gaps between images can seem wordy and prolix, with prepositions and articles that make the lines fluid but dilute them in the process. The addition of a few parts of speech or an unfortunate choice of punctuation can significantly alter the translation and affect the reading experience.

While it is difficult to translate economically from a language that typically eliminates articles and pronouns, one can nevertheless attempt to create a translation that reads as cleanly and concisely as possible. We consider it a great success if we can translate a five-character line of Chinese poetry into a five- or six-word line in English, though this is not always possible. Too often translators will translate a seven-character line into two full lines of poetry in

English, which makes the poem read like Walt Whitman, when the Chinese is much closer to Emily Dickinson.

The poetry of Wang Wei—the poet I've translated most extensively from the Chinese—is often spare and clean, like "River Snow." Each character resonates in emptiness like the brief bird-calls he records in one of his poems. The inventor of the monochrome technique, Wang Wei was the most famous painter of his day. In his work, both painting and poetry were combined through the art of calligraphy—poems written on paintings. As Su Shi said of him, "His pictures are poems and his poems pictures," and as Francois Cheng has pointed out, painting and calligraphy are both arts of the *stroke*, and both are created with the same brush. I like to imagine each character in "River Snow" sketched on the page: a brushstroke against the emptiness of a Chinese painting—like the figure of the old man himself surrounded by all that snow.

The most famous piece by Zen-influenced composer John Cage was titled "4'33"" (1952). The audience came in and sat down, and for four minutes and thirty-three seconds nothing happened. The audience was the music. Their rustlings, coughs, chatter, the creaking of seats, perhaps the rain on the roof of the auditorium—all this was the music. In classical Chinese painting the white space defines what forms emerge, and in Buddhism emptiness is wholeness. The perfect man's mind, according to Zhuangzi, is empty as a mirror, and according to the Daoist aesthetics of Chinese painting, each stroke of the brush is *yin* (blackness, woman) upon *yang* (light, whiteness, man). All the empty space reacts to one brushstroke upon the page. Each additional stroke makes the space adjust itself into a new composition, in much the way each great poem makes all of literary history readjust itself, as T. S. Eliot wrote. To make a Chinese poem in English we must allow silence to seep in around the edges, to define the words the way the sky's negative space in a painting defines the mountains.

As I stated earlier, I think the poem in translation must carry on a conversation with other poems in order to discover itself. For me, "River Snow" calls to mind Japanese Zen poems and poems of the English Romantics in addition to poems from the Chinese tradition, and it is this conversation that allows me to hear its silence.

Consider these lines from the poem "People's Abuse" by Japanese Zen poet Muso Soseki (1275–1351), translated by W. S. Merwin and Soiku Shigematsu:

> Don't look back
>   to this world
>   your old hold in the cellar
> From the beginning
>   the flying birds have left
>   no footprints on the blue sky.

In Soseki's image, the flying birds pass through the sky without leaving a trace, as in "River Snow," which also shares with Soseki's lines a distinction between the human world and the natural world. Now consider these lines from Zhu Xizhen's poem "Fisherman, to the Tune of 'A Happy Event Draws Near,'" in which the fisherman

> spins his boat around at will
> traceless like a bird across sky.

The fisherman on the water is like the birds in the sky, whose trackless flight is a symbol of the enlightened mind's passage through the world without grasping or holding or desiring. Compare "On Nondependence of the Mind," a poem by Dogen (1200–1253)—founder of the Soto school of Japanese Zen Buddhism—translated by Brian Unger and Kazuaki Tanahashi:

> Water birds
> going and coming
> their traces disappear
> but they never
> forget their path.

The mind that doesn't depend on the world leaves no traces, just as the "water birds" don't forget their path—a path we can understand as a mystical Way. In these lines from Wordsworth's *Prelude*, he describes his hike through the Alps:

> Like a breeze
> Or sunbeam over your domain I passed
> In motion without pause; but ye have left
> Your beauty with me
>
> *(Book 6, lines 675–78)*

Because Wordsworth is in tune with the natural setting, his meditative mind passes through nature without leaving tracks. The inverse parallelism he sets up (of his trackless passage through nature's landscape versus nature's beautiful inscription in his mindscape) is implicit in "River Snow" as well. "River Snow" is also a poem in which the mind is washed clean, like the sky empty of birds, the paths empty of humanity. Zhuangzi asks, "Where can I find a man who has forgotten words so I can have a word with him?" The fisherman in "River Snow" is that man.

Although I felt it necessary in "River Snow" to make a literal, word-for-word translation to get at the heart of the poem, in other cases I've translated lines in unusual ways to get at the poem behind the poem: the urgent image, the quiet mood, the sound that I felt resided in the Chinese poem and needed emphasis to be felt in English. Sometimes I've deviated slightly from a literal translation in order to get an effect that I believe is truer to the poet's vision. There are no fast rules; the translator has to feel it. To illustrate this, I'd like to discuss a translated line that is much more problematic than the ones above.

First, though, I need to discuss what—somewhat idiosyncratically, perhaps—I call deep-image lines in Chinese poetry. There are times when Chinese poets create such strange and evocative nature imagery that it is almost surreal. To learn how to re-create these lines in English, I think it's helpful to look at the school of deep-image poets in America. Most famous among them are Robert Bly and James Wright, although I would classify contemporary Native American poet Linda Hogan as deep image as well (in her practice, as opposed to her literary history). Bly and Wright were deeply influenced by the combination of personal and impersonal perspectives and tones in Chinese and by Chinese rhetorical parallelism, clarity of image, and focus on implication. They blended these characteristics with a late strain of surrealism derived from Trakl, Vallejo, Lorca, and Neruda. It is precisely this mélange of influences on Bly and Wright that opens up a space in American poetry for a blend of the Chinese tradition and the surreal—and that provides a model for translators.

Here are two examples of deep-image lines, the first from Linda Hogan:

> Crickets are pulsing in the wrist of night.

and the second from James Wright:

> A butterfly lights on the branch
> Of your green voice.

How do these lines work? They invert your expectation, blending the human and the natural or engaging in synesthesia (as in Su Shi's great line "With cold sound, half a moon falls from the painted eaves"). Similarly, in Wang Wei's poems "In the Mountains" and "Sketching Things," nature does strange things; the world is so lush that its green color becomes a liquid that wets his clothes:

> No rain on the mountain path
> yet greenness drips on my clothes.

and

> I sit looking at moss so green
> my clothes are soaked with color.

The strange beauty of James Wright's image taps into a profound psychological mystery and opens up a space in the imagination that Wang Wei's lines also reach. Wright makes it possible for us to *see* Wang Wei's synesthesia, and to *see how* to translate him into English.

As with the Wang Wei lines above, the human and the natural are intertwined in Linda Hogan's line, which imagines the world as a body through which the blood pulses, an intermittent action that is also a sound, the *ba-dump* of the heartbeat. The cricket sound is similarly an intermittent, two-beat sound, and it brings the night into our bedrooms, making it as intimate as our bodies—a small, internal event, like a pulse.

Of course, I was thinking of Linda Hogan when translating one of my favorite lines of Wang Wei in which he sets himself the task of getting at the action-pulse of the cricket's song. Wang Wei's line comes from "Written on a Rainy Autumn Night After Pei Di's Visit": "The urgent whir of crickets quickens." I like the sound qualities here, the onomatopoeia, the internal off-rhymes, and the sense that the line is just beyond comprehension, yet intuitively right. However, this line as I translated it—in collaboration with Willis Barnstone and Xu Haixin—is extremely problematic, an example of translation as reinvention. Literally, the line reads, "cricket cry already hurried" (促織鳴已急), so why did we translate it as "The urgent whir of crickets quickens"? The first two characters, 促織, refer to the house cricket and mean "to urge" + "weave," or "urgent" + "weave" with a sense of "to urgently weave" or "to urge into weaving." The idiom derives from the similarity of a cricket's intermittent, two-beat chirp, produced by rubbing its wings together, to the *shhk-shhhk* of a shuttle on a hand loom, or the whir and whirl of a spinning wheel. In other words, this Chinese idiom for cricket derives from a similarity of sound. The ono-matopoetic element is also present in the English word "cricket," which derives from the French *criquer* ("little creaker"), and suggests the insect's characteristic sound, *cricket, cricket*. We forget this unless the word is heard freshly; the off-rhyme "crickets quickens" is meant to focus our attention on the forgotten music of the word—to make us actively *hear* "cricket," perhaps for the first time.

Now what about "the urgent whir"? Isn't it mistranslating to add this image, using something that is simply an idiom? I don't think so. Idioms such as this add an idiosyncratic beauty to lan-guage, like the pillow talk of Japanese poetics or the kennings of Old English. A translation that rendered Beowulf's "whale path" as "the sea" would be a very dull translation indeed. The Chinese idiom suggests an image that is inherent in the language, much as "foot of the mountain" bears a comparison, long forgotten, of the mountain to a human body.

This idiom allowed me entry to the poem behind the poem, to a sound that was also an action. I wanted to bring alive the complex image of the cricket wings shuttling like a cranky loom or lost in a whirring blur like a spinning wheel, so I had to analyze the phrase for what activated that metaphor: intermittency, quick action, noise. I imagined the blur of cricket wings rubbing themselves into song, and I imagined that song as both continuous and intermittent, both an act and a sound. The word "whir" suggested both the action of spinning—the insect's blur of wings—and the sound of that action: *whir.* I wanted a line that was musical throughout, wanted readers to sense the stuttering trochaic rhythm of a cricket's call (**crick**-et, **crick**-et) when they hear the line's rhyming, emphatic beat: "The **urgent whir** of **crick**ets **quick**ens." I also liked the double meaning of "quickens," which can make the line mean the cricket song comes alive, as if out of silence. This goes beyond the question of whether to be true to the letter or the sense; it's a question of being true to the spirit of the line, which is both image and song. Of course, in doing so I sacrificed other elements. For example, the third character, 鳴, means "cry" but is constructed of the characters for "mouth" 口 and "bird" 鳥, suggesting bird song. Certainly by emphasizing the weaving element with "whir" I sacrificed the sense of singing. Furthermore, I had to make a choice between two different readings of the line. The fourth character, 已, means either "already" or "stop," suggesting in context either that the cricket song pauses and then speeds up urgently, or that the cricket cry is already urgent. In this interpretive translation, I can't say that I truly got this line of Wang Wei's into English, but I do believe that I brought an analogous English poem to life—one closer to Wang Wei's imagination and to the imagination inherent in the Chinese language rather than one merely translated as "the cricket's sound is already hurried."

I have argued elsewhere that Chinese poetry in English has deviated deeply from the form, aesthetics, and concerns of the Chinese originals and that this is the result of willful mistranslation by modernist and postmodern poet-translators. In the first decades of the last century, Chinese poetry was a powerful weapon in the battle against Victorian form. It was brought over into English in forms resembling the free verse that it helped to invent. Rhyme and accentual meter were quietly dropped from the equation because—unlike Chinese use of parallelism, caesura, minimalism, implication, and clarity of image—they weren't useful in the battle for new poetic form. However, we are now in a new century and need no longer be constrained by past literary conflicts. While the elimination of rhyme and meter from translations of Chinese poetry has created a distinguished English-language tradition of "Chinese" free verse—one that has influenced successive generations of American poets—it has also denied the poem its right to sing.

I am just as much to blame for this as other translators of Chinese poetry. The simple truth is that most of the time I am trying to bring across into English poetic effects as well as a literal accuracy that I judge will be damaged by too much attention to sound. However, in recent years I have increasingly attempted to sneak in the pleasures of sound, as in this translation of Du Fu's "Thoughts While Night Traveling," cotranslated with Chou Ping:

> Slender wind shifts the shore's fine grass.
> Lonely night below the boat's tall mast.
> Stars hang low as the vast plain splays;
> the swaying moon makes the great river race.
> How can poems make me known?
> I'm old and sick, my career done.
> Drifting, just drifting. What kind of man am I?
> A lone gull floating between earth and sky.

To emphasize sound in this poem, we cast around for lucky synonyms, choosing for example "splays" in line 3 over our original translation, "broadens," and changing line 6 from "my career over" to "my career done" to get the off rhyme with "known." So we created a loose form in English—four or five beats per line to correspond to the five-character lines of the original, and a use of off and true rhyme to emphasize the parallelism of the couplet structure. Of course, the Chinese *lu shi* (regulated verse) poem doesn't rhyme in couplets. It has a single rhyme in the first couplet that is repeated every other line throughout the poem. Perhaps the next example, "Facing Snow," also by Du Fu, comes a bit closer:

> Battles, sobbing, many new ghosts.
> Just an old man, I sadly chant poems.
> Into the thin evening, wild clouds dip.
> On swirling wind, fast dancing snow.
> A ladle idles by a drained cask of green wine.
> Last embers redden the empty stove.
> No news, the provinces are cut off.
> With one finger I write in the air, *sorrow*.

In our first attempt, below, sound was not a primary concern:

> Battles, sobbing, many new ghosts.
> I sadly chant poems, just an old man.
> Wild clouds dip into the thin evening.
> Fast snow dances in swirling wind.
> A dropped ladle, no green wine in the cask.
> Last embers still redden the empty stove.
> No news, the provinces are cut off.
> With one finger I write my sorrows in the air.

The revision uses the long "o" of "ghosts," "poems," "snow," "stove," and "sorrow" to suggest a regulated verse rhyme scheme. To achieve this we needed to invert the syntax and rearrange elements so the lines in English would end on a rhyme sound. Even so, I am not entirely convinced that the revision for sound is an improvement. As one sinologist pointed out to me, "With one finger I write in the air, *sorrow*" specifies a word that the poet is writing in the air, whereas the original is more ambiguous, closer to "With one finger I write my sorrows in the air," in which the nature of the sorrow is left open and resonant.

What a pleasure it was for me as an American translator to encounter a sonnet sequence by twentieth-century Chinese poet Feng Zhi, written after he fled to the countryside to escape the Japanese bombing of Kunming. In the past Feng Zhi's sonnets have always been translated into free verse in English, but we decided to re-create them as sonnets, preferring to use consonance, assonance, and slant rhyme where possible, instead of true rhyme. Here is one, "Sonnet 16":

> We stand together on a mountain's crest
> projecting vision far across the steppe
> till sight is lost in distance, or else rests
> where paths spread on the plain and intersect.
> How can the paths and streams not join? Tossed
> in sky, can winds and clouds do otherwise?
> The cities, mountains, rivers that we've crossed
> become a part of us, become our lives.
> Our maturation and our grief is near,
> is a pine tree on a hill over there,
> is a dense mist on a town over here.
> We flow inside the waters, blow in air.
> We are footpaths that crisscross on the plain
> and are the people traveling on them.

Translating the poem this way was difficult, certainly more difficult than it would have been to translate it as free verse, and yet in some way it was a relief. How wonderful to know that all the poetic skills I had developed writing sonnets in English could be applied so directly to Chinese poetry. Once I discovered that I could translate Feng Zhi's sonnets as English sonnets with both accuracy and formal integrity, I had found the answer to the question that has vexed me for nearly two decades. Is it worse to pass off free verse translations in English as Chinese poems or to try to maintain meter and rhyme, running the risk of creating sing-songy, jingly, archaic-sounding poems that lose the plain and revelatory power that free verse translations embody so well?

I don't recommend a return to the practice of translating Chinese poems into rhyming iambics (generally, this overwhelms the Chinese poem). But I do think that as much attention should be given to the way the Chinese poem triggers sound as to how it triggers sight, and that translators should use the whole poetic arsenal—syllabics, sprung rhythm, off rhyme, half rhyme, internal rhyme, assonance, consonance, and so forth—to try to give the English version of the poem a deeply resonant life. Too often translators have given Chinese poets the resolution powers of an electron microscope, but have cut off their ears. By being cognizant of the poem's song, we are less likely to be deaf to the poem behind the poem, and less likely to be satisfied with clumsy rhythms and a lack of aural pleasure.

If my examples are notable less for their similarity than for the apparent divergence of the translation principles by which they were created, this is the essence of my argument. There are many roads to China. For the Chinese poem's voice to be heard, the poem behind the poem may require word-by-word fidelity—that is, translators may need to restrain their inventiveness. Or the poem may require a radical departure from convention to arrive where it began. In either case, the translator must keep faith with the deeper need that poetry fulfills in our lives. Like a cricket's song, a poem is an arrangement of sound that is also an action affecting the reader. If we are very quiet, we can feel its tiny pulse fluttering in our wrists. If we listen like Stevens's snow man, if we become nothing long enough, we may discover not what the poem *says* but what it *does*. A poem is a machine made out of words, as William Carlos Williams once wrote, and like a wheelbarrow or a can opener or a telephone, it is a machine reduced to an economic efficiency of parts and designed for a specific function. It doesn't matter whether we take the original poem apart with an Allen wrench or a Phillips screwdriver, or whether we build the translation out of wood or plastic or burnished copper. What matters is that the gears engage and the wheels turn and that the poem's *work* is done in the translation as well. All translation is mistranslation, but a translator's work and joy are to rig something out of the materials at hand that opens cans, or carries hay, or sends voices through the lines. We will never create a truly Chinese poem in English, but in this way we can extend the possibilities of the translation, which may in turn reveal to the imaginations of English-language poets unforeseen continents.

— TONY BARNSTONE

Introduction to Chinese Poetic Form

(as a Function of Yin-Yang Symmetry)

CHINA IS A NATION CREATED BY ITS THOUSANDS OF POETS, who have imagined and extended and redrawn its boundaries as well as the contours of its landscape from year to year, from dynasty to dynasty. For millennia, poetry has played an essential role in shaping its collective consciousness and maintaining the continuity of Chinese civilization. Neither time nor space nor linguistic change restrict free communication in the nation because of the nature of the Chinese written language: a system of pictographs and ideographs that convey their meaning, divorced from their sounds, which, after all, vary according to the time period, the region, and the city or provincial dialect. So when a contemporary Chinese recites a poem written in the Tang dynasty (618–907), the poem remains pure, its meaning virtually constant, even though more than a thousand years have elapsed and the poet's modern speech would be unintelligible to the original author. But the original meaning does not remain intact, of course, since reception, audience, and aesthetics vary according to reader and period, and allusions and expressions that were common in one era might become strange in another. Regional and temporal change in pronunciation also affect the reception of the poem, because Chinese poetry typically uses rhyme and, particularly after the fifth century, has often used tonal prosody (similarly, in the English tradition Chaucer was until recently considered an irregular prosodist, because later generations did not understand how to sound out Middle English). To understand how the Chinese have imagined their poetry, it may help to go back to the earliest Chinese verse and trace its development to its maturity in the Tang dynasty, and then to pursue it further as verse is transformed in later dynasties.

The Book of Songs *and the* Origins *of Chinese Poetry*

The general Chinese term for poetry is *shi* 诗. *Shi* 诗 also refers more specifically to a sort of tonally regulated verse that became popular in the Tang dynasty, as well as to older forms of poetry that were not tonally regulated, such as rhymed prose (*fu* 賦), an elegant and elaborate blending of poetry with prose passages. While verses are normally independent from music, songs can be further classified into folk song poetry (*ge* 歌), lyric songs (*ci* 词), and opera arias (*qu* 曲). We will visit each of these forms in turn, but it is best to begin with the primary source of Chinese poetry, the *Book of Songs*.

Dating back a thousand years before the Tang, the *Book of Songs* is the earliest surviving anthology of Chinese poems. It was collected in Northern China from the eleventh century to the sixth century BCE. For a modern Chinese, the *Book of Songs* is not at all easy to read. Its diction is often archaic, and many of its references need footnotes. Since the pronunciation of some characters has changed over time, the modern ear cannot always detect the original rhyme scheme. Despite these difficulties, the poems have elegant structural characteristics that aid in their reading and enjoyment. Accompanied by music, the short stanzas often contain fully or partially repeated lines to create an effect of refrain. In this early phase of Chinese poetry, verse and music were not clearly separated.

Although line length varies, especially in folk songs, over ninety percent of the lines in the *Book of Songs* consist of four characters. The four-character line is the dominant form in early Chinese poetry. Its use reflects a desire for balance: the standard pattern of rhythm in these songs is two beats per line, with each beat consisting of two characters. There are exceptions, however, with some poems having stanzas consisting of lines with seven or more characters.

Different traditions of poetry coexist in the *Book of Songs*: hymns of religious solemnity, folk songs of emotional spontaneity, and structurally symmetrical literati poetry. Structural symmetry is a crucial element in the evolution of the Chinese poem. It may be seen in the first stanza of the very first poem from the *Book of Songs*:

关关 / 唯 鸠,	guan	guan/	ju	jiu	"Guan-guan" / the ospreys cried
在 河 / 之 洲。	zai	he /	zhi	zhou	on the / riverside.
窈 窕 / 淑 女,	yao	tiao /	shu	nu	A lady / so dignified
君 子 / 好 逑。	jun	zi /	hao	qiu	is a gentleman's / good bride.[1]

Since Chinese characters are monosyllabic, they are ideal for creating visual and aural symmetries. We can imagine the paired lines as mirror images of each other in terms of syllables and rhythm. In this poem every two characters form a beat, every two beats a line, every two lines a pair, and every two pairs a stanza. Each pair forms a complete sentence, and each stanza presents a complete idea. All five stanzas in this poem are structurally identical. As the poems in the *Book of Songs* have a strong tendency to have lines constructed in pairs, their architectural balance offers a perfect example of how the gestalt of yin-yang symmetry in Chinese poetry came into being. It also allows us to trace the ancient psychological and aesthetic need for lines to be paired and balanced into the development of "regulated verse," with its preoccupation with metrical and phonic balance.

Though many songs evince this perfect symmetry, the poems from the *Book of Songs* that we have translated in this volume are primarily folk songs whose forms are often less rigid. These folk songs have been popular, and often imitated, in the Chinese tradition; they also read well in translation because their themes speak to universal human emotions and raise fewer cultural obstacles for their English-language readers. Consider:

---

[1] Literally, the stanza reads:

Guan-guan cry the ospreys
on the riverbank.
Elegant lady,
a gentleman's good bride.

We have rearranged the syntax to allow the poem to rhyme in English.

野有 / 死 麕,	In the wilds / is a dead river-deer.
白茅 / 包之。	White rushes / wrap her.
有女 / 懷春,	A lady yearns / for someone dear.
吉士 / 誘之。	A fine man / seduces her.

林有 / 樸樕,	In the woods / are clustered bushes,
野有 / 死鹿,	and in the wilds / a river-deer is dead
白茅 / 純束。	and wrapped up / in white rushes.
有女 / 如玉。	There is a lady / as fine as jade.

舒而 / 脫脫兮,	Oh! Slow down, / don't be so harsh,
無感 / 我帨兮,	let go / of my girdle's sash.
無使 / 尨也吠。	Shhh! / You'll make the dog bark.

On the surface, the first two stanzas are structured exactly the same as those of the earlier example: two characters form one beat and two beats a line. But they present variations in the relationship between lines. In the first stanza the lines are paired, but each can stand on its own as an independent sentence. The stanza's rhyme scheme is also different, with the rhyme falling on the first and third lines, while the same character repeats in the second and fourth lines. In the second stanza the line relationship is even more complicated, with the first three lines forming a sense group and the last line all on its own. The same rhyme falls on each of the four lines. In the last stanza the diction shifts to direct speech written in five-character lines.[2]

As illustrated by the above poems, we can detect two major Chinese poetic traditions: literati and folk. The literati is characterized by yin-yang symmetry and uniformity while folk songs are generally more spontaneous and less refined. In the evolution of Chinese

---

[2] We tried to create a poem with an equivalent form in English, using homonyms, repeated words, slant rhymes, caesura, and a loose strong stress meter (based on the meter of Old English poems). For the majority of poems in this anthology, we have chosen to be accurate to other levels of the poem—the diction, imagery, implicit thought problems, tone, and/or parallel structure—while abandoning meter and rhyme. For a few select poems, however, we thought it worthwhile to experiment and see what would be gained or lost by approximating Chinese form in English.

poetry, new poetic forms not deriving directly from music would preserve the yin-yang gestalt as a structural backbone in literati poetry, but if music played a major role in the form (as in songs from the Han Dynasty Music Bureau, Song Dynasty Lyrics, and Yuan Dynasty Tunes), the symmetry in paired lines would often dissolve. While in the above folk songs we can find markings of the compilers who tampered with their spontaneity to give a uniform look to the poems in the *Book of Songs*, that spontaneity remains in the structural irregularities noted in the above discussion of "In the Wilds Is a Dead River-Deer."

From the Verses of Chu *to the Han Dynasty*

The next high wave of poetry, the *Verses of Chu*—also known as the *Songs of the South*—came toward the end of the Warring States Period (475–221 BCE) in the south, forming a sharp contrast with the northern tradition as reflected in the *Book of Songs*. Qu Yuan, the most important poet from the South, had a vast vocabulary and a passionate imagination. His works, with the exception of those used in religious rituals, were not set to music. Absorbing influences from prose as well as folk tradition in the Chu state, Qu Yuan had the genius to break with the dominant four-character line tradition without losing a strong sense of yin-yang symmetry. Maintaining two beats in paired lines, Qu Yuan had a free hand in diversifying numbers of characters used in each beat. He employed different characters as beat markers (*xi* 兮, *er* 而, *yi* 以, *zhi* 之, and *yu* 與; *xi* 兮 can be placed either within or between lines while the others can be used only within lines) and achieved changes in tempo depending on the placement of the marker—when it is placed right in the middle of the line, both the line itself and the pair become perfectly symmetrical, and the tempo is comparatively slow; when it is placed between two lines, symmetry is established between the paired lines, speeding up the tempo. Sometimes Qu Yuan placed the marker at an unbalanced location within a line to break the monotony of perfect symmetry.

Qu Yuan not only diversified the symmetrical rhythmic patterns of Chinese poetry but also steered the literati in a new direction. His major contribution was a conscious construction of parallelism in paired lines, which is found throughout his writing; this would become the model for the creation of a multidimensional yin-yang symmetry in regulated verse. For example, in Qu Yuan's major work, *Encountering Sorrow* (*lisao*), we can find lines like "朝搴阰之木蘭兮，夕攬洲之宿莽" ("Mornings I gathered mountain magnolia, / evenings I picked winter grasses on the shoals") and "朝飲木蘭之墜露兮，夕餐秋菊之落英" ("Mornings I drink the dew that drips from the magnolias, / evenings feed on fallen petals of autumn chrysanthemums"). Though these lines are not perfect according to later standards for parallel couplets (for they contain repeated characters and a beat marker between two lines), they do signal an important new dimension. He has made the yin-yang symmetry conceptual as well as rhythmic.

For a long time in the Han dynasty, the period almost immediately after Qu Yuan, Chinese literati were fascinated by Qu Yuan's experiment with language. They directed their creative energy toward the *fu* form (a kind of crossbreed between poem and prose, often translated as "prose poem," "rhyme prose," or "rhymed prose"), inspired by Qu Yuan's new patterns of rhythm combined with parallelism. In our collection, Jia Yi's "The Owl" is a work in this category. In translating it we maintained the rhymes in English. This was not always possible, or even desirable, and so in translating Lu Ji's *Art of Writing*, a very well-known piece of rhymed prose, we rendered it in free verse form, determining that the poem read better as English-language poetry in that format.

While the Han dynasty literati were obsessed with symmetry, the folk tradition during this period was a wide-open field. People tried different line lengths, not only from one poem to the next but also within poems, as in the anonymous poem "The East Gate," presented in this volume as one of the Music Bureau poems. In this time the newly developed five-character poem had become an established form. It represents a key step in the evolution of Chinese verse. One can find five-character lines in both the *Book of Songs* and the *Verses of Chu*, but not really as a sustained form. During the Han dynasty one of the most mature works composed in five-character form was the "Nineteen Ancient Poems," written by scholars who were familiar with the life of the lower classes and who chose to remain anonymous. The Han dynasty also saw a change in the rhythmic pattern of the five-character lines. The old pattern for the division of the two beats, exemplified by the poems in the *Verses of Chu*, was typically three characters/caesura/two characters; it was replaced by two characters/caesura/three characters. This would remain the standard pattern in later periods.

After the Han dynasty many poets contributed to the popularity of the five-character form, among them Cao Zhi, Ruan Ji, and Tao Qian. It became the dominant form among literati writers. The seven-character form was a latecomer; literati poets did not accept it as a standard form until after the fifth-century poet Bao Zhao. There are many theories about its evolution, but the Chinese love of yin-yang symmetry helps to explain it. For quite a long time the seven-character form rhymed on every line, and the lines were not always in a paired relationship.[3] Starting with Bao Zhao, paired lines were used conspicuously in the seven-character form. This form soon became very popular because it provided more space for expression in each line as well as satisfaction of the symmetry gestalt.

Under Sanskrit influence during the Yong Ming reign (483–493), when the Buddhist canons were translated into Chinese, the four tones of classical Chinese were established. Two critics, Zhou Yong and Shen Yue, wrote to promote regulated usage of the four tones in poetry, introducing yet another aspect of elegant symmetry into the construction of the Chinese poem. The old style verse, which did not follow a regulated use of tones, came to be called Ancient Style poetry (*gushi* 古詩), while regulated verse came to be called Modern Style poetry.

The Tang Dynasty and Regulated Verse

During the Tang dynasty (618–907), the golden age of Chinese poetry, a diversity of poetic forms helped poets find their own

---

[3] E.g., from Zhang Heng's (78–139) "Four Sorrowful Poems" to Cao Pi's (187–226) "Songs of Yan." These poets are important historically for their formal innovations, but their poems are not of the highest quality and have not been translated for this volume.

highly individualized voices. Authentic folk poetry continued to exist in its natural, anonymous state and continued to be used by literati poets such as Li Bai, who found it a source of inspiration and a handy form for experiments in writing distinctive poems in the Ancient Style. Also during the Tang, after many years of experiments in earlier dynasties, regulated verse, containing the most exquisite symmetries in poetry, reached its apex. Other important forms flourished as well, such as the quatrain (*jueju* 絕句), a truncated regulated verse poem. The diversity of forms certainly contributed to the glory and the variety of achievement in Tang poetry, but there were other factors as well. The sociopolitical climate attracted talented people to poetry, since excellence in writing poetry had become a necessity for those who wished to achieve high official positions. Poetry brought rewards in terms of social mobility as well as celebrity status, so good poetry was written during the Tang by people from all walks of life, including nuns and monks. The diverse backgrounds of the Tang poets and the sense of writing as a form of competition for fame and power made Tang poetry more vital and powerful than in any preceding or subsequent period.

Much of the best poetry from the period was written in the very difficult regulated verse form. Du Fu's poem "Gazing in Springtime" is a good example of the sort of multidimensional architectural balance that regulated verse poems achieved:

國破山河在。	The empire is shattered but rivers and peaks remain.
城春草木深。	Spring drowns the city in wild grass and trees.
感時花濺淚，	A time so bad, even the flowers rain tears.
恨別鳥驚心。	I hate this separation, yet birds startle my heart.
烽火連三月，	The signal fires have burned three months;
家書抵萬金。	I'd give ten thousand gold coins for one letter.
白頭搔更短，	I scratch my head and my white hair thins
渾欲不勝簪。	till it can't even hold a pin.

This five-character verse consists of four paired lines. Their symmetries can be analyzed on three levels: (1) rhythmic pattern, (2) lexical parallelism, (3) tonal pattern. Rhythmically, this verse employs the standard pattern of five syllables (two syllables, pause, three syllables). With the same rhyme on even lines, the first two characters form one beat while the following three can either be taken as a single beat, or split into two sub-beats if one wants to read the poem slowly. If we transcribe the poem phonetically, its rhythmic symmetry in paired lines is easier to perceive:

> Guo po // shan he / zai,
> Cheng chun // cao mu / shen.
>
> Gang shi // hua / jian lei;
> Hen bie // niao / jing xin.
>
> Feng huo // lian / san yue;
> Jia shu // di / wan jin.
>
> Bai tou // sao / geng duan,
> Huan yu // bu / shen zan.

As required by the form, the two middle pairs have to be parallel couplets. In other words, symmetry also exists on the conceptual level. Therefore, there must be a one-to-one parallelism between characters at the same positions: (1) parts of speech should match; (2) conceptually, the corresponding words should be chosen from the same category as prescribed by tradition. We can use the second pair of lines as an example:

感時花濺淚，   A time so bad, even the flowers rain tears.
恨別鳥驚心。   I hate this separation, yet birds startle my heart.

Touched (by)	time	flowers	splash	tears
Verb	Noun	Noun	Verb	Noun
Hate	separation	birds	startle	heart
Verb	Noun	Noun	Verb	Noun

In comparison with the rhythmic balance and the conceptual parallelism demonstrated above, the tonal symmetry is very difficult to perceive, even for Chinese readers. The tonal qualities of

Chinese characters have undergone a dramatic change since Mandarin was made the standard speech. One of the traditional tones, namely the fifth or the *ru* tone 入聲, is absent in Mandarin and was redistributed into other tones. However, in many dialects the fifth tone still exists. For example, in Changsha 長沙 dialect, there are still five tones: 媽 ma (1), 痲 ma (2), 馬 ma (3), 罵 ma (4), 抹 ma (5), while in Mandarin the fifth tone 抹 ma (5) does not exist and can be pronounced only as a first tone—e.g., 抹布 ma (1) bu (4). According to traditional prosody, the first two tones belong to the category of smooth tones 平聲, while the other three are classified as sharp tones 仄聲.

In regulated verse, the key tonal positions in the five-character lines are 2, 4, and 5. There are two basic rules governing the arrangement of the tones: within a pair of lines, characters placed at the key tonal positions should always form a contrast between a smooth tone and a sharp tone, while between the paired lines, i.e., in the second line of a preceding pair and the first line of the pair to follow, characters placed at positions 2 and 4 should actually share a tone in the same category (either a smooth tone or a sharp tone), though the contrast at the end positions is still maintained. Here is the tonal chart for Du Fu's poem "Gazing in Springtime":

1	2	3	4	5	(character positions)
/	/	--	--	/	(first pair of lines)
--	--	/	/	=	
/	--	--	/	/	(second pair of lines,
/	/	/	--	=	couplets required)
--	/	--	--	/	(third pair of lines,
--	--	/	/	=	couplets required)
/	--	--	/	/	(fourth pair of lines)
/	/	/	--	=	

(/ = a sharp tone; -- = a smooth tone; = = a smooth tone with rhyme)

The musicality of the lines is best explored by their intrinsic tonal qualities since the first rule guarantees a tonal yin-yang balance within a pair, while the second rule helps to break the monotony of repeating the same pattern in the next pair. Depending on the first line, many different tonal charts can be worked out for regulated verse. If it is a seven-character verse, an extra key tonal position (position 6) is added, and the basic rules remain the same. To write regulated verse is often compared to dancing in chains. Many poets enjoyed their chains and wrote great works in this restrictive and elegant form.

After the maturity of regulated verse (both five-character and seven-character forms) in the Tang dynasty, the essence of the verse tradition was stabilized, coming to include both the old forms (unregulated) 古詩 and the new forms (regulated) 新體詩, the long forms 排律 and the short forms 絕句. By the end of the Tang dynasty, regulated verse had become the dominant form in poetry writing, and yet the pleasures of its symmetry began to be out-weighed by the negative impact of its restrictive form. Though *shi* poetry continued to be written in the Song and later dynasties, the stage was set for new forms to gain predominance, and to revitalize the tradition.

The Song Dynasty and Lyric Songs

Verses in the *shi* tradition written in the Song dynasty (960–1279) are manifestly different from Tang poetry. As a reaction to the Tang tradition, Song verses appeal more to human intellect than to emotions. As a result, the poet's individuality often becomes hidden behind the form and wit. On a sociopolitical level, there was also a major change in the notion of poetry: it was now more a vehicle for ideology than an expression of self. Nonetheless, human emotions and individuality always need an outlet in poetry, and so lyric songs 詞 prospered in the Song dynasty. In fact, poets were already experimenting with this new form of poetry in the Tang dynasty, even though they were considered only "leftovers of poetry" (詩餘), composed to fill in fixed tunes. The best-known lyric poet using this form in the transitional period between the Tang and Song dynasties was Li Yu, a Southern Tang emperor who lost his throne and palace to the Song court, was taken captive, and then was poisoned for writing lyric songs mourning his lost state. In the Song dynasty many masters of lyric songs emerged who authentically expressed their personalities and experiences in this form. To illustrate the difference between lyric songs and verses, we should take a close look at a poem written by Li Yu:

虞美人   To the Tune of "Beauty Yu"

春花秋月何時了，	Will spring blooms and autumn moon never end?
往事知多少。	These memories are too much.
小樓昨夜又東風，	Last night east wind pierced my narrow tower again,
故國不堪回首月明中。	and I saw lost kingdoms in the clean bright moon.
雕欄玉砌應猶在，	The carved railings and jade steps must still be there,
只是朱顏改。	though lovely faces must have aged.
問君能有幾多愁，	How much sorrow do I feel?
恰似一江春水向東流。	Like river water in spring it flows to the east.

When we compare this poem to Du Fu's "Gazing in Springtime," there are some obvious differences. With its form determined by specific tunes, a lyric song often consists of a mixture of long and short lines (hence this form is also called long-and-short lines 長短句). Meanwhile, its rhyme scheme does not always fall on even lines. As a lyric song is supposedly to be appreciated by the ear, it is naturally easier to understand than a *shi* verse, which is presented in written form, to be read and reread many times. In comparison with parallel movement prescribed by the paired symmetrical lines in verse, the movement in a lyric song is normally linear and narrated from a fixed perspective. Moreover, the poem is often set at a clearly perceivable geographical location. As a result, the points of entry and and exit in a lyric song are more distinct than those in a verse, which sometimes gives the Western reader a sense of an abrupt beginning followed by an unexpected ending with no fixed location. The high-water mark in poetry of the Song dynasty was reached by lyric songs; however, as with *shi* verse after the

High Tang, lyric songs became too regulated and refined by the end of the Song dynasty, and the momentum and vitality of the form were lost.

The Yuan, Ming, and Qing Dynasties and Operatic Arias

Though China's history is one of unending conquest and invasion, of rising and falling dynasties, sometimes in quick succession, the Mongolian invasion of China in the thirteenth century was a particularly important watershed in Chinese poetic writing. During this period, known as the Yuan dynasty (1280–1367), Confucian scholars and literati poets were ranked number nine on the social ladder, between prostitutes and beggars. For about a hundred years the world of Chinese poetry shrank to its smallest size, even as the actual territory of China expanded considerably. The only literary form encouraged by the Mongolian rulers was Yuan opera, and so opera songs, or arias (*qu* 曲), rose in importance and became the dominant form in poetry writing. The specific term for songs intended to be sung in the theater is "dramatic aria" (*xiqu* 戲曲). Most of the opera songs selected for this anthology were composed as "separated arias" (*sanqu* 散曲), arias written to be totally independent from plays. Here is an example by Ma Zhiyuan:

天淨沙·秋思	Autumn Thoughts, to the Tune of "Sky-Clear Sand"
枯藤老樹昏鴉，	Withered vines, old trees, ravens at dusk.
小橋流水人家，	A small bridge, a flowing brook, a cottage.
古道西風瘦馬。	Ancient roads, west wind, and a lean horse.
夕陽西下，	The evening sun dies west.
斷腸人在天涯。	A broken man at the sky's edge.

This is one of the most famous poems in classical Chinese poetry. Opera songs are typically highly colloquial and direct, though some of them are highly imagistic. In this example the absence of verbs in the first three lines makes them unfold like a series of cinematic scenes, and the juxtaposition of images carries on the Tang tradition. A Chinese reader can learn this poem by heart after reading it just once or twice.

When the Han Chinese regained the throne from the Mongolians in the Ming dynasty (1368–1644), the creative talent was more involved with fiction than poetry, and it took some time for the Chinese to reconnect with their poetic heritage. In the Qing dynasty (1644–1911) the Chinese were again invaded by outsiders, and the Manchus ruled China for about three hundred years. It was a time of literary inquisition, and individuality in poetry writing was stifled. In fact very little innovation can be found in poetry during the Ming and Qing dynasties, as the poets were largely engaged in searching for their roots back in the Tang and the Han dynasties. Although some of the literary output of this period has been reevaluated, it seems unlikely that there will be a rediscovery of a major poet who can match the caliber of the Tang talent.

Ambiguity in Classical Chinese Poetry

To understand the reasons why the move from classical Chinese poetry to the poetry of the modern era is often perceived as a further decline from the tepid and imitative poetry of the Ming and Qing dynasties, a discussion of aspects of ambiguity in the classical Chinese poem is helpful. With the emergence of the five-character line as the dominant form and the increasing employment of parallelisms in the classical Chinese poem, functional words were gradually reduced to a minimum. As a result, the lines often work like a shooting list for a movie director, conveying an amazing sense of cinematic time and space. But for all the gains in intensity of content and imagery, there was a corresponding rise in ambiguity, since words were juxtaposed without any signs of relationship between them. Given the fact that Chinese characters do not have inflections in themselves, it is almost like writing in English with only nouns, verbs, and adjectives and without personal pronouns to indicate speaker. Consequently, classical Chinese poetry, especially Tang poetry, possesses an exceptional intensity and ambiguity.

Ranging from general to specific, various ambiguities exist in classical Chinese poems. One of the most common is the indeterminacy of perspective. Wang Wei's "Birds Sing in the Ravine" is a good example:

鳥鳴澗

Birds Sing in the Ravine

人閑桂花落，
夜靜春山空。
月出驚山鳥，
時鳴春澗中。

At rest, he senses acacia blossoms fall.
Quiet night, the spring mountain empty.
The sudden moon alarms mountain birds
Pulses of song in the spring ravine.

The first character in this poem, 人 *ren* (human), forces a choice in the translation. It refers to the poet himself, and yet the sense is that the speaker observes himself as well as nature from the third-person perspective. In English it is difficult to reproduce the effect of having the speaker himself in the picture yet seen from the outside. In Wang Wei's world, human beings and nature exist in great harmony, and the poet registers activities both in nature and in himself like a monitoring camera. And yet the sensory effects in this poem require more than a camera to discern. The intoxicating sweet smell of the acacia flowers cannot be captured with lenses no matter how powerful they are. Moreover, the tiny acacia petals' landing is rendered with such ambiguity that it cannot be captured with a camera, either. The effect at first seems to be visual, but it is only when the first two lines collide with the last two that the reader realizes that the poet experienced the falling of the petals totally in the dark, before moonrise. This realization intensifies the effect of the first two lines and clarifies the meaning of being "at rest"—the mind must be totally free either to hear the soft landing of the acacia petals on the ground or to feel their weightless impact on one's clothes. The quietness of the night, the emptiness of the mountain, as well as peace in the mind, are all captured in the motion of the falling petals. The poet is there in the picture, and yet he observes himself from outside, with internal and external experience combined. By contrast, the second pair of lines is purely external. The scene is loud and dramatic, even though it is only a description of a chirping bird startled by the rising moon. One can almost see the bird dart across a huge, low moon, followed by an eye-line tele- photo lens tracking the intermittent sound of the bird. In a moment, after the collision of these two pairs of lines, tranquility reigns again, and the sudden movement and sound of the bird only height- ens the emptiness of the mountains. What derives from this ambi- guity in perspective is a new appreciation of nature through a transparent and perceptive Zen mind.

Ambiguity also arises when natural syntax comes up against the expectation of symmetrical structure in paired lines. For example, the couplet " 感時花濺淚, 恨別鳥驚心 " ("A time so bad, even the flowers rain tears. / I hate this separation, yet birds startle my heart."), from Du Fu's "Gazing in Springtime," contains an ambiguity that is often lost in translation. According to the natural syntax, an initial read- ing of the first half of the couplet would be "A time so bad, even the flowers rain tears," taking the flowers as the subject of the whole line. But the second half immediately suggests a different reading. It is very clear that the poet himself was startled by birds, and the symmetrical structure strongly suggests that the subject in the first half is the same person. Thus, when we read the poem again, the first half may be read as "sad about the times, flowers make me shed tears." This ambiguity results from two legitimate readings according to syntax or symmetry. Since it is impossible to keep two interpretations in the translation, we chose personification of the flowers to avoid making the second half of the couplet too expected. This sort of conflict between natural reading and reading for sym- metry can be found in many seemingly unambiguous lines in Chi- nese poetry.

Ambiguities can also be quite local and involve indeterminacy in grammar or definition of words. Two of the lines we discussed ear- lier from the first poem from the *Book of Songs* contain such ambi- guity:

| 窈窕 / 淑女, | yao | tiao / | shu | nu | Full of grace, / the lady |
| 君子 / 好逑。 | jun | zi / | hao | qiu | is a gentleman's / good spouse. |

The last two characters can be read as "*hao* (1) *qiu* (2)" (first tone plus second, meaning "good spouse"). But they can also be pronounced as "*hao* (4) *qiu* (2)" (fourth and second tones). In that case the character *hao* 好 is no longer an adjective modifying the noun *qiu* 逑 (spouse) but rather a word meaning "love to" (*hao* [4] 好) modifying a verb *qiu* 逑 (to marry). In that case the line indicates a man's strong desire for the hand of a lady, and perhaps should be translated: "Full of grace is the lady. / The gentleman is obsessed with marrying her," or ". . . seeks her hand." Although a translation can keep just one of the interpretations, the effect of reading the Chinese is that the text is wavering between readings, a door swinging open and shut.

In contemporary Chinese poetry, much of the elegant ambiguity of the classical Chinese poem is lost. This can explain why a Chinese reader's first reaction to classical Chinese poetry in English or in modern Chinese can be summed up in one word: "diluted." But to leave out in translation most of the functional or connective elements of language in an attempt to re-create the intensity of the original Chinese too often yields a poem that reads like pidgin English.

From Modern to Contemporary

After the last emperor was removed from the throne in 1911 and China entered an era of warlords and revolution, the classical Chinese language and all its forms of poetry quickly became outmoded. The vernacular movement promoted by Dr. Hu Shi and other advocates of modernization introduced a fault line in the poetry tradition as well as a schizoid understanding of poetry: while new poetry was expected to be in sync with the changing times and to emerge from the shadow of classical poetry, many readers continued to evaluate new poetry against the merits of classical poetry—namely musicality, memorability, and intensity of information and imagery. The best of the modern poets, the one who solved the riddle of how to blend classical qualities with modern sensibility, was Mao Zedong; he did so by using classical forms, such as regulated verse and lyric song, in modern ways.

Even though classical Chinese and modern Chinese share the same characters, there are significant differences that influence how they are used in the composition of poetry. Modern Chinese is mainly disyllabic, while classical Chinese is mainly monosyllabic. Many common words are even more than two syllables now, and functional words are often necessary to clarify the relationship between words. As a further complication, many modern poets, rejecting what they saw as an outmoded and failed Chinese cultural tradition, began to draw on the Western tradition. Translated poems became a model of style and resulted in new forms and uses of language. Feng Zhi even tried to introduce the sonnet into Chinese poetry. After about a hundred years of experimentation, the forms of the new poetry are still as open as folk songs in the Han dynasty. Contemporary Chinese poetry, particularly that of the Misty school, whose poets often imbue their work with political messages that can be glimpsed through the mists, is typically a hybrid of classical Chinese parallelism, Western free verse, surrealism, and symbolism, as in these lines by Shu Ting: "A colorful hanging chart with no lines. / A pure algebra problem with no solution" (from "Missing You").

Like other Asian nations, China in the era of modernity suffers from a split consciousness, seeking at once to modernize and to retain a sense of what was traditionally Chinese. Its poets have helped to imagine a China for the twentieth century and for today—one that creates uneasy hybrids between tradition and experimentation, that promotes political movements and is persecuted by them, and that seeks new poetic forms that can express what it means to be Chinese in the new millennium.

—CHOU PING

The Anchor Book of

CHINESE POETRY

ZHOU DYNASTY

(1122–256 BCE)

THOUGH CHINESE CIVILIZATION STRETCHES BACK TO NEO-lithic times, the earliest known dynasty, the Xia, is of limited importance to a discussion of Chinese literature, as there is no evidence that a written language was in use. The succeeding dynasty, the Shang, was a Bronze Age agricultural civilization. During the Shang, characters were written on oracle bones (usually made of turtle shell or cattle shoulder bones, and later on bamboo strips, silk, and bronze), but no literature from this time is extant.

The Shang were overthrown by the king of Zhou, a small dependent nation in the Wei River Valley in the western Shang territory, and thus began the Zhou dynasty, the first great period of Chinese literature. It was during the Zhou dynasty that the doctrine that the Chinese king was exercising a "Mandate of Heaven" developed. It later became an extremely important doctrine both to justify imperial rule and to explain the fall of an empire (should an emperor prove corrupt or weak, heaven would remove his mandate). The Zhou dynasty is the longest of China's many dynasties, and is divided into the Western Zhou (1122–771 BCE) and the Eastern Zhou (770–256 BCE), as the Zhou were forced out of their capital at Xian by barbarian invaders from the north, and moved east to found their new capital in Luoyang. The Eastern Zhou is itself subdivided into the Spring and Autumn Period (770–476 BCE) and the Warring States Period (475–221 BCE). The troubled Warring States Period marked the waning years of the dynasty. Such great thinkers, moralists, and philosophers as Confucius, Mencius, Laozi, and Zhuangzi lived during the Eastern Zhou. It was the time of the Hundred Schools of Thought, the golden age of Chinese philosophy, when the great traditions of Confucianism,

Daoism, Legalism, Militarism, and Mohism developed. In this period, itinerant thinkers traveled with their followers, finding employment with rulers, who would seek their advice on warfare, morality, diplomacy, and government. The Zhou dynasty eventually weakened to the point where it ruled only in name, as seven powerful warring states vied for dominance. In 256 BCE, the Zhou were conquered by the Qin state, but the warfare continued for another thirty-five years. In 221 BCE, the ruler of Qin succeeded in conquering the remaining states and unified China, naming himself Shi Huangdi (the "first emperor") and beginning the Qin dynasty. After eight hundred years, heaven had removed its mandate from the Zhou at last.

The three Zhou dynasty texts presented here are the source of Chinese poetic literature, evolving out of the beginnings of Chinese writing and foreshadowing what was to come in this extraordinary three-thousand-year tradition. Chinese poetry begins with the *Book of Songs*, comprised of folk songs, hymns, and court songs collected largely from ordinary people living along the Yellow River, and putatively edited by Confucius himself (thus the collection is sometimes referred to as the *Confucian Odes*). The fact that the Chinese poetic tradition begins with folk poetry reworked and set to music has meant that the long tradition of Chinese poetry written by the nobility has often striven for a sense of folk authenticity to blend with the master poet's craft and skill, simplicity balancing elegance. The four-character verses in the *Book of Songs* are the model for *shi* poetry, whose variations came to dominate classical Chinese poetry for the next two thousand years.

The *Book of Songs* is one of the Confucian classics, studied throughout Chinese history by the nobility and by those who wished to rise in society as scholar-officials. Poetry is held to be one of the great arts that educated Chinese men (and sometimes women) should know and be able to practice. In fact, poetry has been the mainstream of literary expression in Chinese literature, and so it is often afforded great powers of influence in the Chinese critical tradition. The "Great Preface" to the *Book of Songs* states that poetry is a Confucian rectifier that establishes the proper relationships between spouses, encourages respect and loyalty for the old, strengthens human ties, improves civilizations, and excises bad customs. In the *Analects*, Confucius often mentions the *Songs*. In

Analect 2.2, for example, he states, "There are 300 *Songs*, but they can be summed up with one phrase: let your thoughts be free of depravity." Poetry serves a moral purpose, according to Confucius, "stimulating the reader, and making him observant, sociable, and capable of expressing his grievances," while at the same time "helping him to serve his family and his King" (Analect 17.8). Though the poems in the *Book of Songs* were in fact simply songs of the peasants, they were read as moral allegories, or as analogues to political and historical events.

The second text presented here is the marvelous, riddling, profound, and elegantly difficult *Dao De Jing* of Laozi (better known in the West by an earlier transliteration as the *Tao Te Ching* of Lao Tzu). As the *Book of Songs* stands as one of the key texts that gave birth to the Confucian tradition, so the *Dao De Jing* (along with another great text, the *Zhuangzi*) stands as the source of the great religious and philosophical tradition of Daoism, and ultimately of Chinese Buddhism, which blended with Daoism in a particularly Chinese philosophical and spiritual mélange. Though it is not normally considered to be poetry, the *Dao De Jing* translates as marvelous poetry. A selection from it can help give Western readers an understanding of the concepts that underlie so many of the great Daoist and Buddhist poets in China who were to come later.

The final text in this section is a selection from the great long poem *Encountering Sorrow* by Qu Yuan (c. 340–c. 278 BCE). This poem comes from the *Verses of Chu*, the second great early anthology of Chinese poetry, which included Qu Yuan's poetry, as well as that of a later poet, Song Yu. *Encountering Sorrow* and other poems in the collection tell of how Qu Yuan's dedication to his king was rewarded with banishment, leading him to drown himself in despair. The poems are celebrated for their Confucian dedication to duty. The work of Qu Yuan represents the beginning of an ornate literary tradition in China, which is counterbalanced by the simpler, vernacular, folk tradition of the *Book of Songs*. His poems are also the source of Chinese *fu* poetry, an irregular blend of poetry and prose that was to become an important part of the Chinese tradition. *Fu* poems usually begin and conclude with prose passages, with rhymed poetry in the center.

Qu Yuan is supposedly the first Chinese poet whose name we know (though in fact there are a few cases in the *Book of Songs* in which a poet's name is embedded). That the *Verses of Chu* begins the tradition of named poetry in China is more important than one might think. When one knows a poet's name, and something of his or her life, one gets a powerful sense of human connection to the person behind the poem. As poets name the world, so their own names name something to us as readers—a life and, perhaps more important, a lifework. Though the songs from the *Books of Songs* can often feel personal, they are almost exclusively anonymous and written to set, generic topics. Thus, despite their allusive and elaborate nature, the poems of Qu Yuan are the fountainhead of personal poetry in China.

BOOK OF SONGS

(C. 600 BCE)

The *Book of Songs* is the earliest anthology of Chinese poetry and the thematic and formal source of the Chinese poetic tradition. The Chinese name for the *Book of Songs* is the *Shi Jing*, and the term *shi* (the general term for poetry, like the Japanese term *waka*) derives from its name. Legend has it that its 305 poems were compiled by Confucius (551–479 BCE) from an earlier manuscript of around three thousand songs. The assertion that Confucius was the compiler is questionable, but certainly the anthology was extant in Confucius's time, and it seems likely that the anthology was collected between 1100 and 600 BCE. Confucius refers to the *Book of Songs* in the *Analects*, and it was part of the curriculum of his disciples; it is counted among the Confucian classics that form the basis of Confucian education. The collection was banned in the third century BCE, along with the other Confucian classics, but was reconstructed during the Han dynasty, and the edition that is most complete derives from this time.

The *Book of Songs* contains three basic categories of song: folk songs and ballads, court songs, and sacrificial songs. Like the Sanskrit *Vedas* of India, these songs provide us with a window onto the simple and beautiful life of an ancient time. Heroes and ancestors are praised, love is made, war is waged, farmers sing to their crops, people complain about their taxes, and moral categories are set forth in stark and powerful form. Though these are songs, the music has been lost, and some of them have been revised from folk song roots by court musicians, rhymed and arranged into stanzas. Others were aristocratic songs, songs to be sung to accompany ritual dancing, or to accompany the rites of ancestor worship.

White Moonrise

The white rising moon
is your bright beauty
binding me in spells
till my heart's devoured.

The light moon soars
resplendent like my lady,
binding me in light chains
till my heart's devoured.

Moon in white glory,
you are the beautiful one
who delicately wounds me
till my heart's devoured.

Translated by Tony Barnstone
and Willis Barnstone

Fruit Plummets from the Plum Tree

Fruit plummets from the plum tree
but seven of ten plums remain.
You gentlemen who would court me,
come on a lucky day.

Fruit plummets from the plum tree
but three of ten plums still remain.

You men who want to court me,
come now, today is a lucky day!

Fruit plummets from the plum tree.
You can fill up your baskets.
Gentlemen if you want to court me,
just say the word.

Serene Girl

The serene girl is pretty,
waiting for me at the corner.
She loves me but hides from me.
I scratch my head, walking back and forth.

That serene girl is tender,
she gave me a red straw.
The red straw shines;
I love this beauty.

It was picked in the fields.
It is beautiful and rare.
It isn't the straw that is so beautiful
but that it's a gift from a beauty.

In the Wilds Is a Dead River-Deer

In the wilds is a dead river-deer.
White rushes wrap her.
A lady yearns for someone dear.
A fine man seduces her.

In the woods are clustered bushes,
and in the wilds a river-deer is dead
and wrapped up in white rushes.
There is a lady as fine as jade.

Oh! Slow down, don't be so harsh,
let go of my girdle's sash.
Shhh! You'll make the dog bark.

All the Grasslands Are Yellow

All the grasslands are yellow
and all the days we march
and all the men are conscripts
sent off in four directions.

All the grasslands are black
and all the men like widowers.
So much grief! Are soldiers
not men like other men?

We aren't bison! We aren't tigers
crossing the wilderness,
but our sorrows
roam from dawn till dusk.

Hairy-tailed foxes slink
through the dark grass
as we ride tall chariots
along the wide rutted roads.

Ripe Millet*

Rows and rows of ripe millet,
the sorghum sprouts,
and I take long, slow walks

---

*According to the preface of the *Book of Songs*, the poet is a minister of the Eastern Zhou dynasty (771–256 BCE). He comes to the capital city of the earlier Western Zhou dynasty (1122–771 BCE) and finds all the temples destroyed and the royal palace replaced by rows and rows of millet. Moved by these changes, he improvises this poem.

with a shaking, shaken heart.
My friends say,
"His heart is hurting"
but strangers wonder,
"What can he be looking for?"
O far, far blue heaven
what makes me feel this way?

Rows and rows of ripe millet,
the sorghum is in spike,
and I take long, slow walks
with a drunken heart.
My friends say,
"His heart is hurting"
but strangers wonder,
"What can he be looking for?"
O far, far blue heaven
what makes me feel this way?

Rows and rows of ripe millet,
the sorghum is all grain,
and I take long, slow walks
with a choking heart.
My friends say,
"His heart is hurting"
but strangers wonder,
"What can he be looking for?"
O far, far blue heaven
what makes me feel this way?

I Beg You, Zhongzi*

I beg you, Zhongzi,
don't come into my neighborhood,

---

*This is a poem from the perspective of either an unmarried girl or a young widow.

don't break my willow twigs.
I'm not worried about the willow trees,
I'm afraid of my parents.
I do miss you
but I'm scared
of my parents' scolding.

I beg you, Zhongzi,
don't climb over my wall,
don't break my mulberry branches.
I'm not worried about my mulberry trees,
I'm afraid of my brothers.
I do miss you
but I'm scared
of my brothers' words.

I beg you, Zhongzi,
don't trespass into our orchard,
don't break my sandalwood boughs.
I'm not worried about the sandalwood trees,
I'm afraid of rumors.
I do miss you
but I'm scared
of people's gossip.

When the Gourd Has Dried Leaves*

When the gourd has dried leaves,
you can wade the deep river.
Keep your clothes on if the water's deep;
hitch up your dress when it's shallow.

The river is rising,
pheasants are chirping.

*The ancient Chinese used to tie gourds around their waist as a safety device
when wading.

The water is just half a wheel deep,
and the hen is singing to the cock.

Wild geese are trilling,
the rising sun starts dawn.
If you want to marry me,
come before the river is frozen.

The ferryman is gesturing,
other people are going, but not me,
other people are going, but not me,
I'm waiting for you.

LAOZI

(FOURTH–THIRD CENTURIES BCE)

Laozi was the legendary author of the *Dao De Jing*, a collection
of prose and verse wisdom literature that is considered the semi-
nal work of Daoism. Yet mysteries abound about Laozi and the
Dao De Jing. It is by no means certain that a historical personage
named Laozi ever existed. The collection itself was originally
known simply as *Laozi*; since Laozi also means "old man," and
there is evidence of a body of wisdom literature whose various
book titles all translate as "elder" or "old man," it may be that
this collection is the lone survivor of a lost genre. The title *Dao
De Jing* (*Classic of the Way and Its Power*) was subsequently
given to it. The *Dao De Jing* may be an anthology by diverse
authors of sayings linked by common themes or the work of one
author augmented by later redactors. The traditional Laozi is
said to have been an older contemporary of Confucius (551–
479 BCE), who instructed the younger sage in the rites, but this
story seems not to have circulated until the third century BCE. It is
now thought that the text dates from no earlier than the third or
fourth centuries BCE. In the first century BCE, the famous histo-
rian Sima Qian recounted the Confucius encounter and other sto-

ries about Laozi, which he gathered from sources now lost. The story about Laozi's writing the *Dao De Jing* follows:

> Laozi cultivated the way and virtue, and his teachings aimed at self-effacement. He lived in Zhou for a long time, but seeing its decline he departed; when he reached the Pass, the Keeper there was pleased and said to him, "As you are about to leave the world behind, could you write a book for my sake?" As a result, Laozi wrote a work in two books, setting out the meaning of the way and virtue in some five thousand characters, and then departed. None knew where he went to in the end.[1]

The book itself has more than the five thousand characters mentioned by Sima Qian and is divided into eighty-one chapters in two sections. Unlike the other great source of Daoism, the *Zhuangzi* text, the *Dao De Jing* is not a work of anecdotes and parables; it is a general, didactic work of great poetic beauty, mystery, and ambiguity. Central to the work and to Daoism is the concept of the Dao, which means the way, method, or reason. The Dao is ineffable—it can't be captured in words; it is as small as the essential nature of the smallest thing and as large as the entire universe. The term *De* means "virtue" and refers to the nature of a thing—its inherent virtue and energy. The term *Jing* means "classic," and thus the title of the book translates as *The Classic of the Dao and the De*. The Dao in this work is seen as the source of the world, as everything and, at the same time, nothing. It is fluid, weak, and passive, yet it conquers all and is the source of all action. Its nature is paradoxical because it is so large that it contains both ends of all oppositions. The Dao is also a contemplative method for understanding oneself and for merging with the Dao. Different interpreters see it either as a method of survival through passive resistance written in a time of great insecurity and turmoil or as a more mystical treatise. In any case,

---

[1] D. C. Lau, tr., *Lao Tzu: Tao Te Ching* (Harmondsworth: Penguin, 1963), p. 9. The Wade-Giles transliteration of this quotation has been changed to the Pinyin system.

a number of passages treat the proper behavior of citizen and ruler and suggest that true self-interest lies in selflessness (thus, the ruler must humble himself before the people in order to rule, follow in order to lead).

Like Confucianism, Daoism took on magical elements as it developed, and the longevity of the follower of the Dao (who would live longer in turbulent times) was interpreted as physical immortality. Daoism resembled Western alchemy in its quest for the secret of immortality. It later came to blend with Buddhism. Throughout Chinese literature and intellectual history, Daoism has been a liberating counterbalance to the dogmatic order of Confucianism.

from the *Dao De Jing*

1

The Dao that can be told is not the timeless Dao.
The name that can be named is not the eternal name.
Heaven and earth emerged from the nameless.
The named is the mother of all things.
Lose desire and see the Dao's essence.
Have desire and see the Dao's manifestations.
These two have the same source but different names.
Their sameness is a mystery,
mystery of mysteries,
gateway of untold secrets.

4

Dao is an empty vessel,
used without ever being filled,
unfathomably deep, the source of all things,
where sharpness blunts,
knots untangle,
glare mellows,
dust coalesces.
So hidden, in nonbeing it is being.

Who knows whose child it is,
this ancestor of the gods?

11

Thirty spokes join at one hub;
emptiness makes the cart useful.
Cast clay into a pot;
the emptiness inside makes it useful.
Cut doors and windows to make a room;
emptiness makes the room useful.
Thus being is beneficial,
but usefulness comes from the void.

22

Warp to be whole,
twist to be straight,
hollow out to be full,
fray to be new,
have less and gain more,
have much and be perplexed.
Therefore the sage embraces the One
and is a model for all under heaven.
Not exhibiting himself, he stands out.
Not full of himself, he is acclaimed.
Not boasting, he succeeds.
Not vain, his works maintain. He doesn't strive
and so nothing under heaven strives with him.
The ancients say, "warp to become whole."
These are not empty words.
Return to the source and be whole.

33

Know others for wisdom,
but enlightenment is knowing yourself.
Master others to gain power,
but true strength is mastering yourself.

Wealth is to know you have enough.
Acting with force is willpower,
but stay still to endure.
To die without expiring is longevity.

43

The softest thing in the world
can inundate the hardest thing under heaven,
slipping in formless where there is no breach.
This is why I know nonaction is valuable.
But the lesson taught without words,
the value of doing nothing,
can be understood by few under heaven.

47

Without walking out the door,
know the whole universe.
Without looking out the window,
see the Way of heaven.
The farther you go, the less you know.
Thus the sage knows by staying still,
fathoms without seeing,
achieves through nonaction.

49

The sage doesn't have his own heart.
The people's heart is his heart.
He is kind to the kind
and kind to the unkind since virtue is kind.[1]
He has trust in the trusting
and trust in the trustless since virtue is trust.

---

[1] In lines 4 and 6, two homonyms with the sound of *de* are used in different versions of the text. One character for *de* means "virtue," and the other *de* means "gain." So line 4, for example, could also be read "and kind to the unkind to gain in kindness."

He breathes carefully, not to scare those under heaven.
He seems muddled when he does things for the world
and in the eyes and ears of all
he seems to act like a child.

76

Soft and weak at birth,
a man is rigid hard at death.
Trees and plants are soft and supple alive,
brittle and withered when dead.
Thus the hard and brittle belong to death
and the soft and weak belong to life.
An adamant army may be decimated.
A tree that's too strong will be crooked.
Thus the hard and strong are subjugated
and the soft and weak triumph.

78

Nothing is softer and more yielding than water,
yet nothing is better in attacking the solid and forceful
because nothing can take its place.
Weak conquers strong,
soft conquers hard.
No one doesn't know this,
yet who practices it?
Thus the sage says,
"The state's true master takes on
the country's disgrace
and by taking on the country's misfortunes
is king under heaven."
Straight speech may seem like paradox.

VERSES OF CHU

(THIRD CENTURY BCE)

The *Verses of Chu* is the second great anthology of Chinese poetry. Since it comes from the kingdom of Chu, a Southern state located in the central valley of the Yangtze River, it is often considered representative of a Southern style of poetry, as distinguished from the Northern style of the *Book of Songs*. The two collections have formal elements in common, however, and modern scholars question the adequateness of the Northern/Southern dichotomy.

Most of the poems in the *Verses of Chu* are attributed to Qu Yuan (c. 340–c. 278 BCE), the first Chinese poet whom we know by name, but the anthology itself reached its final form some four hundred years after he lived, in the second century CE. It seems highly unlikely that Qu Yuan composed all the works attributed to him. We know little about the historical Qu Yuan, except that he belonged to the royal house of Chu and served in the court of King Huai (329–299 BCE). As a result of slander from a jealous colleague, Chu fell from the king's graces and was said to have written the extremely important poem *Encountering Sorrow* to show his faithfulness and remonstrate with the king. Qu Yuan was supposed to have warned the king repeatedly against the aggressions of the state of Qin, but he was ignored, and the king was captured by Qin. After the king's death in captivity abroad, his son was inaugurated but proved as gullible and flawed a king as his father. He banished Qu Yuan to the far south, and Qu Yuan drowned himself in the Miluo River in protest. Eventually the state of Chu was swallowed up by Qin. Qu Yuan is a highly influential early figure of the honest retainer who dares to criticize his superiors, along the Confucian model, and his death is the subject of the yearly Dragon Boat Festival in China.

While the *Book of Songs* consists primarily of poems in a lyric mode, the *Verses of Chu* are longer narratives, more dramatic in nature. In addition to the extended narrative poem *Encountering Sorrow*, the collection includes a set of shamanistic ritual songs in which the shaman joins sexually with the deity (the "Nine

Songs"); the "Heavenly Questions," a riddling, gnomic series of questions about the origin of the cosmos, mythology, and Chinese history; "Far Journey," a celestial voyage that bears resemblance to *Encountering Sorrow*; the "Nine Arguments," attributed to Song Yu (fourth to third century BCE), a series of poems that is the origin of later evocations of the melancholy associated with autumn, such as Du Fu's "Autumn Thoughts"; "The Fisherman," a dialogue in which a fisherman advises Qu Yuan not to abandon office and commit suicide; and a series of three poems, two of them shamanistic in nature, that are summons to the soul, or to a virtuous gentleman to come out of retirement.

from *Encountering Sorrow* *

. . . .
Days and months sped by, never halting;
springs and autumns gave way to each other.
I thought how the grass and trees wither and go bare,
and feared that my Fair One, too, would grow old.
Hold fast to youth, cast off what is foul!
Why won't you change your ways?
Harness your fine steeds, gallop abroad!
Come, I'll go before you to lead the way.

So pure the virtue of those three ancient lords
that all fragrant things flocked around them.[1]
With the pepper of Shen they mingled dwarf cinnamon,
had more than mere heliotrope and angelica.[2]
And Yao and Shun, shining in splendor—

---

*Although most of the translations in this book are in the Pinyin transliteration system, in this poem and a few others we have respected the practice of those translators who prefer to use the Wade-Giles system.

[1] Yü, T'ang, and Wu, founders of the Hsai, Shang, and Chou dynasties respectively. For easier reading, I have divided the translation into sections on the basis of content, though there are no such divisions in the original poem.

[2] Here and elsewhere the plant names, usually of aromatic or efficacious plants, are probably intended to represent actual adornments to the hero's dress and at the same time to symbolize his talents and superior moral qualities.

they followed the Way, found the right road;
but Chieh and Chou in depravity
hurried by bypaths, stumbling at each step.[3]
Men of that ilk enjoy stolen pleasures,
their road dark and shadowy, peril all around.
It's not that I tremble for my own safety,
I dread the overturn of my lord's carriage!
Swiftly I will run before and behind it
till we find ourselves in the tracks of former kings.
But he fails to perceive my inner feelings;
instead, heeding slander, he turns on me in rage.
My frank counsels bring me only trouble, I know,
but I must endure it, I cannot desist.
I point to the ninth heaven as witness of my uprightness—
all this I do solely for my Godly One.
Once he talked to me in open words,
but later regretted it and took to other ways.
I'm not afraid to be cut off from him,
only sorrow that my Godly One should be so fickle.

. . . .

With repeated sighs I wipe my tears,
grieved that this life should be so thick with woes.
I do what is just and good, yet they tie and bind me;
I give admonitions at dawn, by evening I am banished.
Banished, I fashion a sash of heliotrope,
add to it angelica I've gathered.
So long as my heart tells me this is right
I will die nine deaths with no regret.
But it wounds me that my Godly One should be so rash and
    heedless;
never will he look into a person's heart.
His other women envy my moth eyebrows;
gossiping, slandering, they say I love wicked ways.[4]

---

[3] Yao and Shun are wise rulers of the time before Yü. Chieh and Chou are the
evil rulers of the Hsia and Shang dynasties respectively.

[4] Moth eyebrows are eyebrows shaped like moth antennae, a mark of femi-
nine beauty. In this passage the hero imagines himself as a beautiful woman.

The clever carpenters who follow the times
reject rule and T square to fashion their own measure,
turn their back on chalk and line in favor of the crooked,
make accommodation their only rule.
Bitterly downcast in my frustration,
in such times I alone suffer hardship and want.
Better to die at once as a wandering exile—
I could never bear to do what those others do!

The swift-winged bird does not travel with the flock;
from times past this has been so.
How can square and round be made to fit together,
how can those who travel different roads plan for one another?
But to humble the heart and curb the will,
suffer censure, put up with shame,
hold fast to purity and whiteness, die for the right—
this the ancient sages heartily extolled.
. . . .
Fording the Yüan and Hsiang, I journeyed south,
visited Ch'ung-hua and stated my case.[5]
"Ch'i's Nine Arguments and Nine Songs—
these the Hsia rulers loved, indulging their desires.
They failed to heed danger, to consider the ages to come,
and so Wu-kuan brought contention to the ruling house.[6]
Yi wandered recklessly, too eager for the chase;
he loved to shoot the big foxes.
But wild and disorderly ways seldom end right,
and Han Cho was there to covet his wife.[7]
Chiao dressed himself in stout armor,
gave way to desires without restraint,

---

[5] The Yüan and Hsiang Rivers in Ch'u, south of the Yangtze. Ch'ung-hua is another name for the sage ruler Shun, said to be buried near the Hsiang.

[6] Ch'i was a son of Yü, founder of the Hsia dynasty. He visited heaven and brought back the pieces of music mentioned here. Wu-kuan was a son of Ch'i.

[7] Yi, noted as a skilled archer, usurped power from the Hsia rulers but spent all his time hunting and neglected government affairs. In time the high minister Han Cho had him murdered and married Yi's wife.

daily losing himself in sport and pleasure,
until his head came tumbling down.[8]
Chieh of the Hsia violated the norms
and thus in the end encountered disaster.
Lord Hsin pickled the flesh of others
and hence the rule of Yin lasted no longer.[9]
T'ang and Yü were solemn, pious, respectful;
Chou[10] expounded the Way and committed no error;
they promoted men of worth, employed the able,
followed the chalk and line without partiality.
August Heaven shows no favoritism;
it sees men's virtue and apportions its aid accordingly.
Only the sages and wise men flourish in action;
they indeed are worthy to rule these lands below.
I have viewed what went before, scrutinized what came after,
observing the standards that guide men's conduct.
Who, if not righteous, can ever rule,
who, if not good, can oversee affairs?
I have placed myself in peril, drawn close to death,
but as I look back at my former ways I have no regret.
Trying to shape a peg without thought for the hole it must fit—
even the ancient worthies met misfortune that way.
I sigh in my gloom and melancholy,
sad that the times I live in are so uncongenial.
Picking tender heliotrope, I wipe away the tears,
tears that wet my collar in wave on wave."

. . . .

I gathered bindweed, bamboo slips for divination,

---

[8] Chiao was the son of Han Cho and Yi's wife. Though he wielded power for a time, he was overthrown by a prince of the Hsia dynastic line.

[9] Lord Hsin is another name for Chou, the evil last ruler of the Shang or Yin dynasty. Pickling the flesh of his associates was only one of the many heinous deeds he is charged with.

[10] Chou here is the dynasty founded by the sage kings Wen and Wu to succeed the Shang dynasty, not the last ruler of the Shang, whose name is written with a different character.

commissioned Ling Fen to tell my fortune.[11]
"Two beautiful ones are certain to come together," he said.
"Who is truly fair and yet lacks admirers?
Consider the breadth and vastness of these Nine Provinces—[12]
why should you think of those women only?
Dare to range farther afield, put off doubt—
who in search of beauty would pass you by?
What region is without its fragrant grasses?
Why must you pine for your old land?"
But the age is benighted, blinded, and confused;
who claims it can discern the good and bad in me?
People may differ in likes and dislikes,
but these cliquish ones—they're a breed apart!
Each one sports mugwort stuffed in his waist
and avers that rare orchids are not fit to wear.
If they're so blind in their discernment of plants,
how could they gauge the worth of precious gems?
They scoop up rotten earth to fill their scent bags
and claim that the pepper of Shen lacks aroma.
. . . .
How rich the rare jewels I wear at my sash,
but the crowd conspires to darken and conceal them.
Among such partisans, none can be trusted;
I fear in their envy they'll smash my treasures.
The times are discordant, too easily they shift—
how can I linger any longer?
Orchid and angelica have changed and lost their fragrance,
sweet flag and heliotrope have turned to mere grass.
Why have the fragrant plants of bygone days
now all gone to common mugwort and wormwood?
How could it be for any other reason?
The fault's that no one cares for beauty!
I thought that orchid could be trusted,

---

[11] Ling Fen is identified as an ancient expert in divination. Stalks were bound
together and then broken to perform the divination.

[12] The nine provinces of ancient China and, by extension, the world at large.

but he proved to have no substance, nothing but boasts.
He spurns beauty to run with the crowd,
yet expects to be ranked with the fragrant ones.
Pepper is all flattery and insolence,
and even prickly ash thinks he can fill a scent bag!
They strive to advance, work to gain admittance,
but what fragrance are they fit to offer?
Yet such, to be sure, is the current of the times—
who can fail to be affected?
If I see pepper and orchid[13] behaving thus,
what can I expect from cart-halt and river sage?
Only this girdle of mine is worthy of respect;
others scorn its beauty, but I go on as before.
Its teeming fragrance never falters,
its aroma to this day has yet to fade.
I will compose myself, think of my own pleasure,
go rambling once more in search of a mate.
Now while my adornments are at their finest
I'll seek her through every land high and low.

Ling Fen had already told me his auspicious augury;
I would choose a lucky day and commence my journey.
I broke a branch of carnelian to serve as food,
pounded carnelian fragments to make rations for the road.
I had flying dragons to draw my vehicle,
a carriage inlaid with jasper and ivory.
How could I band with those of different mind?
I would go far away, remove myself from them.
I turned my course toward the K'un-lan Mountains,
over distant roads rambling on and on,
hoisting clouds and rainbows to shield me from the sun,
sounding the tinkle of jeweled carriage bells.

---

[13] Commentators have attempted to identify "orchid," "pepper," and the other plants censured in this passage with persons at the Ch'u court, though with little evidence to go on.

In the morning I set off from the Ford of Heaven,[14]
by evening I had reached the westernmost limit.
Phoenixes reverently bore my banners,
soaring and dipping in solemn flight.
Suddenly my route took me to the Flowing Sands;
I traced the Red Waters,[15] ambling at my ease.
I beckoned dragons and horned dragons to bridge the ford for me,
commanding the Western Sovereign to let me pass over.[16]
But the trail was long and rank with dangers
so I summoned a host of carriages to come and attend me.
Passing Pu-chou Mountain, I veered to the left,[17]
pointing to the western sea as our destination.
I marshalled my chariots, a thousand in number,
their jeweled hubs aligned as they raced side by side,
my eight dragons drawing me, writhing and turning,
my cloud pennants fluttering and streaming on high.
I tried to curb my will, to slacken my pace,
but my spirit soared upward into distant regions.
I played the Nine Songs, danced the Shao music,[18]
stealing a brief day for enjoyment.
But as I ascended the bright reaches of heaven,
suddenly I looked down and saw my old home.

---

[14] A constellation in the eastern portion of the sky.

[15] The name Flowing Sands probably refers to the desert areas north and west of China; the Red Waters refers to one of the four rivers that flow out of the K'un-lun Mountains, each of a different color.

[16] The Western Sovereign is the mythical ruler Shao Hao, who in Chinese cosmology presides over the western direction.

[17] Pu-chou Mountain serves as a pillar holding up heaven in the northwest sector. When Kung Kung, contending for power with the mythical ruler Chuan Hsü, butted his head against the mountain in rage, he caused heaven to tilt toward the northwest and the earth to sag in the opposite direction.

[18] The Nine Songs of Ch'i: see footnote 6.

My groom was filled with sadness, and the horses in their longing
pulled about in the reins and refused to go on.

Luan[19]

It's over! In this land there's no one, no one who knows me!
Why must I long for my old city?
Since there's no one I can join with in administering just rule,
I will seek out P'eng Hsien in the place where he dwells.[20]

Translated by Burton Watson

---

[19] *Luan* appears to have been a musical term designating the concluding
section of a musical selection. Here and in other works that imitate the Li Sao
it denotes a reprise or summation of the poem.

[20] Since P'eng Hsien is supposed to have committed suicide by drowning,
commentators have traditionally taken the last line to refer to the hero's
determination to do likewise. Ch'u culture abounds in legends of persons who
drowned themselves in a river and thereafter became the tutelary deity of the
river, and the hero of the Li Sao perhaps hopes for a similar apotheosis.

HAN DYNASTY
(206 BCE–220 CE)

THE QIN DYNASTY THAT FOLLOWED THE ZHOU DYNASTY DID NOT last long. The expansionist First Emperor was known for his ruthless repression of dissent in his attempt to unite China, and, seeing the Confucianist nobles as his enemy, famously ordered a burning of the books, and of the Confucian classics in particular. Much ancient literature and wisdom was lost. The Qin was overthrown by a peasant revolt, and the succeeding dynasty, the Han, reformed the tax structure and the treatment of the peasants, leading to an expansion of agriculture.

The Han dynasty is divided into the Western Han, with its capital in Changan, and the Eastern Han, with its capital in Luoyang; these bookended a brief, intermediate dynasty, the Xin, which lasted only from from 8–25 CE. During the prosperous Han dynasty, China expanded to a population of 50 million, and an aggressive foreign policy helped expand its borders east into Korea, south into northern Vietnam, and west into Chinese Turkistan. The expansion of trade led to the creation of the Silk Road, which stretched all the way from China to Europe, and the Great Wall was built as a security measure against the depredations of barbarians. The majority population in China, the Han Chinese, took their name from this dynasty. Though the Han dynasty began as a Legalist state with Daoist elements, under Emperor Wu (157–87 BCE) it became an officially Confucianist state. Emperor Wu also instituted the examination system (125 BCE), in which administrators would have to demonstrate proficiency in the Confucian classics in order to serve. The system lasted until the modern era and insured continuity and a commonality of reference in Chinese culture. It established the basis for a meritocracy and helped to assure that government officials would be literate and learned. During this time the Confucian classics became the base upon which Chinese education was built, and upon which prospective civil servants were tested in the civil service examinations.

The Han saw a flowering in works of history and literature and in the arts, surpassed in China's history only by the Tang and the Song dynasties. In poetry the Han was known for its rhyme prose (*fu*) poems, which developed from the *Verses of Chu*, and for its Music Bureau (*yuefu*) poetry. The elaborate, ornate, elegant, and erudite rhyme prose poems were the poetry of the court. "The Owl," by Jia Yi (200–168 BCE) is an example of the form at its height, as is a later poem, "The Art of Writing" by Lu Ji (261–303), from the Six Dynasties Period. In 193 BCE a Directory of Music was founded, followed under Emperor Wu by a Music Bureau whose job was to collect and copy popular folk songs as well as the music written by scholars. Some of the songs were influenced by Central Asian melodies, and new songs were written under the direction of a musician. Later poems in the Music Bureau style, separated from their musical roots, were not sung and were not accompanied by instrumentation. During the Han, the dominance of the four-word line was shaken in Chinese poetry, and a new five-word line imitating the Music Bureau poems became popular, notably in the "Nineteen Ancient Poems" and in *Southeast the Peacock Flies*, a long anonymous poem written at the end of the Han or in the immediate post-Han period. Imitation of the Music Bureau poems by literati led to the creation of a new poetic form called Ancient Style Poetry (*gushi*).

The Han dynasty was weakened by a peasant revolt led by a secret society known as the Yellow Turbans. It started in 184 CE and continued to plague the empire for decades, until, like the Zhou dynasty, the Han degenerated and fragmented. It was succeeded by a tumultuous period of warring kingdoms, known as the Three Kingdoms Period, and by the long Six Dynasties Period, during which the empire remained in pieces. It was not to be reunited for four hundred years, until the short-lived Sui dynasty (581–618), which paved the way for the golden age of China, the Tang.

NINETEEN ANCIENT POEMS

The anonymous "Nineteen Ancient Poems" were written in the five-character meter, the longest-lasting and most influential form of versification in Chinese literature. They are the earliest poems that we have in this meter, and they helped shape the themes and forms of Chinese poetry for the next two thousand years. They probably represent a now-vanished tradition of first- or second-century poems, of which they are the sole remaining texts. They show aspects of folk song, but have been reworked into literary poems. Melancholy, lovelorn, accessible, and concerned with universal themes of the brevity of life and separation from the loved one, these poems shine out of the deep past of China with an intense and intimate beauty.

Nineteen Ancient Poems

I

Traveling traveling and still traveling traveling,
you're separated from me for life,
ten thousand miles apart,
gone to the other end of the sky.
With your road so long and difficult,
how can we know if we'll meet again?
A northern horse leans against northern wind;
a southern bird nests on southern branches.
This separation lengthens day by day,
and day by day my gown and belt grow slack.
Floating clouds obscure a white sun
and wanderer, you do not return.
Missing you makes age come fast.
Years and months spin past.
No need to mention you abandoned me.
Just take care of yourself and eat enough.

2

Green so green is the river grass,
thick so thick are the garden willow's leaves.
Beautiful so beautiful is the lady upstairs,
shining as she stands by the window, shining.
Pretty in her powdered rouge, so pretty
with her slender, slender white hands.
Once she was a singing girl,
but now is the wife of a womanizer.
He travels and rarely comes home.
So hard to sleep in an empty bed.

3

Green so green are the cypress over the burial mounds.
Boulders upon boulders in the rushing ravine.
Born between heaven and earth,
a man is a long-distance traveler.
Let's take joy from this pitcher of wine
and drink with heart, not thin pleasure.
Whipping slow horses pulling our wagon,
we'll play at Wan and Luo.
It is so noisy and crowded in Luoyang,
officials with caps and belts visit each other,
there are main streets and tributary lanes,
and mansions owned by kings and princes.
The two palaces gaze at each other from afar,
yet their watchtowers seem just a hundred feet apart.
Let's exhaust ourselves in banquets to entertain our hearts!
Sorrows and melancholy—who needs such pressure?

4

At today's great banquet
it's too hard to list all our joys.
The zither vibrates with escaping notes,
a new melody so fine it entrances us.
The talented sing high words,

and we who know music understand.
Our hearts share such wishes,
but they've never poured out like this.
Our being is only one life,
up and gone like floating dust.
Why not whip your horse
ahead of others at the ferry landing?
Staying poor is worth nothing.
It just means long suffering on a rutted road.

5

A tall tower in the northwest,
tall as floating clouds,
with patterned lattice windows
and a pavilion up three flights of steps
where strings and voices are heard,
a sound so plaintive and bitter.
Who could play and sing a song like this
except the wife of Jiliang?[1]
Clear autumn sounds blow through the prelude,
then the main melody shifts and varies,
one strike then repeated phrases
with the lingering force of grief.
I don't regret the singer's sorrow,
but mourn how few truly understand her.
If only we were a pair of singing cranes
beating our wings and soaring high!

6

I cross the river to pick lotus flowers
where fragrant grasses grow in the orchid lake.
But to whom can I send these flowers?
My love is far away on the road.

---

[1] The wife of Jiliang was said to have played her lute before drowning herself
in sorrow after her husband's death in battle.

I turn my head and look home
down the road so long and wide.
We share one heart yet live apart
in sorrow and grief till age takes us.

7

Clear moon pours bright light at night
and crickets sing in the eastern wall.
The Big Dipper's jade handle points to midwinter,
all the stars incredibly clear.
White dewdrops hang to wild grass,
as seasons flow by fast and change.
Autumn cicadas rub their wings in trees.
Where have black swallows migrated to?
Once we studied together,
but you have soared on powerful wings,
forgetting we once held hands.
You abandoned me like old footprints.
The South Basket and North Dipper can't be used
and the Pulling Ox won't bear a yoke.[1]
Indeed, nothing is solid as rock.
What's the use of empty names?

8

Soft and frail is a solitary bamboo
though rooted in the foothills of Mount Tai.
I married you just recently,
a creeper climbing up its host.
There is a time for creepers to spread,
but husband and wife should stay as one.
Three hundred miles away from marriage,

---

[1] "The South Basket and North Dipper can't be used" alludes to Song 203 in
the *Book of Songs*, and the sense of the source, as above, is that these two
constellations can't be used as baskets or dippers, just as the Pulling Ox con-
stellation does not bear a yoke. If the narrator's old friendship is just mere
words, "empty names," then it is similarly useless.

you're past the mountain range.
Missing you makes me old.
Why does your carriage return so late?
Orchid flowers grieve me,
unfolding themselves in bright colors.
If you don't pick them before they are past season,
they'll wither with autumn weeds,
but since you are so faithful to our marriage,
what can I say, humble as I am?

9

There is a wonderful tree in the courtyard,
rich flowers among its green leaves.
Breaking a twig, I pick its blossoms
to send them to the man I love.
The fragrance fills my blouse and sleeves.
You are too far off for me to send them.
Not that these flowers are some great gift;
they give me grief of long separation.

10*

Far and far is the Cowherd Star,
bright so bright is the Weaver Girl.
Slender and white, her hands are moving
click-cluck shuttling over the loom.
She doesn't finish one piece in a day
and her tears spin down as rain.
The Celestial River is clear and shallow;

---

*The poem refers to the mythical story "The Cowherd and the Weaver Girl,"
a common subject in traditional Chinese poetry (see for example Qin Guan's
"To the Tune of 'Magpie Bridge Immortal,'" later in this volume). The
Weaver girl was a granddaughter of the Emperor of heaven. Her job was to
weave cloud embroidery, but after her marriage to the Cowherd she stopped
working. The Emperor of heaven was not happy about this and had them
separated by the Milky Way. Each year they could reunite only once, on the
seventh day of the seventh month, by crossing the Celestial River (the Milky
Way) on a bridge built for them by magpies.

there is no great distance between the two.
Across the brimming water
the Weaver gazes with silent love.

11

I turn my carriage around to return,
slowly, slowly, on a long journey.
I look around and see nothing but uncertainties,
and a hundred plants shaking in east wind.
All that I meet on the road looks unfamiliar.
How can I not age fast?
To rising and falling there is a season,
but I can't stand still being a failure.
A man's life is not made of gold or stones,
so how can he reach longevity?
Suddenly life goes through final transformation.
A great name is a great treasure.

12

The east wall is tall and long,
extending and connecting with itself.
Swirling winds rush up from the earth
and autumn grass is melancholy and yellow;
the four seasons keep changing
and soon it is year's end again!
"Morning Wind" refreshes my longing;
"Crickets" makes me sad about confinement.[1]
I should go wild and let my passions free.
Why should I bind myself so tightly?
In Yan and Zhao beauties abound,[2]
pretty as jade,
and I see a girl wearing a silk dress

---

[1] "Morning Wind" and "Crickets" are two poems from the *Book of Songs*.

[2] Yan is in the area of today's Hebei province, and Zhao is in the area of Shanxi province.

and practicing a *Qingshang* tune in a doorway.[3]
Your music is so sad
the notes so fast and high strung!
My heart flies to you as I tie my robe
pacing back and forth and fantasizing
I am with you, a pair of swallows flying
with mud in beaks to build a nest under your roof.

13

I drive my wagon to the east gate
and gaze at distant tombs north of the city
where poplars sigh and sigh in wind
and pines and cypress line the road.
Underneath are the ancient dead.
Endless, endless is their long evening
in deep sleep under the Yellow Springs.
Through thousands of years they never wake.
Powerfully yin and yang cycle past
and years alive are like morning dew,
human existence just a short trip,
not solid like gold or stone.
Ten thousand generations have seen each other off
and no sage or saint is an exception.
Trying pills and lotions for immortality,
many people poisoned their lives.
Much better to drink great wine
and wear silk and satin clothes.

14

Day by day the dead are receding
and the living coming closer.
Looking straight through the city gate,
I see nothing but burial mounds and tombs,
ancient tombs plowed into fields

---

[3] *Qingshang* tunes are three tunes based on *yuefu* (Music Bureau) songs.

and ancient cypress trees cut down as firewood.
Poplar trees catch sad wind
and rustling, rustling this sorrow kills.
I'd like to return to my home village,
but there is no road to take me there.

15

Man dies within a hundred years
but is filled with a thousand years of grief.
Since day is short and night seems long
why not wander with a candle
seeking joy while you are in time?
Don't wait for your time to come.
The fools who care just for cash
will be sneered at in the future.
So hard to come across a man
like Wang Ziqiao, immortal.

16

Chilly, chilly, the year-end clouds darken.
Mole crickets sing sadly in the evening.
Cold winds are getting sharper,
but traveling man you have no winter clothes.
You left your embroidered quilt at Luopu,
and don't share a gown with me anymore.
I sleep alone through a long night,
and see your face in my dream,
good man who cherishes me, his old joy.
Your carriage came and you gave me marriage ribbons,
saying, "I wish I could smile more often
and come back with you in the same carriage."
You leave my dream so quickly,
do not stay in my chamber.
Since you have no wings to glide on morning wind,
how does the wind carry you back?
I look around to let my heart unfold,
stretch my neck, looking into distance for your gaze.

I stand here seized by grief
and wet my door with tears.

17

A cold current in early winter,
a north wind of bitter shivers.
This grief lengthens night.
I look up, see a million stars arrayed,
a full moon on the fifteenth
but on the twentieth the moon-rabbit's part gone.
From a far land, traveler, you came
and handed me a letter
with a first part about missing me,
a second part mourning long separation.
I put the letter in my sleeve
three years ago. The characters still speak.
My whole heart holds on with a passion.
I fear that you won't understand.

18

A traveler came from afar
and brought me a piece of silk.
Parted by three thousand miles,
my man's heart is unchanging.
I used the pattern of two mandarin ducks,
and cut the silk into a quilt for two,
stuffed it with my missing him
and tied all the knots hard and fast.
When you throw glue into paint,
who can separate the two?

19

Pure and white bright moon,
lighting my silk bed curtains.
I feel such grief I cannot sleep,
just slip on a robe and rise.

Traveling may be a joy,
but early return is better.
I step out of the door and pace
with no one to listen to my sorrow.
Head lifted to sky, I return to my chamber,
clothes wet with tears.

JIA YI

(200–168 BCE)

Jia Yi was a talented politician and poet under the Han dynasty reign of Emperor Wen. After suggesting Confucian reforms that made him enemies in the government, he lost his position as Grand Palace Grandee and became tutor to the King of Changsha, a low and damp malarial region that left him mourning his fate and feeling his life was in jeopardy. He is known for two rhyme prose (*fu*) poems, one on Qu Yuan and the other the one presented below, a poem about an owl (often considered a bird of ill omen) who flew into his room and caused him to meditate from a Daoist perspective upon mortality and mutability and the vicissitudes of a political life.

The Owl

The year of *tan-o*, the first
summer month, on April's first day
with the slant sunlight going fast,
an owl flapped through my window bay
and settled in the corner of my mat.
It seemed at ease and without fear.
I wondered why—why was it that
this strange being had come to roost here?
I read my fortune-telling tome
and found this omen through my art:

"Wild birds fly into a man's home;
the resident will soon depart."
And so I called out to the bird,
please tell me where I'm going, master
owl! If it's good, give me the word,
and if it's bad, name the disaster.
"Please let me know the date," I said.
"Please tell me if it's imminent."
The owl just sighed and raised its head
and flapped its wings. All that it meant
I couldn't tell (it could not talk)
but still I gleaned this implication:
"The world's ten thousand things don't stop
in moving through their transformation,
always they circle and revolve,
and driven off, they may return.
The energies blend and evolve
through forms that they'll slough off in turn.
How deep and endless it all seems!
Who can name all its forms and sides?
Disaster is what fortune leans
on; fortune's where disaster hides.
Joy and grief find the same door, as
good luck and bad find the same seat.
How powerful the Wu State was,
yet Fu Cha ended in defeat.
King Goujian conquered the Wu State
though at Huiqi his men were slaughtered.
Prime minister Li Si was great
yet ended up being drawn and quartered.
Fu Shuo was captured, thrown in prison,
but King Wu Ding made him his aide.
Thus providence and cataclysm
like rope strands twine into one braid.
So who can tell where fortune steers
when no one knows? It never dies.
In rapids water can be fierce,
a strong arm sends an arrow high.

Ten thousand things all swirl around
each other, quiver and transform.
While clouds go up the rain comes down
all tangled up into one storm.
The earth spins round, a potter's wheel
so vast and boundless one can't know
it's end, can't foretell heaven, steal
a glimpse of what's to come through Dao.
Our fates come slow or fast; we strive
but cannot know the fatal date.
The earth and heaven are a stove.
Nature's the craftsman of our fate
and yin and yang are his hot coals.
He melts ten thousand things like brass
or scatters them, and so he doles
out being and nonbeing in one mass.
There are no rules by which to bind
the thousand shifts, ten thousand changes
with no known end. One day you find
they chance to make you human. Strange
fortune that turned you to this form,
but why hold on to it so tight?
In death again you'll be transformed,
so why be worried, why feel fright?
The fool adores himself alone;
disdains all others, hoards his life
but men of wisdom don't disown
the rest, they have a broader sight.
The greedy die for gold in towers,
the heroes die for fame and live
as names, vain men die for power,
but common people just survive.
The driven and the needy are sent
far off, are pushed to east and west.
But the great man will not be bent,
at ease with change, his mind at rest.
The stupid man, bound by conventions,
will suffer like a man in jail; how

free the sage is, with purged attention,
he's unattached, alone with Dao.
The masses live a messy riot
with likes and hatreds in their hearts,
but the immortal man is quiet,
he moves with Dao in peace, apart.
Releasing mind and leaving shapes
behind, he loses self, transcends
and floats without support in space.
He soars with Dao beyond all ends
and sails off on a current, rides
until he finds a river isle
and leaves his body to the tide,
giving up selfhood with a smile.
His life is like a floating weed,
his death is like taking a nap.
He quiet as the void, and freed
to drift, his unmoored boat escapes.
He does not treasure his own life.
His open boat in emptiness
drifts on, and so this man can live
unburdened and without distress.
Be free and have trust in your fate
and be a man who seeks what's true
and though the thorns and weeds may scrape,
what can such trifles mean to you?"

LIU XIJUN

(LATE SECOND CENTURY BCE)

Around 107 BCE a Chinese princess from the Han royal family
was married for political reasons to the chief of the Wusun tribe,
a nomadic band in the northwest of China. When she arrived, she
found her new husband aged and decrepit. They saw each other
once every six months, or once a year, and couldn't communicate

since they had no common language. When her husband grew much older, she was forced to marry his grandson. This song is attributed to her.

Lament

My family married me off to
the king of the Wusun,
and I live in an alien land
a million miles from nowhere.
My house is a tent.
My walls are of felt.
Raw flesh is all I eat,
with horse milk to drink.
I always think of home
and my heart stings.
O to be a yellow snow goose
floating home again!

ANONYMOUS FOLK SONGS
FROM THE MUSIC BUREAU

(C. 120 BCE)

The *yuefu* refers to the Bureau of Music, which was set up around 120 BCE by Emperor Wu of the Han dynasty and abolished in 6 BCE by Emperor Ai. At the time of its dissolution, it employed 829 people. Its function was to collect songs by the common people, in part as a way of judging their reactions to the imperial government. The Music Bureau employees also performed rites and created sacrificial music. The collected songs came to be called *yuefu* songs, and in the history of Chinese poetry this term now describes a type of poem written in imitation of *yuefu* themes. As with the songs in the *Book of Songs*, the

popular themes of the folk songs have proved to be more endur-
ing and affecting than the ritual hymns or the eulogies in praise of
the dynasty. Though the majority of the poems fall into regular
lines, there are also poems of irregular meter. In the Tang dynasty,
"new Music Bureau" songs were created by Bai Juyi and Yuan
Zhen that deviated from *yuefu* form and content, seeking formal
freedoms and often satirizing the abuses of the ruling classes.

The East Gate

I stride out the east gate
and don't look back.
The next moment I'm in our doorway,
about to break down.
There's no rice in our pot.
I see hangers but no clothes.
So I draw my sword and again head out the east gate!
My wife grabs me by the shirt and sobs
"I'm not like other wives. I could care less for gold or rank.
I'm happy to eat gruel if I'm with you.
Look up! The sky is a stormy ocean.
Look down! See your small son's yellow face?
To go now is wrong."
"Bah!" I say,
"I'm going now
before it's too late.
We can barely survive as it is
and white hairs are raining from my head."

A Sad Tune

I sing a sad song when I want to weep,
gaze far off when I want to go home.
I miss my old place.
Inside me, a dense mesh of grief.
But there's no one to go back to,
no boat across that river.

This heart is bursting, but my tongue is dead.
My guts are twisting like a wagon wheel.

He Waters His Horse Near a Breach in the Long Wall*

Green so green is the river grass,
and I can't stop thinking of that far road,
can't bear thinking of that far road.
Last night I saw him in my dream,
dreamed him standing by my side.
Suddenly I was in another land,
another land and a different country.
I tossed and turned and woke apart.
The gaunt mulberry knows the sky's wind
and waters of the sea know cold heaven.
When travelers return in joy
not one has a word for me.
From a far land a traveler came
and left me two carp.
I asked my children to cook the fish
and inside they found a silk letter.
I knelt long and read the letter.
What did that letter say?
It started, *Try to eat.*
and ended, *I miss you always.*

At Fifteen I Went to War

At fifteen I went to war
and I'm eighty now, coming home at last.

---

*Compare this poem to the "Nineteen Ancient Poems," especially numbers 1, 2, 16, 17, and 18. The letter in the carp refers either to wooden fish-shaped letter cases or to actual fish, since in Chinese tradition people sometimes sent secret things packed inside of fish (maps, daggers, letters, and so on).

I meet a man from my village
and ask who lives in my home now.
"Your house is over there,
where pine and cypress crowd the grave mounds."
Rabbits scurry in the dog door,
pheasants fly among the rafters,
wild grain burgeons in the yard,
and sunflowers blossom by the well.
I beat the grain to make gruel,
pick sunflowers to make soup,
but when the gruel and soup are cooked
no one is there to serve the food.
I go to the east door and stand gazing
while tears soak my clothes.

An Ancient Poem Written for the Wife of Jiao Zhongqing

(Southeast the Peacock Flies)

The peacock flies southeast
but every few miles it lingers, circling.

"I wove silk at thirteen
and learned to tailor at fourteen.
At fifteen I played the many-stringed harp,
and at sixteen recited the *Book of Songs* and *Book of Documents*.
I became your wife at seventeen,
but my heart's core was often bitterly sad.
You worked as a governmental clerk;
I guarded my virtue and my passion never shifted.
I stayed in an empty chamber,
rarely able to see you.
I'd start to weave when the rooster crowed,
night after night without rest.
In three days I finished five bolts,

but Big Mother chose to complain that I was slow.[1]
It wasn't that I didn't work fast enough,
but it's hard to be a wife in your home.
I can't bear being used this way.
There's no use in staying any longer.
So please tell your parents,
to send me back home soon."

The clerk heard these words,
and begged his mother in the hall:
"I have a meager income,
and am fortunate to have her as my wife.
Once we bound our hair as children, we shared pillow and sheets,[2]
and will stay friends even in Yellow Springs, where the dead go.[3]
We've been together just two or three years,
not much time at all.
Her behavior is not wayward,
so why treat her unkindly?"

The mother said to the clerk:
"That's just too much! Such nonsense.
This woman is not polite,
her behavior is so free and headstrong
it's made me furious for a long time.
How dare you seek to have your way!
There's a nice girl, our east-side neighbor,
named Qin Luofu.
She has a beautiful figure, without rival.
As your mother, I will ask for her for you.
Just send your other wife away,
send her fast, without delay."

---

[1] "Big Mother," literally "Big Person" (*da ren*), a title of respect, like "Your Honor"; in this context, a term for the mother-in-law.

[2] "Once we bound our hair," meaning after we came of age. Thus the term for the first wife is the "bound hair wife."

[3] Literally, the line ends "even in Yellow Springs."

The man knelt down and answered:
"I just want to let you know, mother:
if you send this woman away,
I will never marry again!"

The mother heard this
and beat the bed in fury:
"Little one, you better take care.
How dare you defend this woman!
She has already lost my favor,
and I will never approve your request!"

The man fell silent,
kowtowed to her and returned to his room.
He tried to talk to his wife
but fell sobbing and his voice failed.
"I don't want to send you away,
but my mother forces me.
Please just go home for a while,
let me report back to my office today.
I will come home again soon
and come for you to welcome you back.
Don't worry, this is my intent,
so please do as I say."

The woman replied to her man:
"Please don't go over these tangled questions.
In the past, early one spring,
I said farewell to my home and came to your honored door.
My actions always followed your parents' wishes.
I didn't dare take a step on my own.
Day and night I worked with industry,
alone and suffering terrible hardship.
I committed no offenses,
just served and tried to show gratitude.
But when even so I'm still to be sent away,
how can you talk about my return?
I have an embroidered silk jacket

so bright it shines with its own light
and red silk curtains for my bed
with scented bags hanging in the four corners,
sixty or seventy covered chests
tied with green and black silk ropes,
countless different kinds of boxes,
and within are treasures of every sort.
Since I am so humble, my belongings are also humble,
hardly good enough to serve the new woman.
But I'll leave them here in case you can give them away.
Since we will never see each other again
they might give you some comfort.
As time unfolds, don't ever forget me."

The rooster crowed and it was the crack of dawn.
The woman rose and did her makeup.
She put on her silk padded skirt,
and carefully checked herself four or five times.
She slipped a pair of silk shoes on her feet
and on her head a glowing hawksbill turtle comb,
a flowing white silk sash around her waist,
and on her ears bright moon earrings.
Her fingers were slender white scallion roots,
her lips red as if she'd sucked on cinnabar.
She walked with tiny elegant steps
with a beauty matchless in this world.
She went to the hall and kowtowed to her mother-in-law,
who listened without interrupting her:
"When I was a girl before marriage
I was brought up in the fields.
I did not have a good education
and I am sorry to have humbled your son.
I know I've received much money and silk from you,
and yet I cannot bear the way you use me.
Today I'm returning home,
and I worry you'll have too much work without me."
Then she said good-bye to her husband's little sister
while her tears rolled down like stringed pearls:

"When I first came as a young woman
you held the bed's edge in order to stand up.
But now that I am being sent away
you are just as tall as I am.
Use your heart and take care of your parents
and take care of yourself.
On the seventh and twenty-ninth[4]
don't forget how much fun we had."

She walked out and climbed into the carriage,
shedding a hundred lines of tears.
The man's horse trotted away,
and her carriage set off later.
Click-clack and rambling and rumbling,
the horse and carriage met again at a large crossroads.
Dismounting, the husband entered the carriage,
lowered his head and whispered in her ear:
"I vow I will not abandon you.
You just go home for the time being.
I must return to my office
but will come back soon.
I swear before heaven I will not forsake you."

The woman answered the clerk:
"I thank you for your concern.
If you truly hold me so near to your heart
I expect you to come soon.
You will be the rock
and I will be a reed.
Reeds can be tough as silk,
but don't let the rock move!
I have a father and many brothers
with tempers explosive as thunder.
I fear they won't let me follow my will.
The thought of it makes my heart sizzle."

---

[4] The seventh and twenty-ninth were days of rest.

They raised their hands long in farewell
two of them loving and sad, unwilling to depart.

She passed through the gate and into the hall of her home,
hesitant and feeling shame.
Her mother clapped her hands in anger:
"I never expected to see you sent back home!
I taught you how to weave at thirteen
how to tailor at fourteen
how to play the many-stringed harp at fifteen
and rules and good manners at sixteen.
I married you off at the age of seventeen
and you vowed you wouldn't be wayward.
Now what offense have you committed,
that you return home without invitation?"
But Ah Lan said, "I am sorry to humiliate you mother,
yet I really did nothing wrong,"
and then her mother felt a deep sorrow.

About ten days after her return,
the county head sent a matchmaker over, who said,
"The governor has a third son
handsome without peer.
He is only eighteen or nineteen
and he shows great eloquence and talent . . ."

The mother said to her daughter,
"You should take this offer."
But her daughter replied in tears:
"When I was coming home,
the clerk urged me again and again
and we vowed not to separate.
If I go against emotions and integrity
I'm afraid this matter will turn out badly.
Please send the messenger away,
and let's take time to talk about this matter."
The mother told the matchmaker:
"Our daughter is poor and humble,

and she was just sent home to her parents.
If she was not good as a clerk's wife,
how can she be good for your gentleman?
You should go and inquire in other houses.
I cannot give you my consent now."

After the matchmaker had been gone a few days
the governor sent over another official:
"Since people know Lan Zhi's family
has long served as government officials,
and since the fifth son of the governor
is handsome and unmarried,
I'm sent to be a matchmaker.
I talked to your local secretary
and told him about the governor
and this fine young man.
We intend to propose a marriage
so we are here at your honored door."
The mother thanked the matchmaker:
"My daughter has already made a vow;
how dare I mention it again?"

When the brother learned about this,
his heart was puzzled and annoyed.
He questioned his sister:
"Why don't you think about it carefully?
Your first marriage was only to a clerk,
but for a second marriage you could get a lord!
It's like changing earth for heaven.
It is enough to give you high status. If you don't want this
    marriage,
what are you going to do in the future?"

Lan Zhi held up her head and replied:
"You are right, brother.
I left home to serve my husband,
yet midway had to return to my brother's door.

I should follow my brother's wishes.
How should I follow my own will?
Though I have an agreement with the clerk,
there's no chance we will be together again."
And at the moment she agreed,
ready to accept this marriage.

The matchmaker rose up from the couch,
and repeatedly said yes and yes.
He returned to tell the governor:
"I took your orders and conferred with them,
the outlook seems very promising."
When the governor heard this
his heart was full and happy.
He consulted his books and astrological calendar
and said, "It is best for them to marry in this month.
The six elements are all in the right combination.
The lucky date is the thirtieth,
and today is already the twenty-seventh.
You can go and arrange the wedding."

Orders were soon given to have things prepared,
errand runners came one after another like floating clouds.
There were green peacock boats and white swan boats
with dragon banners decorating their four corners
and turning gracefully with wind,
gold wagons with jade wheels
and piebald horses prancing,
their gold saddles decorated with tassels,
a dowry of three million coins
all strung along green threads,
three hundred bolts of varied silks,
delicacies from seas and mountains of Jiao and Guang provinces,
and four or five hundred servants
crowded out from the governor's gate.

The mother said to the daughter:
"I just received the governor's letter,

they will come and take you tomorrow.
Why aren't you making your wedding dress now?
Please don't ruin the whole thing."
The daughter remained silent,
weeping with a handkerchief over her mouth,
tears coming down like torrents.
She moved her glazed table
and placed it by the front window.
With scissors and ruler in her left hand,
and gauzes and silks in her right hand
she made herself an embroidered padded skirt by morning
and by evening her silk blouse was done.
The gloomy sun was darkening out
when in grief she stepped out of the gate to weep.

The clerk heard how unexpectedly things had changed,
and asked for leave to come home.
About one mile from Lan Zhi's place,
his horse sensed his sadness and neighed.
The woman recognized the horse's whinny,
stepped into her shoes and went to see.
Looking sadly into the distance,
she knew it was her husband.
She raised her hand and beat the saddle,
lamenting with a hurt heart:
"Since you were separated from me,
things have happened unexpectedly
and nothing we wished for has turned out,
though you may not understand the reasons.
I have my parents
and my brothers who have pressured me,
promising me to another man.
And now you're here, expecting what?"

The clerk replied to the woman:
"Congratulations! Congratulations on your rise!
The rock is square and solid,
it stays put for a thousand years

but rushes are tough for just a moment,
changing between dawn and dusk.
Your life will improve day by day,
while I go alone to the Yellow Springs."
The woman said to her man,
"Why do you say things like this?
We both were forced
—you just the same as I was.
We'll meet down in the Yellow Springs.
Don't go back on what you said today!"
They held hands and then went each their own way,
returning to their homes.
Although alive, they were parted as in death
with bitterness beyond words.
They were determined to leave this world;
its ten thousand things could not pull them back.

The clerk returned to his home
and greeted his mother in the hall:
"Today's high wind is cold,
it has destroyed many trees
and heavy frost encases the orchid.[5]
Your son is sunsetting,
leaving you alone behind.
I make this bad move by my own choice;
don't complain to gods or ghosts.
I wish you a long life like rock in the South Mountain,
with all your limbs healthy and straight."

The mother heard the son's words,
her tears came down immediately.
"You are a son from a great family,
a family that has held high offices.
Do not take your life for a woman,
between the noble and the humble, love is nothing!

---

[5] The "orchid" refers to his wife, Lan Zhi, whose name means "orchid."

There is a fine lady from our east neighbor,
her beauty charms the whole city.
Your mother will seek the lady for you,
she will be yours before morning becomes evening."

The clerk kowtowed again and withdrew,
sighing and sighing in his empty bedroom
even more determined to see out his plan.
He turned his head to the door,
and felt the pressure of anxious sorrow.

That day cows lowed and horses neighed
as the newly wed woman entered the green tent.
Dark and dark, late in the evening,
quiet, so quiet, all the people settled, she said,
"My life is going to end today,
the soul will leave the body behind."
Lifting her skirt and taking off her silk shoes,
she jumped into a green pond.
When the clerk heard about this,
his heart knew she'd taken the long departure.
He walked back and forth under a tree in the courtyard,
and hanged himself from the southeast branch.

The families decided to bury them together.
They were buried by Flower Mountain.
On the east and west sides, pines and cypress were planted,
left and right, parasol trees,
branches and branches holding hands,
leaves and leaves touching each other
and in the center a pair of flying birds,
the kind called mandarin ducks.
They'd look up and sing to each other
every night till the fifth beat of the drum,
making travelers stop and listen
and widows get up at night and pace.
This is a warning to people of the future:
learn this lesson and never forget this story!

SIX DYNASTIES PERIOD

(220–589)

AFTER A REVOLT BY A SECRET SOCIETY OF DAOISTS KNOWN AS the Yellow Turbans, the Eastern Han dynasty ruled in name, but three warlords held the true power. Though the great military leader Cao Cao tried to rule through a puppet emperor, he was confronted by two powerful enemies, Liu Bei and Sunquan. In 220, Cao Cao's son proclaimed himself the emperor of the Kingdom of Wei, in 221 Liu Bei became the king of Shu, and in 229 Sunquan became the king of Wu, ushering in a period of great disorder and disunity known as the Six Dynasties Period, which stretched from the end of the Han dynasty in 220 to the reunification of China in the Sui dynasty in 589.

The Six Dynasties Period opens with the Three Kingdoms Period (220–260), as the three powerful kingdoms, the Wei, the Xu, and the Wu, each vied for military dominance. These short-lived empires soon gave way to a dizzying array of kingdoms and dynasties, none of which could manage to reunify China, with the exception of the brief Western Jin dynasty, which was overrun within decades of its founding by northern barbarians. Northern China, the traditional core of Chinese civilization, was given over to foreign rule, and the Chinese retreated to the south, beginning the period known as the Northern and Southern Kingdoms. Only with the Sui dynasty did China attain something like its former extent and glory, and although the Sui did not last long, it laid the foundation for the extraordinary cultural and economic golden age of the Tang dynasty that followed.

During the Six Dynasties Period the Han dynasty state cult of Confucius declined, Daoism developed into a full-blown religion, and Buddhism was introduced and rapidly spread throughout China.

Folk songs were popular and continued to be adapted by the literati, as they had during the Han dynasty under the direction of the Music Bureau. Literary poetry also flourished, marked by the five-character line that the Music Bureau had popularized. There were wonderful rollicking drinking songs, elegant poems of nature and of spiritual questing, and, of course, political poetry as well. Cao Cao, the ruler of the Kingdom of Wei, was a notable literary poet and patron of poetry, as were his two sons. In this tumultuous time, as J. D. Frodsham notes, "Life may not have been nasty and brutish; but it was undoubtably short. In perusing the biographies of the officials of this epoch, one is struck by the frequency with which the phrases 'executed in the marketplace,' 'permitted to strangle himself,' 'was killed by marauding soldiery,' and the like, write finish to many a career. A violent and bloody end was a commonplace of the time. . . . Small wonder then that the poetry of this period is deeply concerned with the terrors of old age and death."[1]

Perhaps it is no surprise that in an era of such upheaval, some of the finest poetry was written by Tao Qian (also called Tao Yuanming), whose work is known for its Daoist, romantic celebration of retreat from the cares of the world into nature. Tao Qian does have an aspect of what Burton Watson calls "thanatophobia, the morbid fear of death," particularly in his elegies, the coffin-puller songs, based (as Watson notes) upon "the dirges sung by the men of Han times as they pulled the hearse to the graveyard."[2] Tao Qian's poetry is known for its plain diction, spiritual and imaginative depth, and celebration of the ordinary, and its Daoist reverence for the spiritual aspect of nature deeply influenced later poets—notably Wang Wei, the great Tang dynasty poet of pastoral Buddhism.

---

[1]J. D. Frodsham and Ch'eng Hsi, *An Anthology of Chinese Verse: Han Wei Chin and the Northern and Southern Dynasties* (London: Oxford University Press, 1967), p. xxiv.

[2]Burton Watson, *Chinese Lyricism: Shih Poetry from the Second to the Twelfth Century* (New York: Columbia University Press, 1971), p. 49.

CAO CAO

(155–220)

Cao Cao, the founder of the Wei Kingdom, was an important warlord who carved his kingdom from the fragments of the Han dynasty in the north of China. He was also an important prose writer and poet whose literary reputation has grown in recent centuries. He was descended from a powerful palace eunuch, who adopted his father and left him wealth and assured political positions. Cao Cao's sons were also literary: Cao Pi (187–226), who upon his father's death accepted the abdication of the Han emperor and ruled as Emperor Wen, first emperor of the Wei dynasty, was an important poet, but he was jealous of his half brother Cao Zhi (192–232), an even more talented and imaginative poet, and kept him in isolation. Cao Cao, his sons, and the Seven Masters of the Jianan Period all made up a school of writing called the Jianan Period. A champion of literature as a Confucian rectifier in morally decadent times, Cao Cao is particularly noted for his ballad-form (*yuefu*) poems. Around twenty-two of his poems survive.

Watching the Blue Ocean

I go to the east coast cliff
to watch the blue ocean.
How vast the water's waves and waves
while widespread cliffs and isles jut up.
Trees and bushes cluster
and a hundred weeds grow rampant.
The autumn wind grieves
as billows rise one by one.
The journey of the sun and moon
starts out there in the middle.
The scintillating River of Stars
spills upward out of it.
How lucky I am to be standing here
feeling such passion I must chant this poem!

Song of Bitter Cold

> Going north up Taihang Mountain,
> how rugged and tall is the road
> twisting like goat intestines
> and ruining the wagon wheels.
> The trees are keening
> as the north wind grieves.
> A bear squats right in my path
> and tigers and leopards growl to either side.
> People are few in this valley
> and the snow swirls down heavily.
> Stretching my neck I utter a long sigh.
> I miss many people on this long journey.
> My heart is so low,
> I wish I could just return to the east,
> but the water is deep, the bridge broken,
> and I pace back and forth midway,
> confused, having lost my old road.
> Dusk and I have no place to stay
> as slowly the sun sails away.
> Both horse and rider are hungry
> as I shoulder my pack and gather firewood,
> hack ice with an axe to make porridge,
> thinking, as the song "East Mountain"[1]
> echoes, echoes in my grief.

RUAN JI

(210–263)

Ruan Ji was born in what is today Weishi County, Henan province. He was an official of the Wei dynasty, the son of Ruan

---

[1] "East Mountain": a poem from the *Book of Songs* about an official's return after a long absence.

Yu, an important official and poet. Considered one of the "Seven Sages of the Bamboo Forest" (a famed group of writers of the Wei and Jin dynasties), he had a reputation as a Daoist wild man and drunkard, and his verse is often concerned with the mystical questions that Daoism raises.

This poem is from his long and darkly cynical sequence "Chanting My Thoughts," which encodes an elliptical protest against the general turbulence of his times and against the rise of the Sima family and the gradual decline of the Cao family to whose rule he was loyal. Though not explicitly a political poet, Ruan Ji managed, like the twentieth-century Misty Poets, to express quite a bit of political content through obscure reference and poetic sleight of hand and through the satire and pessimism of many of his works. Often in China, this sort of subtlety has been an essential survival skill for poets who are also politicians and whose words may come back to haunt them when the political winds shift.

from Chanting My Thoughts

1

At night I can't fall asleep,
get up and sit to play my zither.
Through thin curtains I see bright moon
as light breeze flaps my garment.
A lonely wild goose shrieks from far wilderness;
gliding birds call in the Northern Woods.
I pace my room hoping to see what?
Alone, longing, sorrow hurts my heart.

FU XUAN

(217–278)

Fu Xuan was a poet of the Western Jin dynasty who wrote primarily in the Music Bureau style. Sixty-three of his poems survive. He was known to have been extraordinarily prolific, but most of his work has been lost. Despite being impoverished and orphaned as a child, he became rich and famous, largely because of his literary genius.

In the Chinese tradition it is common for male writers to write in a female voice. The author usually assumes the mask of a particular female character—a vain, ambitious woman, a nouveau riche, a ceremonial goddess, or a wife separated from her spouse. Rarely, however, does the male poet achieve the compelling and enlightened sympathy for the maltreatment of women that is one of the hallmarks of Fu Xuan's poetry. The devaluation of women in Chinese society rests in part on economics, and these attitudes are likely to be shared by women as well as men. As one woman from today's Sichuan province puts it, "Girls are no use. They can't inherit your house or your property. You struggle all your life, but who gets your house in the end? Your daughters all marry out and belong to someone else."[1] Such attitudes are deeply rooted in Chinese culture. As the female hero of a Six Dynasties folktale states, "My unhappy parents have six daughters but no son . . . so they have no real descendants. . . . Since we cannot work to support them, but are simply a burden to them and no use at all, the sooner we die the better."[2]

[1] W. J. F. Jenner, and Delia Davin, eds., *Chinese Lives: An Oral History of Contemporary China* (New York: Pantheon Books, 1987), p. 130.

[2] Chen Jianing, *The Core of Chinese Fiction* (Beijing: New World Press, 1990), p. 24.

To Be a Woman

It is bitter to be a woman,
the cheapest thing on earth.
A boy stands commanding in the doorway
like a god descended from the sky.
His heart hazards the four seas,
thousands of miles of wind and dust,
but no one laughs when a girl is born.
The family doesn't cherish her.
When she's a woman she hides in back rooms,
scared to look a man in the face.
They cry when she leaves home to marry—
just a brief rain, then mere clouds.
Head bowed, she tries to compose her face,
her white teeth stabbing red lips.
She bows and kneels endlessly,
even before concubines and servants.
If their love is strong as two stars
she is like a sunflower in the sun,
but when their hearts are water and fire
a hundred evils descend on her.
The years change her jade face
and her lord will find new lovers.
Once as close as body and shadow,
they will be remote as Chinese and Mongols.
Sometimes even Chinese and Mongols meet
but they'll be far as polar stars.

ZI YE

(THIRD–FOURTH CENTURIES)

The songs of "Lady Midnight," or Zi Ye, were attributed to a
young woman who lived during the Jin dynasty. The sexual frank-
ness of her work suggests that she was a singing girl (courtesan).

The *History of the Tang* states that her songs were sung with intense grief, and the music to which they were set was supposed to have been deeply plaintive.

There are 117 poems called Zi Ye poems in the great anthology of Music Bureau poems. Whether there was one woman who wrote these poems or whether the Zi Ye poems represent a whole tradition is a question that remains unresolved. Nevertheless, the set of poems creates a powerful and unified effect, and they have been imitated by great poets such as Li Bai. Their direct, punning, erotic nature carries across the centuries with undiminished fire.

Three Songs

1

At sundown I step out my front door
and see passing by—you,
your face so dazzling, hair mesmerizing,
perfume filling all the road.

2

Last night I didn't comb my hair.
Like silk it tangles down my shoulders
and curls up on my knees.
What part of me is not lovely?

3

The night is forever. I can't sleep.
The clear moon is so bright, so bright.
I almost think I hear a voice call me,
and to the empty sky, I say *Yes?*

Four Seasons Song: Spring

Spring forest flowers are so charming.
Spring birds pour out grief.
Spring winds come with exuberant love—
they lift up my silk skirt.

Four Seasons Song: Autumn

> She opens the window and sees the autumn moon,
> snuffs the candle, slips from her silk skirt.
> With a smile she parts my bed curtains,
> lifting up her body—an orchid scent swells.

LU JI

(261–303)

Lu Ji was born at the end of the Three Kingdoms Period in the state of Wu, at the family estate at Huading in the Yangtze Delta. He came from a family with a long and distinguished military tradition. His grandfather Lu Sun was a famous general who won the throne for the first emperor of Wu, for which he was awarded the title of duke and the estate at Huading. His father and two older brothers all had commands on the Northern frontier, but the weak Emperor Hao ignored Lu Ji's father's warnings of dangers from the neighboring state of Jin and lost his empire in a decisive river battle. Both of Lu Ji's brothers were killed in this battle. Lu Ji and his younger brother escaped to Huading, where they remained in virtual house arrest for ten years, devoting themselves to scholarship, poetry, and the study of Confucian and Daoist thought. At the age of twenty-nine, Lu Ji and his brother went to the Jin court and succeeded in launching themselves once again into official and military careers. In his forty-second year Lu Ji was a general for Prince Yin, who was engaged in battling his brother, Prince Yi. Because of the treachery of another general who refused to support Lu in a key battle, Lu's troops were decisively routed, and the river was choked with their bodies. His enemies denounced him to Prince Yin, and he was executed on trumped-up charges of treason. His two sons were also executed. It is said that the night before his death, Lu Ji dreamed he was confined in a carriage draped with black curtains, from which he could not escape. His last words were said to be, "Will I never hear the call of the cranes at Huading again?"

Lu was a prolific writer, but his only major work was a rhyme prose piece of literary criticism titled "The Art of Writing" (*wen fu*). Its influence on Chinese literary thought cannot be overestimated. "The Art of Writing" sets out to "comment on elegant classics and talk about how strong and weak points find their way into our writings," but it does much more than that. It is valued equally for its critical contribution and its literary merit. Its evocation of the writer's preparation and of the generation of new poems from readings of the classics culminates in a spirit journey of the imagination in which the poet summons great Daoist powers to conduct him through internal and external space and through the literary past.

"The Art of Writing" is both a cosmic treatise and an immensely practical one. From the internal journey of the imagination emerges writing in all its styles and genres, many of which Lu Ji catalogues. His *ars poetica*'s sophisticated treatment of the process of writing is its own best exemplar, embodying the virtues and qualities that it champions. In addition to questions of style and genre, Lu Ji treats the question of revision and of key words that "will whip the writing like a horse and make it gallop." In the preface he writes, "To learn writing from classics is like carving an axe handle with an axe—the model is right in your hand," and yet the relationship of the writer to works of the past is complicated: what may inspire your work will also kill what you write if you fail to "make it new." Lu Ji gives writing tips and discusses tone, high and low registers, poetic form, the "dead river" of writer's block, and the "thought wind" of inspiration. His spiritual view of the writing process is mirrored by his faith in the universal power of literature: "With heaven and earth contained in your head / nothing escapes the pen in your hand."

Written largely in rhymed verse interspersed with prose passages and in lines paired in a kind of rhetorical parallelism, rather like Western poetry's use of chiasmus, "The Art of Writing" is commonly compared with Alexander Pope's *Essay on Poetry* (and with Pope's model, the *Ars Poetica* of Horace) as a great example of literary criticism in verse. The comparison takes on particular relevance when one compares the balanced rhetoric of Pope's rhymed heroic couplets with Lu Ji's parallelism. With characteristic humility, Lu Ji doubts his ability to get at the essence of writing ("this art can't be captured by the finest words"), but this ineffable quality of writing itself expresses writing's spiritual nature. Writing can't express what writing is because it is more than itself; it is a spiritual voyage that connects impulse and action, word and music, and the self to the world.

Translating this notoriously ambiguous text poses special problems. A tortured and embattled critical commentary has built up around it, as many passages are riddles that have countless contradictory solutions. It would be possible to burden the text with footnotes; some translators have been known to produce ten lines of commentary for each line of poetry. Such valuable scholarship distracts from the poem, however, as each word or phrase becomes a trapdoor that drops you into a hypertext of criticism and linguistic exegesis. Our interest has been to chart a middle path between alternative readings and warring commentaries, to make difficult choices and produce a text that reads fluidly, fluently, and, most important, as a poem in English.

from The Art of Writing

Preface

After reading many talented writers, I have gained insights into the writing craft. The ways that words and expressions ignite meaning, varied as they are, can be analyzed and critiqued for their beauty and style. Through my own efforts I know how hard it is to write, since I always worry that my ideas fail to express their subject and my words are even further removed from insufficient ideas. The problem is easy to understand; the solution is more difficult. So I started writing this rhymed essay to comment on elegant classics and talk about how strong and weak points find their way into our writings. Someday, I hope, I will be able to capture these subtle secrets in words. To learn writing from classics is like carv-

ing an axe handle with an axe—the model is right in your
hand, but the spontaneous skills needed to carve a new cre-
ation are often beyond words. What can be said, however, is
verbalized in what follows.

1. The Impulse

A poet stands between heaven and earth
and watches the dark mystery.
To nourish myself I read the classics.
I sigh as the four seasons spin by
and the swarm of living things kindles many thoughts.
In rough autumn it hurts to see leaves stripped away,
but how tender the soft sprigs in budding spring.
Morning frost is awe in my heart,
my ambition floats with high clouds,
I devote songs to ancestors
and sing the clean fragrance of their virtue.
I roam the classics through a forest of treasures
and love their elegant balance of style and substance.
Inspired, I lay down the book I was reading
and let words pour out from my brush.

2. Meditation

At first I close my eyes. I hear nothing.
In interior space I search everywhere.
My spirit gallops to the earth's eight borders
and wings to the top of the sky.
Soon, misty and brightening like the sun about to dawn,
ideas coalesce and images ignite images.
When I drink the wine of words
and chew flowers from the Six Books,
I swim freely in the celestial river
and dive into the sea's abyss.
Sometimes words come hard, they resist me
till I pluck them from deep water like hooked fish;

sometimes they are birds soaring out of a cloud
that fall right into place, shot with arrows,
and I harvest lines neglected for a hundred generations,
rhymes unheard for a thousand years.
I won't touch a flower already in morning bloom
but quicken the unopened evening buds.
In a blink I see today and the past,
put out my hand and touch all the seas.

3. Process

Search for the words and sphere of thought,
then seek the proper order;
release their shining forms
and tap images to hear how they sing.
Now leaves grow along a branching thought.
Now trace a current to its source.
Bring the hidden into light
or form the complex from simplicity.
Animals shake at the tiger's changing pattern
and birds ripple off when a dragon is seen;
some words belong together
and others don't join, like jagged teeth,
but when you're clear and calm
your spirit finds true words.
With heaven and earth contained in your head
nothing escapes the pen in your hand.
It's hard to get started at first,
painful like talking with cracked lips,
but words will flow with ink in the end.
Essence holds content as the trunk lifts the tree;
language is patterned into branches, leaves, and fruit.
Now words and content match
like your mood and face—
smile when you're happy
or sigh when your heart hurts.
Sometimes you can improvise easily.
Sometimes you only bite the brush and think.

4. The Joy of Words

Writing is joy
so saints and scholars all pursue it.
A writer makes new life in the void,
knocks on silence to make a sound,
binds space and time on a sheet of silk
and pours out a river from an inch-sized heart.
As words give birth to words
and thoughts arouse deeper thoughts,
they smell like flowers giving off scent,
spread like green leaves in spring,
a long wind comes, whirls into a tornado of ideas,
and clouds rise from the writing-brush forest.

9. The Riding Crop

Sometimes your writing is a lush web of fine thoughts
that undercut each other and muffle the theme:
when you reach the pole there's nowhere else to go;
more becomes less if you try to craft what's made.
A powerful phrase at the crucial point
will whip the writing like a horse and make it gallop;
though all the other words are in place
they wait for the crop to run a good race.
A whip is always more help than harm;
stop revising when you've got it right.

10. Making It New

Perhaps thoughts and words blend together
into a lucid beauty, a lush growth;
they flame like a bright brocade,
poignant as a string orchestra.
But if you fail to make it new
you can only repeat the past.

Even when your own heart is your loom
someone may have woven that textile before,
and to be honorable and keep integrity
you must disown it despite your love.

11. Ordinary and Sublime

Flowering forth, a tall rice ear
stands proudly above the mass,
a shape eluding its shadow,
its sound refusing echoes.
The best line is a towering crag.
It won't be woven into an ordinary song.
The mind can't find a match for it
but casts about, unwilling to give up.
After all, jade in rock makes a mountain shimmer,
pearls in water make the river seductive,
green kingfishers give life
even to the ragged thornbrush,
and classic and folk songs
blend into a fine contrast.

18. The Well-Wrought Urn

My heart respects conventional rules
and laws of composition.
I recall the great works of old masters
and see how my contemporaries have failed—
poems from the depth of a wise heart
may be laughed at by those who are blind.
Poems fine as jade filigree and coral
are common as beans on the plain,
endless like air in the world's great bellows,
eternal as the universe;
they grow everywhere
but my small hands hold only a few.

My water jar is often empty. It makes me worry.
I make myself sick trying to expand my pieces.
I limp along with short poems
and patch up my songs with common notes.
I'm never happy with what I've done,
so how can my heart be satisfied?
Tap my work: I fear it clunks like a dusty earthen bowl
and I'm shamed by the song of musical jade.

19. Inspiration

As to the flash of inspiration
and traffic laws on writing's path,
what comes can't be stopped,
what leaves will not be restrained.
It hides like fire in a coal
then flares into a shout.
When instinct is swift as a horse
no tangle of thoughts will hold it back:
a thought wind rises in your chest,
a river of words pours out from your mouth,
and so many burgeoning leaves sprout
on the silk from your brush,
that colors brim out of your eyes
and music echoes in your ears.

20. Writer's Block

But when the six emotions are stagnant,
the will travels but the spirit stays put,
a petrified and withered tree,
hollow and dry as a dead river.
Then you must excavate your own soul,
search yourself till your spirit is refreshed.
But the mind gets darker and darker
and you must pull ideas like silk from their cocoon.

Sometimes you labor hard and build regrets
then dash off a flawless gem.
Though this thing comes out of me,
I can't master it with strength.
I often stroke my empty chest and sigh:
what blocks and what opens this road?

21. The Power of a Poem

The function of literature is
to express the nature of nature.
It can't be barred as it travels space
and boats across one hundred million years.
Gazing to the fore, I leave models for people to come;
looking aft, I learn from my ancestors.
It can save teetering governments and weak armies;
it gives voice to the dying wind of human virtue.
No matter how far, this road will take you there;
it will express the subtlest point.
It waters the heart like clouds and rain,
and shifts form like a changeable spirit.
Inscribed on metal and stone, it spreads virtue.
Flowing with pipes and strings, each day the poem is new.

PAN YUE

(247–300)

Pan Yue, along with Lu Ji, was among the finest poets of his time,
but only twenty of his poems have survived the centuries. He was
born in today's Henan province to a family of officials, and he
himself held a succession of important official posts. As legend
has it, his extraordinary beauty was such that he was mobbed by
crowds of women when driving through the streets of the capital.
His involvement in a political scheme against the crown prince

led to his execution in 300. His three poems to his dead wife are
his most famous works, though he was also renowned as a writer
of rhyme prose (*fu*).

In Memory of My Dead Wife*

Slowly winter and spring fade away;
cold and heat suddenly flow and change.
She has returned to the underground spring,
separated forever from me by heavy soil.
Secretly I want to join her there, but I can't,
so what is the use?
I'll obey the imperial order
and return to my old official position.
Yet seeing our house I remember her.
Our life together haunts the four rooms.
I cannot find her behind the curtains or drapery,
only her ink calligraphy.
Her fragrance lingers,
her things still hang on the walls.
In a trance I sometimes feel her presence.
It hurts to return to my senses.
We were a pair of birds nesting in the woods.
One woke in the morning to find himself alone.
We were a pair of fish swimming eye to eye.
Halfway one found the other gone.
Spring wind sneaks in through a gap in the door.
The eaves weep a morning flow in the gutter.
I can't forget her, trying to sleep in our bed.
My sorrow piles deeper each day.
I hope this grief will fade till like Zhuangzi after his wife died
I can beat on a jug and sing.[1]

---

*According to ancient regulations, an official should remain in mourning for
his wife for a year before starting to work again. This poem was written when
the mourning period was just over.

[1] The Daoist sage Zhuangzi had a very unconventional understanding of
death—that it could be a good thing in disguise. When his wife died, he did
not mourn; instead he sang a song while beating a jar with a stick.

TAO QIAN

(C. 365–427)

Daoist poet Tao Qian (also known as Tao Yuanming) is famous for his prose "Preface to the Poem on the Peach Blossom Spring" and for his remarkable poems celebrating a return to nature and an epicurean love of wine. He lived during the politically unstable Six Dynasties Period (220–589), and his work expresses the anxiety and weariness of that time. He held a succession of official posts, working as a military adviser and a magistrate, but he was unsatisfied with this life and retired to the country, where he lived out his remaining years as a farmer. His work reflects this life: he is primarily known as a poet of nature, China's first great landscape poet, contrasting nature's purity and simplicity (exemplified by his own self-representation as a farmer-sage) with the "dusty" world of the court and the marketplace: "After all those years like a beast in a cage / I've come back to the soil again." Like Thoreau in his beanfield, Tao Qian became the quintessential model of the official who has escaped "the world's net" for a life closer to spiritual values. While countless later poets (notably Wang Wei) echo his lines when they write about the country life, Tao Qian was not appreciated in his own time. The dominant mode of poetry in his day was flowery and artificial. The great poets of the Tang and Song dynasties, however, came to treasure Tao's poetry for its measured simplicity, its lack of adornment, and its conscious use of common words. Approximately 130 of his poems survive.

Return to My Country Home

(Five Poems)

I

When young I couldn't bear the common taste,
I loved the mountains and the peaks,
yet I fell into the world's net

and wasted thirteen years.
But trapped birds long for their old woods
and fish in the pool still need deep waters,
so I'm breaking earth in the south field,
returning to the country to live simply,
with just ten acres
and a thatch roof over some rooms.
Elm and willow shade the back eaves,
rows of peach and plum trees by the front hall.
A distant village lost in haze;
smoke twines from neighbors' houses.
From deep in the lanes, dogs bark;
a cock chuckles high up in a mulberry tree.
No dust or clutter within my courtyard door,
just empty rooms and time to spare.
After all those years like a beast in a cage
I've come back to the soil again.

2

No social events in the fields,
no carriage wheels whir through these back roads.
Bright sun, but I close my cane door
and empty myself in empty rooms.

Sometimes I meet the peasants
going here and there in palm-leaf raincoats,
but we speak of nothing
except how the crops are doing.

Each day my hemp and mulberries grow taller
and my land gets wider every day
but at any time the frost or hail
could beat them flat as a field of weeds.

3

I plant beans under South Mountain.
The weeds flourish but not bean sprouts.
Morning, I get up to weed the fields.

I return, shouldering the moon and my hoe.
On narrow paths through thick grass and brush,
evening dew soaks my clothes,
but wet clothes don't bother me
so long as I follow my heart.

4

After so long away from these mountains and lakes,
today I'm wildly pleased in the woods and fields.
Now nephews and nieces hold my hands
as we part brush and enter the wild ruin of a town.

We search through hills and grave mounds
and the lingering signs of ancient houses,
scattered wells and traces of hearths,
rotten stumps of bamboo and mulberry groves.

I ask a man gathering wood here,
"What happened to all these people?"
The woodsman turns to me and says
"They're dead, that's all, there's not one left!"

In thirty years, at court or market, all things change.
I know now these are not empty words,
that we live among shadows and ghosts
and return at last to nothingness.

5

I was upset, walking home alone with my staff,
zigzag through brush and weeds
and by a mountain brook clear and shallow,
just deep enough to wash my feet,
but now I filter the new-made wine
and cook a chicken to entertain neighbors;
the room darkens as the sun sets,
we use firewood as bright candles,
all is joy, the night seems too short,
and it's dawn before we know it.

Begging for Food

Hunger came and drove me on,
though I didn't know where to go,
walking, walking till I hit a village.
I knocked on a door, short for words,
but the owner of the house saw my need,
gave me aid, didn't let me come for nothing.
We talked in harmony till sunset,
raised cups and drained them dry.
Happy to have a new friend,
I improvise this poem.
I'm moved that you treated me like the washerwoman
who fed Han Xin,[1] and wish I were as talented as him.
Deep in my heart I know how to thank you:
I will repay you after death.

I Stop Drinking

My home is where the town stops.
Carefree and alone, I stop then walk
then stop and sit in the shade of tall trees.
My path stops within my brushwood gate.
The best taste is to stopper my mouth with garden vegetables.
My greatest joy stops with my youngest son.
All my life I have not stopped drinking.
I'm never happy when I stop.
If I stop at night I cannot sleep well;
if I stop in the morning, I cannot get up.
Every day I tried to stop drinking,

---

[1] Refers to the story of Han Xin in the "Historical Records" by Sima Qian. Han Xin was very poor when he was young. While he was fishing, an old woman washing clothes noticed his hunger and provided him with food. When Han Xin became the king of Chu, he looked for the old woman and gave her a thousand pieces of gold. After the old woman's death, he had her buried in a position in symmetry with that of his mother.

but my energy flow stopped and became disordered.
I only knew that abstinence stops pleasure
without knowing that to stop has benefits.
Now I truly realize how good it is to stop drinking,
and am really going to stop this morning.
I will stop from now on,
till I reach the Isle of Immortals where the sun stops
till my old face stops and a clear face returns.
I won't be satisfied till I've stopped for ten thousand years.

Drinking Alone When It Rains Day After Day

All creatures start and end in death.
Since ancient times this has been true.
It's said there were immortals like Song and Qiao,[1]
but where are they now?
An old man gives me a present of wine
and says drink will make me live forever.
A few sips and one hundred emotions recede.
More cups and I forget the heavens.
Have the heavens really dissolved in this?
Let me be as natural as nature, and nature as natural as me.
The cranes in clouds have amazing wings;
in a flash they touch the universe's eight corners.
Since I embraced my own true nature
I have worked for forty years
and long ago transformed my body,
but my mind still exists, and what else is there to say?

---

[1] Song refers to Chi Songzi (Red Pine), the legendary Rain Master who worked for the sage-king Shen Nong in ancient times, and Qiao refers to Wang Ziqiao, a prince who practiced on Song Mountain to become an immortal. Both of them supposedly achieved immortality.

Scolding My Kids

> My hair is gray on both sides,
> my muscles and skin no longer firm.
> Though I have five sons,
> none of them is fond of ink brushes and paper.
> Ah Shu is twice eight years old;
> no one can match his laziness.
> Ah Xuan is the age to be devoted to study
> yet does not like writing at all.
> Yong and Duan are both thirteen;
> they cannot tell six from seven.
> The youngest son Tong is almost nine
> and only cares to scrounge for pears and nuts.
> Since that is what heaven decrees for me,
> let me finish the thing in my cup!

Fire in the Sixth Month in 408 CE

I had my thatched cottage built in a poor lane,
willing to give up elegant carriages,
but in June a long violent wind rushed
and woods and cottage caught fire in a second.
My house went up, all rooms gone,
so I live in twin boats moored in shade by the gate.
Vast is the night sky of a new autumn.
Soon the moon will be high and round.
Fruit and vegetables have come back to life,
but the startled birds haven't yet returned.
At midnight I stand still and let my thoughts roam;
with one glance they travel nine heavens.
Since I tied my hair up as a teen, I've stuck to my own path.
Now I'm already past forty.
My body changed according to the law of nature,
while my spirit house remained solitary and unused,
true to its own inner nature.
Jade and stone cannot match that firmness.

I look up at the sky and recall the time of King Donghu,[1]
when surplus food was left in the fields.
With stomachs filled, people had no worries,
rising in the morning, coming home at night to sleep.
Since I was not born in such days,
let me just water my own garden.

from Twenty Poems on Drinking Wine

Introduction

I live a retired life with little joy,
and worse, the nights are lengthening.
Occasionally I get hold of some famous liquor,
and I drink every evening,
gazing at my shadow, soaking up what's in my cup.
Without knowing it I get drunk again
and since I'm already drunk,
I often write a few lines to make myself happy.
The sheets of inked paper have accumulated,
never put together in any order,
so I asked my friends to make a neat copy
to let all of us have some fun.

5

I built my hut near people
yet never hear carriage or horse.
"How can that be?" you ask.
Since my heart is a wilderness, the world fades.
Gathering chrysanthemum by the east fence,
my lazy eyes meet South Mountain.

---

[1] Donghu refers to Donghu Jizi, a legendary king who lived in ancient times. It is said that during his reign times were so good that food was in abundance and one could leave one's things lying about on the roadside and no one would bother them.

Mountain air is clean at twilight
as birds soar homeward wing to wing.
Beneath these things a revelation hides,
but it dies on the tongue when I try to speak.

9

Early this morning I heard someone knock,
and rushed to the door with my clothes upside down.
I called out, "Who's there?"
A kindhearted old farmer
bringing me a pot of wine from far away.
He thought I was not moving with the times.
"To stand under thatched eaves in rags—
that is not the high branch where you should nest.
All the world is moving in the same direction.
Please go with the muddy flow."
I was deeply touched by the villager's words,
but by nature I'm in harmony with no one.
Though it's true I can learn to turn my wagon around,
won't I be lost if I act against my nature?
Let's just enjoy this wine.
My wagon will not turn around!

14

Old friends appreciate my pastime
and come with a pot of wine.
We sit on strewn rushes under a pine tree.
A few rounds later we are drunk.
Old people start babbling,
confusing the toast order.
When oblivious to your own existence,
how can you know what things to value?
If you are so long attached to things,
how can you know the taste of wine is deep?

Elegies

(Three Poems)

1

There is life and there must be death.
Early death does not mean life is rushing.
Last night I still was a human being;
this morning I'm in the book of ghosts.
Where is the soul after its dispersal?
Only my dry corpse is trusted to the coffin.
Little sons are crying for their father,
good friends touch me and weep.
I will never again know gain, loss,
or the right, wrong, of the human world.
After a thousand autumns,
who can tell glory from disgrace?
I regret only one thing:
I didn't drink enough when I had breath.

2

In the past I had no wine to drink;
now the cup is filled in vain.
Foam rises on the surface of spring wine.
When can I taste it again?
A table of food is laid out before me.
Family and friends cry by my side.
No sound comes when I try to speak.
No light in my eyes when I try to look.
I slept in a hall last night.
Now I sleep in the country of weeds.
One day I left my house,
and on no day can I come back.

3

Wild grasses are vast and boundless
and white poplars rustle in wind.
Heavy frost comes in mid-October,

when I am carried off to a far neighborhood.
There is no one living around me,
only tombs stand tall.
Horses neigh up to the sky
and wind is whining for me.
After the dark chamber is closed,
I won't see sun for thousands of years.
No sun for thousands of years,
and even a wise man can't help it.
All the people who carried me here
return now to their homes.
Relatives may still have leftover sorrow,
but others are already singing.
Dead and gone, what can I say?
I just trust my body to the mountains.

SU XIAOXIAO

(LATE FIFTH CENTURY)

Su Xiaoxiao, also known as Su Xiaojun, came from Qiantang
and was the sister of Su Pannu. She lived during the Southern
Song dynasty, which was centered in Hangzhou in the Northern
and Southern Dynasties Period of 420–589 (not to be confused
with the later Southern Song dynasty 1127–1279). She was a
well-known singing girl (courtesan), reputed to be beautiful, tal-
ented, and affectionate. Her poems can be found in *Flowers and
Grass Selection* (*huacao cuibian*), vol. II, as well as in *Complete
Song Lyric Songs* (*quan songci*). Her poem "The Song of the
West Tomb" became extremely famous and was the inspiration
for many future poems. Su Xiaoxiao herself became the subject
of many later literary works (see, for example, Li He's poem "Su
Xiaoxiao's Tomb"). "The Song of the West Tomb" appears in a
collection of Music Bureau poems (*yuefu shiji*) under the title of
"Song of Su Xiaoxiao," and though she is sometimes considered
more of a literary character than a real historical figure, tombs

associated with her are found by the West Lake in Hangzhou and
elsewhere.

Emotions on Being Apart

Thousands of miles off, behind countless mountain passes,
you make me grieve.
Do you even know that?
Since you left
I've counted the leftover days in winter, waited out spring.
Still not one word.
All the flowers have bloomed
and you are still gone.

The Song of the West Tomb

I ride in an oil-paper carriage,
you ride a black steed.
Where are we going to tie our heart knot?
Under the cypress at the West Tomb.

To the Tune of "Butterflies Adore Flowers"

I live by the Qiantang River.
Flowers fall, bloom again, but I don't care about flowing years.
Swallows have carried spring off in their beaks.
A few yellow plum blossoms shower my gauze window.

With a slant unicorn comb in my half-loosened hair
I gently play my hardwood clappers
and sing about gold thread,
about my dream interrupted, colorful clouds nowhere to be found,
a bright moon deep in the night emerging over the south river
    mouth.

BAO ZHAO

(C. 414–466)

Bao Zhao was born in Donghai (modern Changshu, Jiangsu province) to a family of poor gentry. Though he didn't have access to a high official career, he held a post as a magistrate. He was murdered by mutinous soldiers while in military service to the prince of Linhai. His "Rhyme Prose on the Desolate City" is one of his most famous works; in it, he meditates on the ruined city of Guangling, which he visited after the revolt of 459 in which a feudal lord raised a rebellion but found his armies crushed, the city leveled, and more than three thousand inhabitants massacred. Bao Zhao's literary talent earned him patrons, and he is considered the most important poet who wrote in the *yuefu* form in the Six Dynasties Period. His literary influence extends into the Tang dynasty and was particularly important to the work of Li Bai and Du Fu. Of his Music Bureau poems, his "Variations on 'The Weary Road'" sequence is the most celebrated and imitated.

from Variations on "The Weary Road"

5

Don't you see how grass on the riverbank
in winter withers and dies, yet in spring floods the road?
Don't you see how the sun above the walls
evaporates to nothing at dusk
yet tomorrow at dawn is reborn?
But how can we achieve that?
When dead we're dead forever, down in Yellow Springs.
Life has lavish bitterness, is stingy with joy,
and only the young are filled with endless zeal.
So let's just meet whenever we can
and always keep wine money ready by our beds.

Who cares for rank and fame inscribed on bamboo and silk?
Life, death, acclaim, obscurity—leave them to heaven.

6

Facing the table I have no appetite,
draw my sword and hack at a pillar. Then I sigh long.
Life in this world is so brief.
How can I take small steps with drooping wings?
No, I'll give up my official position
and return home to relax.
I said good-bye to my family just this morning,
and in the evening I'm already back.
I play with my son by the bed,
and watch my wife working the loom.
Since ancient times sages have been poor and humble,
especially when like me they are shut out and speak too much.

On the Departure of Official Fu

You—a light swan goose, playing by a riverside,
me—an isolated wild goose nesting on a shoal.
A chance meeting brought us close,
and we couldn't stop missing each other.
But as wind and rains travel east or west,
our separation is instantly thousands of miles.
Recalling the time when we nested there,
my heart fills with your face and voice.
The setting sun makes the river and shoals cold
as sad clouds wrap up the sky.
My wings are too short to soar—
I can only circle around in the mist.

BAO LINGHUI

(FL. C. 464)

Bao Linghui was the younger sister of Bao Zhao (c. 414–466). Six of her poems survive because they were included in a compilation of Bao Zhao's works. Although little is known of her life, Zhong Rong (469–518) writes of her in his work of literary criticism *Poetry Gradings*: "Linghui's songs and poems often stand out and are pure and well made. Her poems in imitation of the ancient style are particularly good."[1]

Sending a Book to a Traveler After Making an Inscription

Since you left,
I never smile by the window,
clubs to beat clothes clean are still at night,
and the high gates are closed all day.
Fireflies swim in the fine net.
Purple orchid blooms in the courtyard.
In dry poplar leaves I see the seasons change.
When wild geese return I know your journey's cold.
You'll roam until late winter ends,
but I expect you back by spring.

PRINCESS CHEN LECHANG

(SIXTH CENTURY)

The story of Six Dynasties Period Princess Chen Lechang, as told in Meng Qi's Song dynasty compilation *Poetry Stories*, goes like

---

[1] Kang-I Sun Chang and Haun Saussy, eds., *Women Writers of Traditional China: An Anthology of Poetry and Criticism* (Stanford, California: Stanford University Press, 1999), p. 720.

this: "A man named Xu Deyan married Princess Chen Lechang. When the Country of Chen was on the verge of being conquered, the man told his wife: 'When the country falls, you will certainly be taken into a powerful man's house. If your love for me doesn't die, I hope we will have the chance to be together again.' So, the lovers broke a mirror into two halves and promised to sell their mirror halves at the capital's market on the 15th of January in an attempt to meet again. Eventually, Chen was overrun and Princess Lechang was taken to be the woman of Yang Su, a duke from the country of Yue. Xu wrote a poem:

> The mirror and the person are gone.
> The mirror returns. The person doesn't.
> I don't see the Moon Lady's shadow,
> Bright and empty moonlight lingers.

The princess received this poem and wept without end. When Yang Su learned of this, he sent for Xu Deyan in order to return his wife. But first he ordered Princess Lechang to write a poem about this situation." The poem that follows is the poem she wrote.

Letting My Feelings Go at the Farewell Banquet

> I feel so frantic today.
> New husband faces old
> and I don't dare laugh or cry.
> How hard it is to be a woman.

TANG DYNASTY

(618–907)

THE TANG DYNASTY WAS CHINA'S GOLDEN AGE, A TIME OF extraordinary achievement in science, medicine, art, music, and calligraphy. But the Tang is especially known for the amazing number of poets it produced from every walk of life and for the extremely high level of achievement of these poets. Tang poetry is particularly famed for its "regulated verse" (*lu shi*), though wonderful verse was written in other forms as well. The Tang represents the apex of Chinese poetry, a time when all the verse forms of the past were practiced and their uses extended as variations on them as well as wholly new forms were developed. In the words of Liu Wu-chi, "Tang China, like Elizabethan England, was virtually a nation of singing birds." The Qing dynasty collection *The Complete Anthology of Tang Poetry* contains more than fifty thousand poems by more than two thousand poets.

While Tang poetry opened itself up to a wider range of themes and emotions than had been explored in previous dynasties, much of Tang poetry is of the occasional sort, written to celebrate a meeting or event or to mark a separation from a friend. According to Burton Watson, "The Chinese, aware that profundity and originality are hardly to be expected in such conditions, have usually been content to settle for grace and technical skill in place of greatness. . . . Verse has been for many Chinese writers the medium for recording not only life's moments of intense feeling and conviction, but the countless minor events and scenes of everyday existence as well. They have used it as writers of other cultures have used the diary, the autobiography, or the sketchbook. . . ." [1]

---

[1]Burton Watson, *Chinese Lyricism: Shih Poetry from the Second to the Twelfth Century* (New York: Columbia University Press, 1971), p. 139.

It took a while for Tang poetry to reach its height, and the poetry of the Early Tang (the seventh century) was typically less innovative than later work. It has been accused of being overly mannered and ornate and imitative of the worst aspects of the Six Dynasties and Sui dynasty styles. Although the Tang was a period of great wealth and stability, particularly the Early Tang, it was the poets who suffered through the An Lushan Rebellion and other disasters in the declining years of the dynasty who truly opened up Chinese poetry to the world. The social commentary and narrative abilities of such poets as Bai Juyi and Du Fu give their work great pathos and emotion.

The High Tang (713–765), represented by the three giants of the Tang, Li Bai, Du Fu, and Wang Wei, was the period of the greatest accomplishment in Chinese poetry. This period largely overlaps with the ill-fated reign of the Tang emperor Xuangzong (685–762, ruled 713–756). Xuangzong was among China's greatest emperors, but he neglected his rule once he met the famous beauty Yang Guifei and took her to be his concubine. Worse, Yang Guifei's adopted son, An Lushan, a Turkic general, led a rebellion in 755 that devastated the empire and sent many of the poets of this period into exile. Yang and her brother, the prime minister, were blamed and killed, and later Xuangzong abdicated the throne. The story is beautifully recounted in Bai Juyi's long poem *Song of Everlasting Sorrow*.

Later Tang poetry declined in quality, becoming at times shrill and pessimistic, probably in response to the uncertainty of life in the twilight of the dynasty, but wonderful poets wrote at this time as well. Li He and Li Shangyin wrote poetry the likes of which China had never seen before, ghostly, obscure, strange, and extraordinary. One of the finest poets of the Tang was the last Tang emperor, Li Yu, who wrote marvelous poems in a new form of song (*ci* poetry) intended to be performed by singing girls. Though such lyrics were most often a kind of erotic boudoir poetry, Li Yu marvelously extended the uses of the form, using it to sing about the sorrows of losing his kingdom. In the Song dynasty that followed the Tang, this form of lyric poetry came to be the dominant form, in which the finest work was written.

WANG BO

(649–676)

Wang Bo, together with Yang Jiong, Lu Zhaolin, and Luo Bin-
wang, was one of the "Four Eminent Men of the Early Tang
Dynasty," a group of poets from two generations who moved
past the conventional forms and images of early Tang court
poetry (in which individuality and emotion were submerged to
craft). Wang Bo is also admired as a master of ornate, rhymed,
rhetorically structured prose. Born in what is today Shanxi
province, he was considered a child genius and was presented to
the emperor, whereupon he was taken into the service of a prince.
Despite this auspicious beginning, he did not become a major
official. The emperor took offense at a spoof Wang wrote about a
cockfight and had him dismissed from his post in the capital. He
became a minor provincial official and was convicted of murder-
ing a slave girl he had helped escape from prison, sentenced to
death, and later granted amnesty. He died, probably by drown-
ing, on a trip to Vietnam, where his father had been exiled after
Wang's arrest.

On the Wind

It shushes, shushes, and a cold landscape forms
as coolness clarifies woods and valley,
it chases smoke, seeks out the gate of a ravine,
carries mist out of mountain columns,
comes and goes and leaves no trace,
moves and pauses as if with emotion,
as sun dies and mountain water quiets
it makes pines sing in waves for you.

HE ZHIZHANG

(659–744)

He Zhizhang came from Yuezhou-Yongxing (in what is today Xiaoshan County, in Zhejiang province). He was one of a group of poets from the Lower Yangtze Basin known as the "Four Scholars from Wuzhong" that included Zhang Ruoxu (whose work is also included in this volume), Zhang Xu, and Bao Rong. A career politician, He Zhizhang retired from politics at age eighty-five to become a Daoist hermit near Lake Jinghu in Zhejiang province. He was a great friend of Li Bai and in fact gave him the appellation "Banished Immortal." He was himself called one of the "Eight Immortals of the Winecup" by Du Fu, and his idiosyncrasies earned him the name "Crazy Zhang." Known for his openhearted love of the lower classes and for his freethinking, he is presented in later Daoist tales as a man who achieved immortality. Only nineteen of his poems remain.

Willow

> Green jade decorates a tall tree,
> thousands of emerald ribbons hanging down.
> Who cut those tiny leaves so fine?
> The March wind like scissors.

ZHANG RUOXU

(C. 660–C. 720)

Little is known about Zhang Ruoxu. Along with He Zhizhang he achieved fame as one of a group of four poets from the Lower Yangtze Basin known as the "Four Scholars from Wuzhong." Only two of his poems survive. On the basis of one of them,

"Spring, River, and Flowers on a Moonlit Night," he has become
a famous poet.

Spring, River, and Flowers on a Moonlit Night

> The tide in the spring river meets the flat ocean.
> On the sea a bright moon is born from the tide
> and shimmers waves for thousands of miles.
> Nowhere on the spring river is without bright moon.
>
> The river meanders through fragrant fields
> and in the flowering woods moon makes everything snow,
> until even frost flowing in space is invisible
> and on the shores white sands disappear in light.
>
> River and sky merge in one dustless color.
> Bright, bright sky, with only the moon's wheel.
> Who first saw the moon on this riverbank?
> What year did this river moon first shine on men?
>
> Generations keep passing without end,
> but the river moon looks the same year after year.
> I don't know for whom the river moon is waiting;
> I only see the long river seeing off the flowing water.
>
> One scarf of white cloud fades into distance,
> leaving unbearable sorrow in the estuary's green maples.
> Whose husband is drifting away in a flatboat tonight?
> Who is missing her lover in a moonlit tower?
>
> What a pity, the moon wandering through the tower;
> it should light the mirror stand of the traveler.
> She cannot roll it up in the jade door's blinds,
> or wipe it from the rock where she beats clothes clean.[1]

---

[1] Traditionally, Chinese women wash clothes by a stream or river by beating
them on a rock with a wooden club. In Chinese poetry the sound of beating
clothes is typically associated with homesickness.

At this moment, they see the same moon, but cannot hear each
   other.
She wishes she could flow with the moonlight onto him.
The wild goose flying off cannot escape this light.
When fish and dragons leap and dive I read patterns in the waves.

Last night she dreamed of fallen petals in a still pool;
what sorrow: with spring half over, the man hasn't returned.
The current has almost washed the spring away
and the setting moon tilts west again in the river pool.

The slanting moon sinks deep, deep into the sea fog.
Between Brown Rock and the Xiang River is a long way
and I don't know how many people ride the moonlight home.
The setting moon fills the river trees with shivering emotion.

MENG HAORAN

(689–740)

Meng Haoran came from present-day Hubei province. He lived
for a time as a recluse at Deer Gate Mountain after failing to pass
the official examinations. Though he was older than such great
poets of the Tang dynasty as Wang Wei and Li Bai, he was their
friend and was himself considered a supremely successful poet.
Despite his failure to pass the imperial exam and become an offi-
cial, he made friends with other major poets of the High Tang
period during his visit to the capital to take the test. Some years
later he was hired to be the assistant to the writer-official Zhang
Jiuling, but he retired from the appointment within the year. He
is well known for his nature poems and for his poems of recluse,
and for the personality that suffuses his poetry.

Parting from Wang Wei

I'm lonely alone, expecting whom?
Each morning I return empty, lone.
I'm ready to go looking for fragrant grass,
but lament this parting, old friend.
On the Way who will help me?
It's rare to find a soul mate
so I should guard my solitude,
just go home and close the gate.

Spring Dawn

Sleeping in spring, I don't feel the dawn
though everywhere birds are singing.
Last night I heard sounds, blowing, raining.
How many flowers have fallen down?

Spending the Night on Jiande River

I moor my boat by the misty shore.
Sunset renews the wanderer's sorrow.
A plain so vast the sky dwarfs trees.
Clear river water brings the moon close.

WANG CHANGLING

(C. 690–C. 756)

Wang Changling was born in Changan, the Tang dynasty capital.
Though he passed the imperial examinations, he served only in
minor posts. He was, however, considered to be the premier poet
of his time and was well represented in anthologies. Banished to
Guangdong in 728, he was later murdered during the An Lushan

Rebellion. His poetics center on an aesthetic of intense focus, and his work was praised for its vitality and zest. Although his critical work, *Definitions of Poetry*, was lost in China, the Japanese monk Kukai quoted extensively from it, thus preserving his thoughts on aesthetics.

Song from the Borders

> Crossing the autumn river I let my horse drink.
> The water's cold, wind a sharp blade.
> Sun is not yet sunk on the sand horizon
> and in the darkening distance I see Lintao
> where we fought near the Great Wall,
> filled with high morale.
> Now yellow dust fills present and past.
> White bones lie chaotic in the weeds.

WANG WAN

(693–751)

Wang Wan was the police chief of Luoyang, the city of his birth, in present-day Henan province. His work appears in the famous anthology *300 Poems of the Tang Dynasty*, but most of it has been lost.

Stopping at Beigu Mountain

> Man on a road through green mountains.
> A boat sails the green waters.
>
> The banks grow when the tide stills.
> One sail taut in the wind.

The ocean sun emerges from broken night.
Spring flows in rivers as the year ages.

How can my letter find its way home
to Luoyang where the geese fly?

WANG WEI

(701–761)

Wang Wei is considered, with Du Fu and Li Bai, one of the three
greatest poets of the Tang dynasty. He was also a talented musi-
cian and a famous landscape painter who founded the Southern
school of landscape painters. The central conflict in Wang Wei's
life was between his career as a successful official and his devo-
tion to Daoism and Chan Buddhism. Born Wang Mojie, he took
the courtesy name Wei; the two names together (Wei Mojie) make
up the Chinese transliteration of the Buddhist saint Vimalakirti,
who affirmed the lay practice of Buddhism. Many of Wang Wei's
poems express his desire to retreat from the "dusty, busy" world
of the court to his estate at Wang River, the setting for his famous
Wang River sequence of poems, whose almost purely objective
landscape descriptions are subtly infused with a Buddhist con-
sciousness or, more accurately, lack of consciousness. Wang Wei's
poems often allude to Tao Qian (c. 365–427), whose own her-
metic retreat was a model for future poets. Of all Chinese poets,
Wang Wei is the one who comes closest to Zhuangzi's description
of the perfect man: "Be empty, that is all. The Perfect Man uses
his mind like a mirror—going after nothing, welcoming nothing,
responding but not storing." One of his most famous poems
begins with "the empty mountain" as the landscape symbol for
the annihilation of consciousness: "Nobody in sight on the empty
mountain." Yet Wang Wei always keeps one foot in the real
world, and with simplicity, an accurate eye, and piercing social
judgment, he portrays the military, the court, the rebellious
Daoist drunkard, and the lonely rooms of women whose hus-

bands are fighting on the Northern frontier. His poems work with few words, often treating traditional themes, yet the mind behind these words is so fresh and authentic that each simple line takes on the quality of originality, of having been uttered on the first morning of speech. His poems are often described as spoken paintings, his paintings as silent poems. As Robert Payne observes, he "can evoke a whole landscape in a single line."

Born in what is today Shanxi province, Wang Wei passed the imperial examinations in 721. He had a series of appointments of increasing importance in Changan, the Tang dynasty capital, from assistant director of the Imperial Music Office to right assistant director of the Department of State Affairs, his most important post, which he attained in 759. Early in his career he was sent into a brief exile to the provinces and turned to the tradition of exile poetry which Li Bai and Du Fu were also to practice and in which he was to excel. In 755 An Lushan led a rebellion that captured Changan, and Wang Wei was imprisoned in a temple, where he attempted suicide. He was later sent to Luoyang and forced to serve in the rebels' puppet government. When the rebellion was put down, Wang Wei's life was in danger because of his collaboration, but the fact that during his imprisonment he had written a poem denouncing the dismemberment of a court musician who refused to play for the rebels at Frozen Emerald Pond persuaded Emporer Suzong to restore him to his former office. Wang Wei never did give up the world of the court for religious practice. But the conflict between his worldly career and his desire to be without desire is central to his most moving poems.

The following poems by Wang Wei were translated by Tony Barnstone, Willis Barnstone, and Xu Haixin.

Watching the Hunt

> Strong wind. The horn bow sings.
> The generals are hunting in Wei Cheng.
>
> In withered grass, the falcon's eye is sharper.
> In melting snow, horse hooves are light.
>
> They've just passed New Harvest Market
> yet are already home at Willow Branch.
>
> They look back. They shot the vulture
> in a thousand miles of twilight clouds.

Walking into the Liang Countryside

The village has just three houses with old people.
A settlement at the frontier doesn't have neighbors on all four sides.
Trees wind-dance by the temple of the field god.
Flutes and drums. People worship the deity,
pouring wine on straw dogs,
burning incense as they bow before a wooden figure.
Holy women circle in a never-stopping dance,
kicking up dust with their silk shoes.

A Young Lady's Spring Thoughts

Unbearable to watch these endless silk threads rain through the sky.
Spring wind pulls them apart and intensifies this separation.
Leisurely flowers fall to the green mossy earth.
Only I can know this. No one comes to see me all day.

For Someone Far Away

All year I stay alone in my bedroom
dreaming of Mountain Pass, remembering our separation.
No swallow comes with letters in its claws.
I see only the new moon like the eyebrow of a moth.

Climbing the City Tower North of the River

Wells and alleys lead me to the rocky hills.
From a traveler's pavilion up in clouds and haze
I watch the sun fall—far from this high city—
into blue mountains mirrored by distant water.
Fire on the shore where a lonely boat is anchored.
Fishermen and evening birds go home.
Dusk comes to the silent expanse of heaven and earth
and my heart is calm like this wide river.

Deep South Mountain

Taiyi Mountain[1] is close to the capital
and its peaks tumble down to the sea.
White clouds come together as I look back
but when I enter blue mist it vanishes.
From the middle peak I see other wild fields,
a valley of shadows, another of sun.
Needing to lodge someplace among people,
I shout across a brook to a woodcutter.

---

[1] Taiyi is another name for Deep South Mountain, south of Changan (now the city of Xian), the capital city of the Tang dynasty. It lies in central China, in Shanxi province, far from the ocean. Only in the eyes of the poet, of course, do the mountains extend to the ocean.

Living in the Mountain on an Autumn Night

After fresh rain on the empty mountain
comes evening and the cold of autumn.
The full moon burns through the pines.
A brook transparent over the stones.
Bamboo trees crackle as washerwomen go home
and lotus flowers sway as a fisherman's boat slips downriver.
Though the fresh smell of grass is gone,
a prince is happy in these hills.

Drifting on the Lake

Autumn is crisp and the firmament far,
especially far from where people live.
I look at cranes on the sand
and am immersed in joy when I see mountains beyond the clouds.
Dusk inks the crystal ripples.
Leisurely the white moon comes out.
Tonight I am with my oar, alone, and can do everything,
yet waver, not willing to return.

Cooling Off

Clear waters drift through the immensity of a tall forest.
In front of me a huge river mouth
receives the long wind.
Deep ripples hold white sand
and white fish swimming as in a void.
I sprawl on a big rock,
billows nourishing my humble body.
I gargle with water and wash my feet.
A fisherman pauses out on the surf.
So many fish long for bait. I look
only to the east with its lotus leaves.

Return to Wang River

Bells stir in the mouth of the gorge.
Few fishermen and woodcutters are left.
Far off in the mountains is twilight.
Alone I come back to white clouds.
Weak water chestnut stems can't hold still.
Willow catkins are light and blow about.
To the east is a rice paddy, color of spring grass.
I close the thorn gate, seized by grief.

Written on a Rainy Autumn Night After Pei Di's Visit

The urgent whir of crickets quickens.
My light robe is getting heavier.
In freezing candlelight I sit in my high house.
Through autumn rain I hear a random bell.
I use white laws to handle mad elephants[1]
and unearthly words to test old dragons.
Who would bother to visit my weedy path?
Though nothing like the hermits Qiu and Yang,[2]
in my refuge I am lucky and alone.

To Pei Di, While We Are Living Lazily at Wang River

The cold mountain turns deep green.
Autumn waters flow slower and slower.
By the lattice gate, I lean on my cane;
we hear cicadas in the wind at dusk.

---

[1] Some Buddhist texts refer to benevolent laws as the "white laws" and evil laws as the "black laws."

[2] Qiu and Yang were ancient scholars who declined offers of official salaries and earned their living by making carts and carriages.

The failing sun rests on the dock
and lonely smoke rises from the village.
You are as drunk as legendary Jie Yu[1]
madly singing in front of Five Willows.[2]

Birds Sing in the Ravine

At rest, he senses acacia blossoms fall.
Quiet night, the spring mountain empty.
The sudden moon alarms mountain birds.
Pulses of song in the spring ravine.

Sketching Things

Slender clouds. On the pavilion a small rain.
Noon, but I'm too lazy to open the far cloister.
I sit looking at moss so green
my clothes are soaked with color.

from The Wang River Sequence

Preface

My country estate is at Wang River Ravine, where the scenic
spots include Meng Wall Hollow, Huazi Hill, Grainy Apricot
Wood Cottage, Deer Park, Magnolia Enclosure, Lakeside
Pavilion, Lake Yi, Waves of Willow Trees, Luan Family

---

[1] Jie Yu was known as the "madman of Chu" and was supposed to have
feigned madness to avoid having to serve in government. He appears in the
Analects and in the classic Daoist text, the *Zhuangzi.*

[2] "Five Willows" is often used in Wang Wei's poems to represent a peaceful
and secluded life. The term comes from Tao Qian, the great poet of the fifth
century, known for his retreat from officialdom to a life of pastoral simplicity.
Tao Qian called himself "Master of Five Willows" after the willows that grew
at his country cottage.

Rapids, White Pebble Shoal, Magnolia Basin, etc. Pei Di and I
spent our leisure writing quatrains about each of these places.

1. Deer Park

>Nobody in sight on the empty mountain
>but human voices are heard far off.
>Low sun slips deep in the forest
>and lights the green hanging moss.

2. House Hidden in the Bamboo Grove

>Sitting alone in the dark bamboo,
>I play my lute and whistle song.
>Deep in the wood no one knows
>the bright moon shines on me.

3. Luan Family Rapids

>In the windy hiss of autumn rain
>shallow water fumbles over stones.
>Waves dance and fall on each other:
>a white egret startles up, then drops.

4. White Pebble Shoal

>White Pebble Shoal is clear and shallow.
>You can almost grab the green cattail.
>Houses east and west of the stream.
>Someone washes silk in bright moonlight.

5. Lakeside Pavilion

A light boat greets the honored guests,
far, far, coming in over the lake.
On a balcony we face bowls of wine
and lotus flowers bloom everywhere.

6. Magnolia Basin

On branch tips the hibiscus bloom.
The mountains show off red calices.
Nobody. A silent cottage in the valley.
One by one flowers open, then fall.

Things in a Spring Garden

Last night's rain makes me sail in my wooden shoes.
I put on my shabby robe against the spring cold.
As I spade open each plot, white water spreads.
Red peach flowers protrude from the willow trees.
On the lawn I play chess, and by a small wood
dip out water with my pole and pail.
I could take a small deerskin table
and hide in the high grass of sunset.

Answering the Poem Su Left in My Blue Field Mountain Country House, on Visiting and Finding Me Not Home

I live a plain life in the valley's mouth
where trees circle the deserted village.
I'm sorry you traveled the stone path for nothing
but there is no one in my cottage.
The fishing boats are glued to the frozen lake

and hunting fires burn on the cold plain.
Temple bells grieve slowly and night monkeys
chatter beyond the white clouds.

About Old Age, in Answer to a
Poem by Subprefect Zhang

In old age I ask for peace
and don't care about things of this world.
I've found no good way to live
and brood about getting lost in my old forests.
The wind blowing in the pines loosens my belt.
The mountain moon is my lamp while I tinkle my lute.
You ask, how do you rise or fall in life?
A fisherman's song is deep in the river.

To My Cousin Qiu, Military Supply Official

When young I knew only the surface of things
and studied eagerly for fame and power.
I heard tales of marvelous years on horseback
and suffered from being no wiser than others.
Honestly, I didn't rely on empty words;
I tried several official posts.
But to be a clerk—always fearing punishment
for going against the times—is joyless.
In clear winter I see remote mountains
with dark green frozen in drifted snow.
Bright peaks beyond the eastern forest
tell me to abandon this world.
Cousin, like Huilian[1] your taste is pure.

---

[1] Xie Huilian (397–433) was the valued cousin of the famous Northern and
Southern dynasties poet Xie Lingyun (385–433). Huilian was a talented
young man who began to write at the age of ten. Later poets often referred to
him when praising their cousins or brothers.

You once talked of living beyond mere dust.
I saw no rush to take your hand and go—
but how the years have thundered away!

On Being Demoted and Sent Away to Qizhou

How easy for a lowly official to offend
and now I'm demoted and must go north.
In my work I sought justice
but the wise emperor disagreed.
I pass houses and roads by the riverside
and villages deep in a sea of clouds.
Even if one day I come back,
white age will have invaded my hair.

For Zhang, Exiled in Jingzhou,
Once Adviser to the Emperor

Where are you? I think only of you.
Dejected I gaze at the Jingmen Mountains.
Now no one recognizes you
but I still remember how you helped me.
I, too, will work as a farmer,
planting, growing old in my hilly garden.
I see wild geese fading into the south.
Which one can take you my words?

Seeing Off Prefect Ji Mu as He Leaves Office
and Goes East of the River

The time of brightness is long gone.
I, too, have been passed over.
It's fate. No complaint colors my face.
The plain life is what I enjoy.

Now that you brush off your sleeves and leave,
poverty will invade the four seas.

Ten thousand miles of pure autumn sky.
Sunset clarifies the empty river.
What pleasure on a crystal night
to rap on the side of the boat and sing
or share the light with fish and birds,
leisurely stretched out in the rushes.

No need to lodge in the bright world.
All day let your hair be tangled like reeds.
Be lazy and in the dark about human affairs,
in a remote place, far from the emperor.
You can gather things smaller than you;
in the natural world there are no kings.

I will also leave office and return,
an old farmhand, plowing the fields.

Winter Night, Writing About My Emotion

The winter night is cold and endless
and the palace water clock drums the hour.
Grass is white clouds of heavy frost
and aging trees reveal a bright moon.
Beautiful robes frame my wasted face.
A red lamp shines on my white hair.
Now the Han emperor[1] respects only the young.
I look in my mirror, ashamed to go to the court.

---

[1] The Han emperor Wu Di (meaning "military emperor") once saw an old
courtier named Yan Si and asked why he was so old but still held a low offi-
cial rank. "In the time of your grandfather Wen Di [meaning 'literary
emperor'']," the old man answered, "I was a military man and thus was not in
favor. Then your father Jing Di [meaning 'emperor of scenery'] trusted only
the old people and I was young. Now you like militant young people, but I
am old." Wu Di was moved by this answer and raised the old man to a higher
rank.

Seeing Zu Off at Qizhou

>Only just now we met and laughed
>yet here I'm crying to see you off.
>In the prayer tent we are broken.
>The dead city intensifies our grief.
>Coldly the remote mountains are clean.
>Dusk comes. The long river races by.
>You undo the rope, are already gone.
>I stand for a long time, looking.

A White Turtle Under a Waterfall

The waterfall on South Mountain hits the rocks,
tosses back its foam with terrifying thunder,
blotting out even face-to-face talk.
Collapsing water and bouncing foam soak blue moss,
old moss so thick
it drowns the spring grass.
Animals are hushed.
Birds fly but don't sing
yet a white turtle plays on the pool's sand floor under riotous spray,
sliding about with the torrents.
The people of the land are benevolent.
No angling or net fishing.
The white turtle lives out its life, naturally.

Song of Peach Tree Spring*

My fishing boat sails the river. I love spring in the mountains.
Peach blossoms crowd the river on both banks as far as sight.
Sitting in the boat, I look at red trees and forget how far I've come.
Drifting to the green river's end, I see no one.

Hidden paths wind into the mountain's mouth.
Suddenly the hills open into a plain
and I see a distant mingling of trees and clouds.
Then coming near I make out houses, bamboo groves, and flowers
where woodcutters still have names from Han times
and people wear Qin dynasty clothing.
They used to live where I do, at Wuling Spring,
but now they cultivate rice and gardens beyond the real world.

Clarity of the moon brings quiet to windows under the pines.
Chickens and dogs riot when sun rises out of clouds.
Shocked to see an outsider, the crowd sticks to me,
competing to drag me to their homes and ask about their native
    places.
At daybreak in the alleys they sweep flowers from their doorways.
By dusk woodcutters and fishermen return, floating in on the waves.

They came here to escape the chaotic world.
Deathless now, they have no hunger to return.
Amid these gorges, what do they know of the world?
In our illusion we see only empty clouds and mountain.
I don't know that paradise is hard to find,
and my heart of dust still longs for home.

---

*Peach Tree Spring refers to a tale by the great poet Tao Qian (also known as
Tao Yuanming) recounting how a fisherman lost his way and sailed into a
Peach Grove. Curious to sail to the end of the wood, he lost all sense of time
and came to a narrow opening at the foot of a mountain. He sailed through
and found himself in the vast stretch of land inhabited by a people whose life
had been cut off from the world since the Qin dynasty (221–207 BCE). Once
the fisherman had returned home, he couldn't find his way back again. This
tale of a lost world of people living a natural life in the mountains is, of
course, a Daoist fable of retreat from the "dusty" world of the court.

Leaving it all, I can't guess how many mountains and waters lie
    behind me,
and am haunted by an obsession to return.
I was sure I could find my way back on the secret paths again.
How could I know the mountains and ravines would change?
I remember only going deep into the hills.
At times the green river touched cloud forests.
With spring, peach blossom water is everywhere,
but I never find that holy source again.

Sitting Alone on an Autumn Night

> Sitting alone I lament my graying temples
> in an empty hall before the night's second drum.
> Mountain fruit drop in the rain
> and grass insects sing under my oil lamp.
> White hair, after all, can never change
> as yellow gold cannot be created.
> If you want to know how to get rid
> of age, its sickness, study nonbeing.

Green Creek

> To find the meadows by Yellow Flower River
> you must follow Green Creek
> as it turns endlessly in the mountains
> in just a hundred miles.
> Water bounds noisily over the rocks.
> Color softens in the dense pines.
> Weeds and water chestnuts are drifting.
> Lucid water mirrors the reeds.
> My heart has always been serene and lazy
> like peaceful Green Creek.
> Why not loaf on a large flat rock,
> dangling my fishhook here forever?

Visiting the Mountain Courtyard of the Distinguished Monk Tanxing at Enlightenment Monastery

> He leans into twilight on a bamboo cane,
> waiting for me at Tiger Creek.[1]
> Hearing tigers roar, he urges me to leave,
> then trails a pouring brook back to his cell.
> Wild flowers bloom beautifully in clusters.
> A bird's single note quiets the ravine.
> In still night he sits in an empty forest,
> feeling autumn on the pine forest wind.

Questioning a Dream

> Don't be fooled. Why bother with the shallow joys of favor
>   or worry about rejection?
> Why flounder in the sea helping others, or being
>   abandoned?
> Where can you dig up a Yellow Emperor or Confucius
>   to consult with?
> How do you know your body isn't a dream?

Weeping for Ying Yao

> How many years can a man possess?
> In the end he will be formlessness.
> Friend, now you are dead

---

[1] Tiger Creek is located at Lou Mountain. According to legend, in the Eastern Jin dynasty (317–420) the distinguished monk Fayuan lived at Donglin Monastery by the side of Tiger Creek. When he went beyond the creek, tigers would growl, so he never went farther when seeing friends off. One day he was walking with the poet Tao Qian and with Lu Jingxiu, a Daoist. Absorbed in their conversation, they crossed the creek, unaware of what they were doing. Suddenly, all of the tigers began to roar. The three of them laughed and went away. Later, a pavilion was built on the spot and called "Three Laughter Pavilion."

and thousands of things sadden me.
You didn't see your kind mother into the grave
and your daughter is only ten.
From the vast and bleak countryside
comes the tiny sound of weeping.
Floating clouds turn to dark mist
and flying birds lose their voices.
Travelers are miserable
below the lonely white sun.
I recall when you were alive
you asked me how to learn nonbeing.
If only I'd helped you earlier
you wouldn't have died in ignorance.
All your old friends give elegies
recounting your life.
I know I have failed you,
and weep, returning to my thorn gate.

Suffering from Heat

The red sun bakes earth and heaven
where fire clouds are shaped like mountains.
Grass and woods are scorched and wilting.
The rivers and lakes have all dried up.
Even my light silk clothes feel heavy
and dense foliage gives thin shade.
The bamboo mat too hot to lie on,
I dry off, soaking my towel with sweat.
I think of escaping from the universe
to be a hermit in a vastness
where a long wind comes from infinity
and rivers and seas wash away my turbulence.
When I see my body holding me here
I know my heart is not enlightened.
Abruptly I enter a gate of sweet dew
where there is a medicine to cool me.

LI BAI

(701–762)

Li Bai is probably the best-known Chinese poet in the West. He and Du Fu are considered the finest poets of the Tang dynasty. Li Bai has attracted the best translators and has influenced several generations of American poets, from Ezra Pound to James Wright. Yet there is considerable confusion surrounding something as basic as his name. He is best known in the West as Li Po, though he is also called Li Pai, Li T'ai-po, and Li T'ai-pai, all of these being Wade-Giles transliterations of variations on his Chinese names ("Pai" and "Po" are different English transliterations of the same character). For each of these names there is a new English version, according to the now-accepted Pinyin transliteration system (Li Pai = Li Bai). To add to the confusion, Ezra Pound, in *Cathay*, his famous sequence of Chinese poems in translation, refers to him as Rihaku, a transliteration of the Japanese pronunciation of his name.

The facts of Li Bai's life come to us through a similar veil of contradictions and legends. Where he was born is unknown. There are those who say he was of Turkic origin, but it seems he was probably born in central Asia and raised in Sichuan province. His brashness and bravado are characteristic of a tradition of poets from this region, including the great Song dynasty poet Su Shi. Li Bai claimed to be related to the imperial family, though this is probably spurious. Perhaps in his teens he wandered as a Daoist hermit; certainly Daoist fantasy permeates his work. We do know that he was alone among the great Tang poets in never taking the imperial examination and that he left his home in 725 and wandered through the Yangtze River Valley, hoping to gain recognition for his talents. During this period he married the first of his four wives. In 742 he was summoned to the capital of Changan (modern Xian) and was appointed to the Hanlin Academy (meaning "the writing brush forest") by Emperor Xuanzong. During his time in the capital he became close friends with

Du Fu, who addresses a number of poems to him. Within a few years he was expelled from the court and made to leave Changan, and he began presenting himself as an unappreciated genius, or as one friend named him, a "banished immortal." In 755 the An Lushan Rebellion took place, in which a Turkic general led his group of Chinese border armies against the emperor. Li Bai was forced to leave Hunan for the South, where he entered the service of the Prince of Yun, sixteenth son of the emperor, who led a secondary revolt. Eventually, Li was arrested for treason, sent into exile, and later given amnesty. He continued his wanderings in the Yangtze Valley, seeking patrons, until his death at sixty-two.

About one thousand poems attributed to Li Bai have come down to us, though some were probably written by imitators. While most of his poems were written for specific occasions, others incorporated wild journeys, Sichuan colloquial speech, and dramatic monologues. Perhaps the most remarkable subject for his poems, however, was himself. He portrays himself as a neglected genius, a drunk, a wanderer through Daoist metaphysical adventures, and a lover of the moon, friends, and women. His colloquial speech and confessional celebration of a sensual flamboyance and fallible self made him the best-loved and most-imitated Chinese poet in English. Translations of Li Bai helped to establish a conversational, intimate tone in modern American poetry. Ezra Pound's *Cathay* put him at the center of the revolution in modern verse. All these qualities, plus an extraordinary lucidity of image, made him extremely popular in China as well, both in his day and to this day. A number of his poems are in the Han dynasty *yuefu* form, which allowed him to indulge in radically irregular lines that gave his imagination free play. He was an influential figure in the Chinese cult of spontaneity, which emphasized the poet's genius in extemporizing a poem: "Inspired, each stroke of my brush shakes the five mountains."

Among the many legends about Li Bai, the most enduring is the account of his death. Like Ishmael in the crow's nest, wanting to penetrate the illusory world that he saw reflected in the water, Li Bai was said to be so drunk in a boat that he fell overboard and drowned, trying to embrace the moon reflected in the water.

Since the "man in the moon" is a woman in Chinese myth, the legend of Li's death takes on an erotic meaning, mixing thanatos and eros. As in *Moby-Dick*, to "strike through the mask" and see the face of truth is to embrace death.

> *Unless otherwise noted, the following poems by Li Bai were translated by Tony Barnstone, Willis Barnstone, and Chou Ping.*

A Song of Zhanggan Village

My hair was still cut straight across my forehead
and I was playing, pulling up flowers by the front door,
when you rode up on a bamboo horse
and danced round the bench, monkeying with the green plums.
And we lived together in the village of Zhanggan,
two small people without hate or suspicion.
At fourteen I became your wife,
so bashful I never laughed.
I lowered my head and faced the dark wall.
You called me a thousand times but I couldn't look at you.
At fifteen my tortured brow calmed
and I wanted to be with you like ashes in dust.
I'd die waiting for you, embracing a pillar,
so why must I climb the widows' tower?
At sixteen you left
for Qutang Gorge where floodwaters crush against Yanyu Rock
and I haven't touched you for five months.
Now I hear monkeys screeching into the sky
and mosses drown the place by our door
where your feet sank in the earth when you left,
moss so deep I can't sweep it away.
It's a windy autumn. The leaves are falling early.
In the eighth month butterflies dart in pairs
through high grass in the west garden.

They hurt my heart.
I grow older, my face ruddy with pain.
If you are coming down through the Three Gorges
please write me
and I will come out to meet you
even as far as Long Wind Sands.

Grievance at the Jade Stairs

The jade steps are whitening with dew.
My gauze stockings are soaked. It's so late.
I let down the crystal blind
and watch the glass clear autumn moon.

Seeing a Friend Off at Jingmen Ferry

When you sail far past Jingmen
you enter the land of Chu
where mountains end and flat plains begin
and the river pours into a huge wilderness.
Above, the moon sails, sky mirror,
and clouds weave and swell into a sea mirage of terraces.
Below your wandering boat, water from the home you love
still sees you off after ten thousand miles.

Watching the Waterfall at Lu Mountain

Sunlight steams off purple mist from Incense Peak.
Far off, the waterfall is a long hanging river
flying straight down three thousand feet
like the milky river of stars pouring from heaven.

Hearing a Flute on a Spring Night in Luoyang

Whose jade flute secretly soars in the night?
Spring wind scatters sound all over Luoyang.
The midnight flute keens a farewell song, "Snap the Willow Branch."
Thinking of my old home and garden, I break.

River Song

Magnolia oars. A spicewood boat.
Jade flutes and gold pipes fill the air at bow and stern.
We have a thousand jugs of tart wine
and singing girls who drift with us on the waves.
Like a Daoist immortal floating off on a yellow crane,
my wandering mind empties and soars with white gulls.
Qu Yuan's poems hang overhead with sun and moon
but the Chu king's palace is an empty mountain.
Inspired, each stroke of my brush shakes the five mountains.
The poem done, I laugh proudly over the hermit's land.
If fame and money could last forever
the Han River would flow backward.

I Listen to Jun, a Monk from Shu, Play His Lute

The Shu monk carries a green silk lute
west down Omei Mountain
and each sweep of his hand
is the song of a thousand pines in the valley.
Flowing water cleans my wanderer's heart
and the sound lingers like a frosty bell
till I forget the mountain soaking in green dusk,
autumn clouds darkly folding in.

Seeing a Friend Off

Blue mountains past the north wall,
white water snaking eastward.
Here we say good-bye for the last time.
You will fade like a hayseed blowing ten thousand miles away.
Floating clouds are the way of the wanderer.
The sun sets like the hearts of old friends.
We wave good-bye as you leave. Horses neigh and neigh.

Drinking Alone by Moonlight

A pot of wine in the flower garden,
but no friends drink with me.
So I raise my cup to the bright moon
and to my shadow, which makes us three,
but the moon won't drink
and my shadow just creeps about my heels.
Yet in your company, moon and shadow,
I have a wild time till spring dies out.
I sing and the moon shudders.
My shadow staggers when I dance.
We have our fun while I can stand
then drift apart when I fall asleep.
Let's share this empty journey often
and meet again in the milky river of stars.

Seeing Meng Haoran Off to Guangling
at the Yellow Crane Tower

From Yellow Crane Tower you sail
the river west as mist flowers bloom.
A solitary sail, far shadow, green mountains at the empty end of
vision.
And now, just the Yangtze River touching the sky.

Saying Good-bye to Song Zhiti

Clear as empty sky, the Chu River
meanders to the far blue sea.
Soon there will be a thousand miles between us.
All feelings distill to this cup of wine.
The cuckoo chants the sunny day;
monkeys on the riverbanks are howling evening wind.
All my life I haven't wept
but I weep here, unable to stop.

Song

The whole forest is a blur
woven by fog.
Cold mountain is color of melancholy,
mauve.
Twilight comes into a tall house.
Someone is unhappy upstairs.
Standing on the jade steps,
a woman is wasting time, nothing to do.
Birds wing off for home
but what road can take me there?
Pavilion after pavilion join far, far, far.

In Memory of He Zhizhang

People in his homeland thought him mad
so He Zhizhang wandered with rivers and winds.

When we first met in Changan
he dubbed me the "Banished Immortal."

He loved good talk and his cup,
who lies under bamboo and pine.

Through a veil of tears, I see
poor He hocking his ring for wine.

Translated by Sam Hamill

Confessional

There was wine in a cup of gold
and a girl of fifteen from Wu,
her eyebrows painted dark
and with slippers of red brocade.

If her conversation was poor,
how beautifully she could sing!
Together we dined and drank
until she settled in my arms.

Behind her curtains
embroidered with lotuses,
how could I refuse
the temptation of her advances?

Translated by Sam Hamill

Zazen on Jingting Mountain

The birds have vanished down the sky,
and now the last cloud drains away.

We sit together, the mountain and me,
until only the mountain remains.

Translated by Sam Hamill

Questioning in the Mountains

You ask me why I live in the jade mountains.
I smile, unanswering. My heart is calm.
Peach petals float on the water, never come back.
There is a heaven and earth beyond the crowded town below.

Missing the East Mountains

It's long since I've gone to the East Mountains.
How many seasons have the tiny roses bloomed?
White clouds—unblown—fall apart.
In whose court has the bright moon dropped?

Having a Good Time by Myself

Facing wine, not aware it's getting dark,
I've been sitting so long my gown brims over with petals.
Drunk, I rise to follow the moon in the brook
long after birds and people have gone home.

Drinking Wine with the Hermit in the Mountains

We raise our cups where mountain flowers bloom.
One cup, another cup, and another cup.
I'm drunk and want to sleep. Leave me now.
Tomorrow, if you feel good, come with your lute.

Sent Far Off

This room was all flowers when my beauty was here.
Gone now. Only an empty bed.
The embroidered quilt is folded up. I can't sleep.

Three years gone, yet I still smell her fragrance.
Why doesn't the fragrance dissipate?
Why doesn't my beauty come back?
I miss her until yellow leaves drop
and white dawn moisture soaks the green moss.

Inscription for Summit Temple

About to sleep a night in Summit Temple
I raise my hand and touch the stars.
I have to whisper just to keep
from bothering people in heaven.

Summer Day in the Mountains

Lazy today. I wave my white feather fan.
Then I strip naked in the green forest,
untie my hatband and hang it on a stone wall.
Pine wind sprinkles my bare head.

Brooding in the Still Night

Bright moonlight before my bed.
At first I think the floor is all frost.
I gaze up at the mountain moon,
then drop my head in a dream of home.

Singing by Green Water in Autumn

Green water washes the plain moon clean.
The moon's brightness startles egrets into day flight.
A young man listens to a woman collecting water chestnuts.
They walk back together at night, singing.

Drunk All Day

To live in this world is to have a big dream;
why punish myself by working?
So I'm drunk all day.
I flop by the front door, dead to the world.
On waking, I peer at the garden
where a bird sings among the flowers
and wonder what season it is.
I think I hear him call, "mango birds sing in spring wind."
I'm overcome and almost sigh.
But no, I pour another cup of wine,
sing at the top of my lungs and wait for the bright moon.
When my song dies out, I forget.

Song on Bringing in the Wine

Can't you see the Yellow River
pours down directly from heaven?
It sprints all the way to the ocean
and never comes back.
Can't you see the clear hall mirror
is melancholy with our gray hair?
In the morning our braids are black silk.
In the evening they are snow.
When happy, be happy all the way,
never abandoning your gold cup
empty to face the moon alone.

Heaven gave me talent. It means something.
Born with genius, a failure now, I will succeed.
Although I waste a thousand ounces of gold
they will come back.
We butcher cows, cook lambs,
for a wild feast, and must drink
three hundred cups at a time.
Friends Chengfuze and Danqiuchen,

bring in the wine
and keep your mouths full.
I'll sing for you. I'll turn
your ears. Bells and drums,
good dishes and jade are worth
nothing. What I want
is to be drunk, day and night,
and never again sober up.

The ancient saints and sages are forgotten.
Only the fame of great drunks
goes from generation to generation.
In the Temple of Perfect Peace
Prince Cheng once gave a mad party,
serving ten thousand pots of wine.
Long ago. Tonight, let no one
say I am too poor to supply
vats of alcohol. I'll find
my prize horse and fur coat
and ask my boy to sell them
for fine wine. Friends, we'll drink
till the centuries
of sorrowful existence dissolve.

On My Way Down Zhongnan Mountain I Passed by Hermit Fusi's Place and He Treated Me to Wine While I Spent the Night There

I descend a green mountain at dusk,
the moon following me home.
Looking back at my path,
darkly, darkly I see a blue mist hanging.
You take my hand and lead me to your farmer cottage
where a boy opens the thorn-branch gate.
Green bamboo leads into a quiet footpath;
emerald vines brush my passing clothes.

Happily chatting while enjoying our rest,
we share a gorgeous wine.
We sing about wind through pines
and don't stop till the stars are scarce.
I'm drunk and you are happy.
Enraptured, we forget the world.

Song of the North Wind

The fire dragon lives at Ice Gate
and light comes from its eyes at night,
yet why no sun or moon to light us here?
We have only the north wind howling furiously out of heaven.
On Yen Mountain snowflakes are as big as a floor mat
and every flake drops on us.
The woman of Yo Zhou in December
stops singing and laughing. Her eyebrows tighten.
Lounging against the door she watches people pass by
and remembers her husband at the north frontier
and the miserable cold.
When he left he took his sword to guard the border.
He left his tiger-striped quiver at home,
with its white-feathered arrows, now coated
with dust on which spiders spin their traps.
The arrows remain, useless. Her husband is dead
from the war. He won't return.
The widow won't look at the arrows.
Finally, it's too much, and she burns them to ashes.
Easier to block the Yellow River with a few handfuls of sand,
than to scissor away her iron grief
here in the north wind, the rain, the snow.

War South of the Great Wall

Delirium, battlefields all dark and delirium,
convulsions of men swarm like armies of ants.

A red wheel in thickened air, the sun hangs
above bramble and weed blood's dyed purple,

and crows, their beaks clutching warrior guts,
struggle at flight, grief glutted, earthbound.

Those on guard atop the Great Wall yesterday
became ghosts in its shadow today. And still,

flags bright everywhere like scattered stars,
the slaughter keeps on. War drums throbbing:

my husband, my sons—you'll find them all
there, out where war drums keep throbbing.

Translated by David Hinton

Hunting Song

Frontier sons are lifelong illiterates
who know only how to hunt big game and brag about being
    tough guys.
They feed their Mongolian ponies white grass
to make them plump and strong in the autumn.
They race proudly on their horses, chasing the sun's shadows.
They brush snow off with the crack of a gold whip.
Half drunk, they call their falcon and wander far to hunt.
They stretch their bows like a full moon and never miss.
One whistling arrow flies and two gray cranes fall.
The desert spectators step back in dread.
These virile heroes shake the sands.
Confucian scholars are no match for them.
What good is it to lock one's doors and read books till one is gray?

CHU GUANGXI

(707–C. 760)

Chu Guangxi's family came from Yanzhou, Shandong, though he himself came from Jiangsu and lived in the Tang dynasty capital, Changan, where he was friends with Wang Wei and other poets. He failed the imperial examinations at first, after which he traveled and might have lived in Henan. He eventually passed the imperial examinations in 726, returned to Jiangsu in 737, and in 755–766 was captured by the forces of An Lushan during the An Lushan Rebellion and pressed into service. After the rebellion failed, he was put in prison. Although he was pardoned, he was banished to the south for his collaboration. He died in the south, in Guangdong. He writes often of peasant and farming life.

from Jiangnan Melodies

2

Floating with the current I pull waterweed leaves.
Along the banks I pick tender reed shoots.
To avoid disturbing two mandarin ducks,
I let my painted boat slide gently.

DU FU

(712–770)

If there is one undisputed genius of Chinese poetry, it is Du Fu. The Daoist Li Bai was more popular, the Buddhist Wang Wei was sublimely simple and more intimate with nature, but the Confucian Du Fu had extraordinary thematic range and was a master and innovator of all the verse forms of his time. In his lifetime he never achieved fame as a poet and thought himself a failure in his worldly career. Perhaps only a third of his poems survive due to his long obscurity; his poems appear in no anthology earlier than one dated 130 years after his death, and it wasn't until the eleventh century that he was recognized as a preeminent poet. His highly allusive, symbolic complexity and resonant ambiguity are at times less accessible than the immediacy and bravado of Li Bai. Yet there is a suddenness and pathos in much of his verse, which creates a persona no less constructed than Wang Wei's reluctant official and would-be hermit or Li Bai's blithely drunken Daoist adventurer.

Most of what we know of Du Fu's life is recorded in his poems, but there are dangers to reading his poems as history and autobiography. By the time he was in his twenties, he was referring to his long white hair—in the persona of the Confucian elder. As Sam Hamill notes, "It was natural that many a poet would adopt the persona of the 'long white-haired' old man—this lent a younger poet an authority of tone and diction he might never aspire to otherwise." Du Fu is sometimes called "the poet of history" because his poems record the turbulent times of the decline of the Tang dynasty and constitute in part a Confucian societal critique of the suffering of the poor and the corruption of officials. He also records his own sufferings, exile, falls from grace, and the death of his son by starvation, but some critics have suggested that the poems on these themes are exaggerated and self-dramatizing.

Du Fu was born to a prominent but declining family of scholar-officials, perhaps from modern-day Henan province, though he referred to himself as a native of Duling, the ancestral home of the Du clan. In the Six Dynasties Period his ancestors were in the service of the Southern courts; his grandfather Du Shenyan was an important poet of the early Tang dynasty, and a more remote ancestor, Du Yu (222–284), was a famed Confucianist and military man. In spite of family connections, however, Du Fu had difficulty achieving patronage and governmental postings and twice failed the imperial examinations, in 735 and 747. He was a restless traveler, and the poems of this early period show him to be a young man given to revelry, military and hunting arts, painting, and music. In 744 he met Li Bai, forming the basis for one of the world's most famed literary friendships; the two poets devote a number of poems to each other. In 751 Du Fu passed a special examination that he finagled through submitting rhyme prose works directly to the emperor, but it wasn't until 755 that he was offered a post—a rather humiliating one in the provinces—which he rejected, accepting instead the patronage of the heir apparent. In the winter of that year, however, the An Lushan Rebellion broke out, and the emperor fled to Sichuan and abdicated, and the heir apparent became the new emperor in Gansu province. Meanwhile, the rebels seized the capital, and Du Fu, attempting to join the new emperor in the distant northwest, was captured by the rebels. He was detained for a year but managed to escape and, after traveling in disguise through the occupied territory, joined the emperor's court in the position of Reminder. He was arrested soon after for his outspokenness in defending a friend, a general who had failed to win a battle, but was pardoned and exiled to a low posting in Huazhou. He quit his job there and moved to Chengdu, where he and his family depended upon the kindness of friends and relatives and moved again and again to avoid banditry and rebellions. In spite of this instability, Du Fu's poems show a serenity in this period, particularly from 760–762, when he lived in a "thatched hut" provided by a patron and friend named Yan Yu, who hired him in the years that followed as a military adviser. After Yan's death in 765, Du Fu left Chengdu and traveled down the Yangtze River, finding patrons and dreaming of a return to Changan, but being prevented by invasions from Tibet. He spent his final three years traveling on a boat, detained in sickness, and finally winding down to his death as he journeyed down the Yangtze, apparently accepting the withering away of his health and life.

Facing Snow

> Battles, sobbing, many new ghosts.
> Just an old man, I sadly chant poems.
> Into the thin evening, wild clouds dip.
> On swirling wind, fast dancing snow.

A ladle idles by a drained cask of green wine.
Last embers redden the empty stove.
No news, the provinces are cut off.
With one finger I write in the air, *sorrow*.

Gazing in Springtime

The empire is shattered but rivers and peaks remain.
Spring drowns the city in wild grass and trees.
A time so bad, even the flowers rain tears.
I hate this separation, yet birds startle my heart.
The signal fires have burned three months;
I'd give ten thousand gold coins for one letter.
I scratch my head and my white hair thins
till it can't even hold a pin.

Ballad of the War Wagons

Carts grumble and rattle
and horses whinny and neigh
as the conscripts pass, bows and quivers strapped to their waists.
Parents, wives, and children run to see them off
till dust clouds drown the bridge south of Changan.
Tugging at soldiers' clothes, they wail and throw themselves in the
     way,
their cries rising into the clouds.

On the roadside a passerby asks what's happening.
The soldiers only say, "We're called up often,
some went north at fifteen to guard the Yellow River
and still at forty are farming frontier settlements out West.
We left so young the village chief wrapped our turbans for us;
we came back white haired but now we're off to fortify the frontier!
The men there have shed a salt ocean of blood,
but the warlike emperor still lusts for empire.

My lord, haven't you heard how in two hundred districts east of
   China's mountains
countless villages grow just weeds and thorns?
Even if a stout wife tries to plow and hoe,
east to west the crops grow wild over broken terraces.
The Qin soldiers are fierce warriors,
but they are driven forth to battle like chickens or dogs.

You, sir, can ask questions
but conscripts don't dare complain.
This winter, for example,
they haven't released the Guanxi troops
but officials still press for the land tax.
Land taxes! How are we to pay that?
The truth is it's a sour thing to have sons.
Better to have a daughter—
at least she can marry a neighbor.
Our sons lie unburied in the grass.
My lord, have you seen the Blue Sea's shore
where the old white bones lie ungathered?
New ghosts keen and old ghosts weep
jiu, jiu like twittering birds as rain sifts from the bleak sky."

Moonlit Night*

> In Fuzhou tonight there's a moon
> my wife can only watch alone.
> Far off, I brood over my small children
> who don't even remember Changan.
>
> Her satin hair dampens in fragrant mist,
> jade arms chilled by clear moonlight.
> When will we lean together between empty curtains,
> beaming as tear tracks dry on our faces?

---

*Written while captive in Changan, separated from his family.

Thinking of My Brothers on a Moonlit Night

Curfew drums cut off a traveler's road.
At the border, autumn comes with a wild goose's shriek.
From this night on, dew will whiten to frost.
The moon looks brighter at home.
My brothers are scattered now.
Who can tell me if they live or die?
I send letters but no word arrives,
and the war goes on and on.

Broken Lines

River so blue the birds seem to whiten.
On the green mountainside flowers almost flame.
Spring is dying yet again.
Will I ever go home?

Thoughts While Night Traveling

Slender wind shifts the shore's fine grass.
Lonely night below the boat's tall mast.
Stars hang low as the vast plain splays;
the swaying moon makes the great river race.
How can poems make me known?
I'm old and sick, my career done.
Drifting, just drifting. What kind of man am I?
A lone gull floating between earth and sky.

A Hundred Worries

I remember I had a child heart at fifteen,
healthy as a brown calf running wild.
In August, when pears and dates ripened in the courtyard
I'd climb the trees a thousand times a day.

All at once I am fifty,
and I sit and lie around more than I walk or stand.
I force smiles and small talk to please my patrons,
but a hundred worries tangle my emotions.
Coming home to the same four empty walls,
I see this grief mirrored in my old wife's glance.
My sons don't treat their father with respect.
They greet me by the door with angry screams for rice.

Standing Alone

A bird of prey above the sky
and two white gulls over the river
gliding on wind. A good time to attack,
while they roam about relaxed.
The grasses are balled with dew
and the spiderweb is not yet closed.
Heaven's secret plan is like human designs.
I stand alone with a thousand worries.

To Wei Ba

In this life we never meet,
orbiting far like polar stars,
so what evening is this
where I can share your candlelight?
Youth is just a few slim hours,
and now our hair and sideburns are gray.
Last time I came, half our old friends were ghosts.
I moaned in shock, my guts on fire.
How could I know that after twenty years
I'd enter your hall again?
When we parted you were unmarried.
Now your sons and daughters form a line,
sweetly show respect for their father's friend
and ask me where I'm from.

With their questions still flying,
you send them for wine and plates,
for spring chives fresh cut in the evening rain
and rice steamed in with yellow millet.
"How hard it is for us to meet!" you cry,
and one toast grows to ten.
After ten cups I'm still not drunk,
just warmed by our old friendship.
Tomorrow mountains will come between us,
and we'll be lost in the world like mist.

Dreaming of Li Bai

I've swallowed sobs for the lost dead,
but this live separation is chronic grief.
From the malarial south of the river
no news comes of the exiled traveler,
but you visit my dream, old friend,
knowing I ache for you.
Are you are a ghost?
No way to tell with the long road between us.
Your spirit comes through green maple woods,
slips home past darkening border fortresses.
You are caught in the law's net,
so how can your spirit have wings?
The sinking moon pours onto the rafters
and your face glows in my mind.
The water is deep, the waves are wide.
Don't let the dragons snatch you!

A Painted Falcon

Wind and frost swirl from white silk:
a painting of a great black hawk,
shoulders braced as he hunts hares,
glancing sidelong with a barbarian glare.

Grasp the gleaming leash and collar,
whistle him down from his bar,
and he'll strike common birds,
spattering the plain with feathers and blood.

New Moon

Narrow rays from the first slice of moon
slant from the trembling edge of the dark orb
which barely crests the ancient fortress
wallowing in the surf of evening clouds.
The river of stars is one eternal color.
Empty cold pours through the mountain pass.
The front courtyard is white dew
and chrysanthemums secretly drenched with dark.

Spring Night Happy About Rain

The good rain knows when to fall.
It comes when spring blossoms.

It steals in on the wind, submerged in night,
moistening all things gently without sound.

Black wilderness, black paths, black clouds;
only a torch on a riverboat sparks.

At dawn I see all things red and wet,
and flowers drown the City of Brocade.[1]

---

[1] A poetic epithet for the city of Chengdu in Sichuan province.

Brimming Water

Under my feet the moon
Glides along the river.
Near midnight, a gusty lantern
Shines in the heart of night.
Along the sandbars flocks
Of white egrets roost,
Each one clenched like a fist.
In the wake of my barge
The fish leap, cut the water,
And dive and splash.

Translated by Kenneth Rexroth

River Village

The clear river curves to embrace the village.
Everything is relaxed here in long summer.
Swallows come and go as they like in the hall,
gulls are necking in the water.
My old wife is drawing a Go board on paper,
my little son is hammering a needle into a fishhook.
As long as old friends give me daily supplies,
what else could my humble body desire?

Looking at Mount Tai

How is Mountain Tai?
Its green is seen beyond State Qi and State Lu,
a distillation of creation's spirit and beauty.
Its slopes split day into yin and yang.
Its rising clouds billow in my chest.
Homecoming birds fly through my wide-open eyes.
I should climb to the summit
and in one glance see all other mountains dwarfed.

Jiang Village

(Three Poems)

1

Red evening clouds are mountains in the west
and the sun's feet disappear under the horizon.
Sparrows noisy over the brushwood door;
I am a traveler home after a thousand miles.
My wife and children are startled to see me alive.
The surprise ends but they can't stop wiping tears.
In the chaotic world I was tossed about;
I've found my way home, alive by accident.
Neighbors crowd over our garden walls.
They are moved, sighing and even weeping.
In deep night we hold candles,
facing each other as if in dream.

2

I live my late years as if I've stolen my life.
Very few joys after I returned home.
My little son never lets go of my knees,
afraid I will go away again.
I remember I liked to chase cool shade,
so I walk under trees by the pond.
Whistling, the north wind is strong,
I finger past events and a hundred worries fry in my mind.
At least the crops are harvested,
wine spurts from the mouth of the flask
and I have enough to fill my cups
and console me in my dusk.

3

A clutter of chickens makes chaos,
fighting each other as guests arrive.
I drive them up bushes and trees,
then hear knocking on my brushwood gate:

four or five village elders greet me
and ask about my long absence.
Each of them brings a gift in hand.
Their wines pour out, some clear, some muddy.
They apologize for their wine, so watery,
as there was no one to grow millet.
Weapons and horses can't rest yet;
the young men are gone on the expedition east.
I offer a song for my old village folks,
feeling deep gratitude.
After singing, I sigh and throw back my head
and tears meander down our faces.

Jade Flower Palace

The stream swirls. The wind moans in
The pines. Gray rats scurry over
Broken tiles. What prince, long ago,
Built this palace, standing in
Ruins beside the cliffs? There are
Green ghost fires in the black rooms.
The shattered pavements are all
Washed away. Ten thousand organ
Pipes whistle and roar. The storm
Scatters the red autumn leaves.
His dancing girls are yellow dust.
Their painted checks have crumbled
Away. His gold chariots
And courtiers are gone. Only
A stone horse is left of his
Glory. I sit on the grass and
Start a poem, but the pathos of
It overcomes me. The future
Slips imperceptibly away.
Who can say what the years will bring?

Translated by Kenneth Rexroth

Newlyweds' Departure

Chinese vines climb up low hemp plants;
the tendrils cannot stretch very far.
To marry a daughter to a drafted man
is worse than abandoning her by the roadside.
"I just did my hair up as a married woman,
haven't even had time to warm the bed for you.
Marry in the evening and depart in the morning
—isn't that too hurried!
You are not going very far,
just to guard the borders at Heyang,
but my status in the family is not yet official.
How can I greet my parents-in-law?
When my parents brought me up,
they kept me in my room day and night.
When a daughter is married,
she has to stay even if she's wed to a chicken or dog.
Now you are going to the place of death.
A heavy pain cramps my stomach.
I was determined to follow you wherever you went,
then realized that was not proper.
Please don't be hampered by our new marriage;
try to be a good soldier.
When women get mixed up in an army,
I fear, the soldiers' morale will falter.
I sigh, since I'm from a poor family
and it took so long to sew this silk dress.
I will never put this dress on again,
and I'm going to wash off my makeup while you watch.
Look at those birds flying up in the sky,
big or small they stay in pairs,
but human life is full of mistakes and setbacks.
I will forever wait for your return."

Old Couple's Departure

The four outskirts are not yet safe and quiet.
I am old, but have no peace.
All my sons and grandsons died in battle,
so what use is it to keep my body in one piece?
Throwing away my walking stick, I walk out the door.
The other soldiers are saddened, pitying me.
I'm lucky to still have all my teeth
but I regret the marrow has dried in my bones.
Wearing a soldier's helmet and armor,
I salute my officers before departure.
My old wife is lying in the road weeping.
The year is late and her clothes thin.
Though I know at heart this is our death farewell,
her shivering in cold still hurts me.
I know I will never come back,
yet hear her out when she says, "Eat more!"
The city wall around Earth Gate is very strong,
and the Xingyuan ferry is hard for the enemy to cross,
so the situation is different from the siege of Ye City,
and I will have some time before I die.
In life we part and we rejoin;
we have no choice, young or old.
I recall my young and strong days,
and walk about leaking long sighs.
War has spread through ten thousand countries
till beacon fires blaze from all the peaks.
So many corpses that grass and trees stink like fish,
rivers and plains dyed red with blood.
Which land is the happy land?
How can I linger here!
I abandon my thatched house
and feel my liver and lungs collapse.

A Homeless Man's Departure

After the Rebellion of 755, all was silent wasteland,
gardens and cottages turned to grass and thorns.
My village had over a hundred households,
but the wild world scattered them east and west.
No one knows about survivors;
the dead are dust and mud.
I, a humble soldier, was defeated in battle.
I ran back home to look for old roads
and walked a long time through the empty lanes.
The sun was thin, the air tragic and dismal.
I met only foxes and raccoons,
their hair on end as they snarled in rage.
Who remains in my neighborhood?
One or two old widows.
A returning bird loves its old branches,
so how could I give up this poor nest?
In spring I carry my hoe all alone,
yet still water the land at sunset.
The county governor's clerk heard I'd returned
and summoned me to practice the war drum.
This military service won't take me from my state.
I look around and have no one to worry about.
It's just me alone and the journey is short,
but I will end up lost if I travel too far.
Since my village has been washed away,
near or far makes no difference.
I will forever feel pain for my long-sick mother.
I abandoned her in this valley five years ago.
She gave birth to me, yet I could not help her.
We cry sour sobs till our lives end.
In my life I have no family to say farewell to,
so how can I be called a human being?

Song of a Thatched Hut Damaged in Autumn Wind

Wind howled angrily in high autumn's September
and tore off three layers of reed from my thatched roof.
The reeds flew over the river and scattered on the bank.
Some flew high and hung from the trees.
Some flew low and swirled and sank into pools.
The kids from the southern village took advantage of my old age,
played pirate and stole my reeds while I watched them
openly carrying armfuls into the bamboo groves.
My lips cracked, my throat dried, and I couldn't yell out.
I returned home and leaned on my stick, sighing.
In a moment the wind stopped and clouds stood ink black,
the autumnal sky stretched into darkness in desert silence.
My cotton quilt is tattered from use and cold as iron.
In an ugly dream, my small son rips the lining with his feet.
The roof is leaking by my bed's headboard and nowhere is dry.
The rain like yarn spins down forever.
I've had little sleep since the An Lushan Rebellion.
Such a wet and long night, when will it end!
I wish I had a house with thousands of rooms
to shelter all the cold people under the sky and give them happy
     faces.
We'd be calm as mountains when it stormed and rained.
Oh, let this big house appear before my eyes
and I will die of cold in my damaged hut, happy.

The Song of a Roped Chicken

My young servant tied up a chicken to sell at market.
Roped tight, the chicken struggled and squawked.
My family hates seeing the chicken eating worms and ants,
not knowing that once sold the chicken will be cooked.
What's the difference between chickens and insects to a human
     being?
I scolded the servant and untied the chicken.
I can never solve the problem of chickens and insects
so just lean against my mountain pavilion, gazing at the cold river.

Poem to Officer Fang's Foreign Horse

> This famous foreign horse comes from Dawan,
> with sharp joints and slender bones.
> Two ears stand firm like bamboo slips,
> wind carries his four hooves lightly.
> Space disappears when he gallops.
> You can trust your life and death to him.
> With strength and speed
> he prances over ten thousand miles.

Qu River

(Two Poems)

1

Spring subtracts itself with each falling petal.
I am sad to see ten thousand dots swirling in wind.
I watch the last petals pass through sight,
but don't complain of suffering when wine passes my lips.
Green birds nest in the small house by the river.
Tall tombs by the flowers, their *qiling* guardian statues[1] decayed.
I meditate on this, decide to live this life with joy.
Why let this body stumble over floating reputation?

2

Each day I return from the court, and pawn spring garments.
Each day I return from the river roaring drunk.
It is nothing to have wine debts wherever I go,
since from ancient times few have lived to seventy.
Deep, deep in the flowers butterflies can be seen.
Dragonflies stop and go, touching the surface of water.
Let my words come to the wind and light, and we'll flow together
for a moment, appreciating each other without disappointment.

---

[1] Originally *qiling* statues. A *qiling* is a Chinese mythical guardian creature, a combination of a dragon, a lion, and a horse, that guards against negative forces and energies.

Leaving in My Boat

A longtime guest in the southern capital, I plow southern fields;
though the north-gate view hurts my spirit, I still sit by the north
    window.
One morning I take my old wife on a small boat
and when it is sunny, watch my little son bathe in the clear river.
Butterflies flying in pairs chase each other.
Twin lotus flowers are blooming on one stalk.
We carry all the tea and sugarcane juice that we need,
and porcelain bottles are as good as jade jars.

Guest's Arrival: Happy About
County Governor Cui's Visit

North and south of my house flow spring waters.
Every day only gulls come to visit me.
I've never before swept petals from the path for guests,
but my wood door is open today for you.
The market is far off so I cook no taste twice.
My poor house offers only unfiltered wine from last year.
If you don't mind drinking with my neighbor as well,
I'll call him over the fence and we'll drain our cups.

A Lone Goose

The lone wild goose doesn't peck or drink,
just flies and cries out, seeking its flock.
Who cares for this tiny piece of shadow
lost in ten thousand layered clouds?
Does he see them where vision ends?
Does he hear them through his deep sorrow?
The wild ravens have no feelings.
They just caw raucously, flapping, flapping.

A Traveler's Night

A traveler's sleep never arrives,
yet the autumnal sky refuses to dawn.
I roll up the curtain and see a shadow of leftover moon,
stack my pillows high and listen to the far off river.
I'm at my wit's end for clothes and food.
At road's end my life depends on friends.
My old wife has brushed many letters to me
and knows the emotion of this unreturned traveler.

from Five Poems About Historical Sites

3 *

Through mountains and valleys I come at last to Jing Gate.
The village where Ming Fei grew up is still there.

She left the Purple Palace for endless desert.
Now only a green tomb remains in the evening sun.

Portraits don't know her face with a smile like spring breeze.
Jade rings echo in emptiness when her ghost returns in moonlight.

For a thousand years her zither makes a foreign song
and the melody sings clearly of her grudge.

---

*In the Han dynasty the Emperor Yuan asked the palace painter to do portraits of all the women in the palace so he could look at the pictures and choose which one to have. Many women bribed the painter to have their portraits done to make them look attractive. Only Ming Fei (also known as Wang Zhaojun) did not bribe the painter, who made her very ugly. When for political reasons the emperor had to marry off one of his palace women to a barbarian tribal leader to the north, he went through the portraits of the thousands of women in his harem and chose Ming Fei. On the day of Ming Fei's departure, the emperor summoned her to his presence. When he realized that she was the most beautiful woman in the palace, he was furious. He couldn't stop the marriage but took his revenge by killing the painter. It is in the Chinese tradition for the poet to talk about his political career from a woman's perspective to avoid offending the emperor.

On Yueyang Tower*

> In the past I heard of Dongting Lake,
> and now I climb Yueyang Tower
>
> and see Wu and Chu unfold east and south.
> Heaven and earth float there night and day.
>
> Not one word from my family and friends,
> I'm old and sick and have just my lonely boat.
>
> War horses charge north of the mountain passes.
> I lean against the railing and sob.

Climbing High

> Gibbons wail into a high sky of wild wind.
> Birds circle a pure isle of white sand.
>
> Leaves drift and shift from countless trees.
> The Yangtze River boils and rolls without end.
>
> I've wandered forever, a thousand miles of autumn woe.
> I climb the terrace alone, sick as always in my lifetime.
>
> Bitter pain has turned my temples to snow.
> I'm so poor I can't even afford muddy wine.

---

*Du Fu is looking down on Dongting Lake from Yueyang Tower and worrying about a Tibetan invasion of Lingwu and Binzhou in October 768, which has kept him from returning to the North.

Traveler's Pavilion

An autumn window still shows the color of dawn
as leafless trees bend further in high wind.
The sun emerges from cold mountains
and the river flows in last night's leftover fog.
No one is abandoned by the celestial court,
but withered and sick, I've become an old man.
What is left for me in what life remains?
I drift helplessly like a rootless tumbleweed.

LIU CHANGQING

(C. 710–C. 787)

Liu Changqing came from a distinguished family who lived in
Hejian, Hebei province. He passed the highest imperial examina-
tions in 733 and held a number of official posts in the provinces
(he was a magistrate and was, by 780, governor of Suizhou), but
his official career was a rocky path: he incurred the emperor's dis-
favor, was sent to prison and demoted, and was demoted again
later in his career under trumped-up charges, banished, and finally
dismissed from office. More than five hundred of his poems sur-
vive. He is often described as a master of five-character verse and
as a poet in the landscape tradition of Wang Wei and Tao Qian.

Spending the Night at Hibiscus Mountain
When It Was Snowing

Dark mountains recede when the sun sets.
So cold the white-thatched cottage seems shabbier.
A dog barks at the firewood gate:
someone approaching in the night storm.

To Official Fei on His Demotion to State Ji

Apes gibber as the guests leave this evening by the river.
For a man with a hurt heart, sorrow flows naturally as water.
We are both exiled, though you are sent farther away:
ten thousand miles of green mountains, and one lonely boat.

JIAO RAN

(730–799)

Jiao Ran was a monk poet from Changcheng in what is today
Changxing County, Zhejiang province. He was the tenth-genera-
tion grandson of Xie Lingyun (385–443), the important Six
Dynasties Period poet and politician. He was born in Zhejiang
and after 785 resided in the Miaoxi Temple on Xu Mountain in
Wuxing. Deeply steeped in the Daoist, Buddhist, and Confucian
traditions, he was considered a very important poet, and his com-
plete works were collected on the emperor's orders. He wrote sig-
nificant literary criticism and was an important influence on the
Ancient-Style Prose Movement of his time.

On Lu Jianhong's Absence During My Visit to Him

You moved to the city outskirts,
on a wild path leading through mulberry and hemp.
Chrysanthemums newly planted by your fence;
it's autumn but they're not in bloom.
No dog barks when I knock on the door.
I go to ask your neighbor to the west:
he says you disappear into mountains
and return through the slanting sunset.

MENG JIAO

(751–814)

Meng Jiao came from Huzhou-Wukang (present-day Deqing County, Zhejiang province) and was the oldest and among the best of the circle of writers who gathered around the great prose master Han Yu in the last decade of the eighth century. He met Han Yu in Changan in 791. A year later Han Yu passed the imperial examinations; Meng Jiao failed, as he did again in 793. He finally passed in 796 but did not receive a position for four years, and even then it was a humiliatingly insignificant post in the provinces. Meng Jiao lost this post within a few years and settled in Luoyang, where he lived for the rest of his life, dependent on patrons and friends. His personal life was one of tragedy and loss: his three sons died young, and he lost his wife as well. Approximately five hundred of his poems survive, most of them in the "old style" (*gu shi*).

Meng Jiao was fairly popular in his own time, but his reputation went into a tailspin some centuries after his death, because his brash, disturbing, and jarring verse was seen to lack grace and decorum. His verse has inspired not so much neglect as active hatred, even in such a distinguished reader as Su Shi, who states baldly in his two poems "On Reading Meng Jiao's Poetry" that "I hate Meng Jiao's poems," which sound to him like a "cold cicada wail." There is no doubt that Su Shi is a master of the literary put-down, and while a number of Meng Jiao's poems do come across as shrill, self-obsessed, and self-pitying, therein lies much of his interest. The great Song dynasty politician and poet Ouyang Xiu admired Meng Jiao precisely because he was a "poor poet . . . who liked to write lines reflecting his hard life." Ouyang writes: "Meng has a poem on moving house: 'I borrow a wagon to carry my furniture / but my goods don't make even one load.' He is saying that he's so poor he hasn't anything to move. He has another poem to express his gratitude to people who have given him some charcoal. 'The heat makes my crooked body straight.' People say one cannot write lines like this without actually experiencing such suffering."[1]

The glaze of decorous objectivity that is so beautiful in much of Chinese poetry is scraped off in Meng Jiao's poems, revealing a didactic would-be Confucian moralist who ends up writing startling, ghostly, and elegiac poems about his sorrows and idiosyncracies, happy to portray himself as despised and sick with illness and self-doubt. If it seems strange to celebrate so fallible a figure, consider his own words: "these sour moans / are also finished verse."

Complaints

> Let's compete with our tears,
> let them pour into a lotus pond;
> then we'll wait this year and see
> whose flowers drown in salt water.

Song of the Homebound Letter

> Tears and ink brushed into a letter
> sent to my family ten thousand miles away.
> My soul leaves with this letter.
> My body becomes a dumb shell here.

---

[1] See *The Art of Writing: Teachings of the Chinese Masters* (Boston: Shambhala Publications, Inc., 1996), translated, edited, and with introductions by Tony Barnstone and Chou Ping, pp. 75–76.

Statement of Feelings in a Shabby Residence on an Autumn Evening

Sleeping in a cold bed, dreams don't go far.
As I listen to autumn, our separation feels sour.
Wind through high and low branches,
thousands and thousands of leaves whisper.
A shallow well won't give enough drink.
Fields of thin soil are unplowed and abandoned.
People don't deal with each other as in ancient times:
no one listens to a poor man's words.

Visiting Zhongnan Mountain

South Mountain fills both earth and sky;
sun and moon emerge from its peaks.
Sunset lingers into night behind a tall summit.
Deep valleys stay dark in broad daylight.
Mountain people are straight and natural,
minds level though the road is rugged.
Long wind drives pine and cypress trees,
skims ten thousand gullies and flows out clear.
At this moment I regret studying books,
morning after morning chasing empty fame.

Frustration

Write bad poems and you're sure to earn a post,
but good poets can only embrace the empty mountains.
Embracing mountains makes me shake with cold.
My face is sad all day long.
They are so jealous of my good poems
swords and spears grow out of their teeth!
They are still chewed by jealousy
of good poets who are long dead.
Though my body's like a broken twig

I cultivate a loftiness and plain austerity,
hoping in vain to be left alone.
The mocking crowd glares at me and howls.

Borrowing a Wagon

I borrowed a wagon to move my furniture,
but my goods don't make even one load.

Don't snap your fingers, wagon owners;
poverty is not worth one sigh.

I run like a servant for my hundred years.
All things bloom and fall like flowers.

After Passing the Highest Imperial Examinations

Why even mention the shabby old days?
This morning I roll free, my thoughts boundless.
Spring wind is joy below my fast horse's hooves
as I race to see all Changan's flowers in just one day.

LADY LIU

(MID-EIGHTH CENTURY)

Lady Liu, according to the Tang story "Biography of Lady Liu,"
was a concubine of a rich man, Mr. Li, who was a good friend to
Han Hong, who was then a poor scholar but was later recog-
nized as one of the ten talented men of letters in the Dali Reign
(he passed the national imperial civil examination in 754). Liu
secretly admired Han Hong. When Mr. Li found out, he married
her to Han. During the An Lushan Rebellion, Liu protected her-
self by hiding in the Faling Temple and cutting her hair to make

herself look ugly. When peace was restored, Han sent people to look for her and sent her a poem. She replied with the lines that appear below. Eventually they were reunited and their story became widely known—recorded not only in *Taiping Records* (*taiping guangji*), vol. 485, but also in Meng Qi's *Narrative Poems: Emotions* (*benshi shi: qinggan*), though the two versions of the story are slightly different.

To the Tune of "Yangliuzhi"*

See the willow twigs
in flowering season:
what a shame each year the twigs are broken as a parting gift.
One leaf releases to wind, suddenly signaling autumn.
Even if you come back this twig is too old to be snapped.

ZHANG JI

(MID-EIGHTH CENTURY)

Zhang Ji was a scholar-poet from Xianzhou who passed the imperial examinations in 753 and held a number of regional and central government posts. His forty-odd poems are not well known, and he is not considered a leading poet of the Tang dynasty, but his short poem "Moored by the Maple Bridge at Night" is extremely popular.

---

*Han's poem, to which Liu's poem was a response, goes as follows:

Willows at the Zhang Platform,
willows at the Zhang Platform,
is the old green spring still there?
Even if the long twigs still hang like in the past,
they must already be snapped by other hands.

Moored by the Maple Bridge at Night

The moon sets, ravens crow, and frost fills the sky.
River maples, fishermen's lanterns. I face sorrow in my sleep.
The Hanshan Temple is outside Gusu City.
At midnight the bell rings—the sound rocks my traveler's boat.

HAN YU

(768–824)

Han Yu was born in Nanyang, Henan province, to a literary family. He is among China's finest prose writers, second only to Sima Qian, and first among the "Eight Great Prose Masters of the Tang and Song." His father died when he was two, and he was raised in the family of his older brother, Han Hui. He taught himself to read and write and was a student of philosophical writings and Confucian thought. His family moved to Changan in 774 but was banished to Southern China in 777 because of their association with disgraced minister Yuan Zai. Han Hui died in 781, leaving the family in poverty; they returned north around 784. In 792, after four attempts, Han Yu passed the imperial exam (*jin shi*). A few years later he went into the service of the military governor of Bianzhou, and then of the military governor of Xuzhou. Finally, in 802, he obtained a post as instructor at the Imperial University, a job that he held periodically between other postings and several periods of exile; ultimately he was made rector of the university. After a number of other distinguished government posts, he died at the age of fifty-six in Changan.

Han Yu was a Confucian thinker and was deeply opposed to Buddhism, a religion that was then popular in the court. As scholar Liu Wu-chi notes, he came close to being executed in 819 for sending a letter to the emperor in which he denounced "the elaborate preparations being made by the state to receive the Buddha's fingerbone, which he called 'a filthy object' and which he said should be 'handed over to the proper officials for destruction by water and fire to eradicate forever its origin.' "[1] He believed that literature and ethics were intertwined, and he led a revolution in prose style against the formal ornamentation then popular, championing instead *gu wen* (old style prose), which was characterized by simplicity, logic, and an emphasis on apt and exact expression. He was at the center of a group of prose writers who adopted this style, a group that included Ouyang Xiu and Su Shi (Su Dongpo) as well as Meng Jiao, whose poetry Han Yu appreciated. While Han Yu's lasting reputation lies as a prose innovator, he was also a fine poet.

Mountain Rocks

Ragged mountain rocks efface the path.
Twilight comes to the temple where bats hover.
Outside the hall I sit on steps and gaze at torrential new rain.
Banana leaves are wide, the cape jasmine is fat.
A monk tells me the ancient Buddhist frescoes are good
and holds a torch to show me, but I can barely see.
I lie quiet in night so deep even insects are hushed.
From behind a rise the clear moon enters my door.

In the dawn I am alone and lose myself,
wandering up and down in mountain mist.
The colors dazzle me: mountain red, green stream,
and a pine so big ten people linking hands can't encircle it.
Bare feet on slick rock as I wade upstream.
Water sounds—*shhhh, shhhh*. Wind inflates my shirt.
A life like this is the best.
Why put your teeth on the bit, why let people rein you in?
O friends,
how can we grow old without returning here?

---

[1] Liu Wu-chi, *An Introduction to Chinese Literature* (Bloomington: Indiana University Press, 1973), p. 126.

Losing My Teeth*

Last year a tooth dropped,
this year another one,
then six or seven went fast
and the falling is not going to stop.
All the rest are loose
and it will end when they are all gone.
I remember when I lost the first
I felt ashamed of the gap.
When two or three followed,
I worried about death.
When one is about to come loose,
I am anxious and fearful
since forked teeth are awkward with food,
and in dread I tilt my face to rinse my mouth.
Eventually it will abandon me and drop
just like a landslide.
By now the falling out is old hat,
each tooth goes just like the others.
Fortunately I have about twenty left.
One by one they will go in order.
If one goes each year,
I have enough to last two decades.
Actually it does not make much difference
if they go together or separately.
People say when teeth fall out
your life is fading.
I say life has its own end;

---

*Written in 803 when Han Yu was thirty-six years old. Zhuangzi tells the story of how he met a woodsman in the mountains who chose not to cut down a tree whose wood was useless. Afterward he visited a friend who wanted to slaughter for him one of his two geese, one of which could sing and one of which could not; he killed the one who didn't greet his guest. His student asked Zhuangzi, "That tree because it's useless was able to survive, but the goose because it couldn't sing was slaughtered. What do you think about that?" Zhuangzi answered, "I stand between the two," meaning you shouldn't be too useful and shouldn't be too useless.

long life, short life, we all die.
People speak of the gaps in my teeth,
and all gaze at me in shock.
I quote Zhuangzi's story—
a tree and a wild goose each has its advantages,
and though silence is better than slurring my words
and though I can't chew, at least soft food tastes great
and I can sing out this poem
to surprise my wife and kids.

Listening to Yinshi Play His Instrument

Softly lovers whisper to each other,
pouring out affection and complaints.
Suddenly the tune becomes daring,
heroes marching to the battlefield.
Floating clouds and willow catkins have no roots;
between heaven and earth they float.
Hundreds of birds chirp and call together
—suddenly only the phoenix is heard.
Now climbing up even one inch is hard,
but then it waterfalls thousands of yards.
I sigh that though I have two ears
they do not understand music.
When you started to play
I couldn't sit or stand still by your side.
I raised my two hands to stop you,
my tears wetting my clothes.
You are a master at this instrument, Yin.
Please don't fill my guts with ice and fire.

Poem to Commander Zhang at the Meeting of the Bian and Si Rivers

Two rivers meet at this corner of the city
where a one-thousand-step polo field is smooth as if planed
and a low wall stretches around three sides.
Drums clatter when red flags are raised.
Before sunrise on a chill early autumn morning,
why are you all dressed up like this?
It's been agreed, teams will be chosen to fight for the win.
A hundred horses draw in their hooves while brushing by each other.
The ball surprises and players gather and disperse with frantic sticks.
There are red pommels made of dyed ox hair and gold bridles.
A player turns aside and reaches over close to the horse belly,
a thunder rolls from his hand and the magic ball runs.
Players retreat and relax on both sides,
but suddenly things shift and they fight again.
The serve is hard, but the receiver is more skillful, such rude
    strength!
Cheers cascade from the surrounding crowd as strong men shout.
This is, of course, for military training, not for fun,
different than sitting calmly moving pieces on a map,
but these days it is hard to find loyal officers,
so please rein in your horses and fight real enemies.

XUE TAO

(768–831)

Xue Tao was a well-respected Tang dynasty poet. She was born either in the Tang capital, Changan, or in Chengdu in present-day Sichuan province, where her father, a minor government official, was posted. A story about her childhood, perhaps apocryphal, suggests that she was able to write complex poems by the age of seven or eight. She may have gained some literary education from her father, but he died before she reached marriageable age. She ended up being a very successful courtesan, one of the few paths for women in Tang dynasty China that encouraged conversation and artistic talent. After the military governor, Wei Gao, became her literary patron, her reputation spread. She is said to have had an affair with another famous literary figure, Yuan Zhen. Late in life she went to live in seclusion and put on the habit of a Daoist churchwoman. More than one hundred of her poems survive. She is often considered (with Yu Xuanji) one of the two finest female poets of the Tang dynasty.

Seeing a Friend Off

> In water lands, night frost on reeds,
> a cold moon the color of the mountains.
> Who says our thousand-mile separation starts tonight?
> My dream can travel to the farthest border pass.

Sending Old Poems to Yuan Zhen

Everyone writes poems in their own manner
but only I know delicacy of wind and light.
When writing of flowers in moonlight, I lean toward the dark.
Of a willow in rainy dawn I write how twigs hang down.
They say green jade should stay hidden deep,
but I write candidly on red-lined paper.
I'm old now but can't stop writing,
so I open myself to you as if I were a good man.

A Spring in Autumn

> Behind a ribbon of evening mist, a chill sky distills,
> and a melody of far waterfalls like ten silk strings
> comes to my pillow to tug feelings,
> keeping me sleepless in sorrow past midnight.

Spring Gazing

(Four Poems)

1

Flowers bloom but we can't share them.
Flowers fall and we can't share our sadness.
If you need to find when I miss you most:
when the flowers bloom and when they fall.

2

I pull a blade of grass and tie a heart-shaped knot
to send to the one who understands my music.
Spring sorrow is at the breaking point.
Again spring birds murmur sad songs.

3

Wind, flowers, and the day is aging.
No one knows when we'll be together.
If I can't tie my heart to my man's,
it's useless to keep tying heart-shaped knots.

4

Unbearable when flowers fill the branches,
when two people miss each other.
Tears streak my morning mirror like jade chopsticks.
Does the spring wind know that?

Willow Catkins

In February, light, fine willow catkins
play with people's clothes in spring breeze;
they are heartless creatures,
flying south one moment, then north again.

Hearing Cicadas

> Washed clean by dew, cicada songs go far
> and like windblown leaves piling up
> each cicada's cry blends into the next.
> Yet each lives on its own branch.

Moon

> Its spirit leans like a thin hook
> or opens round like a Han-loom fan,
> slender shadow whose nature is to be full,
> seen everywhere in the human world.

LIU YUXI

(772–842)

Liu Yuxi came from Luoyang in Henan province. An official who passed the highest imperial examinations when he was twenty, he worked alongside the poet Liu Zongyuan. Demoted for political reasons, he was sent to work for nine years in a minor position in Langzhou in Hunan province. Recalled to the capital, he continued to have political problems, offending officials with his satirical writing and finding himself again exiled to various postings around the country, though he ended his life working in a good position as president of the Board of Rites. An important poet in his day, Lui Yuxi showed an interest in adapting folk songs to poetry (as in the "Bamboo Branch Song" included in this collection) and wrote very strong political poems. His repeated exile was a direct result of the political views evinced in his poetry.

Mooring at Niuzhu at Dusk

When evening wind rises from reeds,
the autumn river is scaled like a fish.
Leftover sunset clouds suddenly shift color
and songs echo after wild geese roam off.
When military drums are no longer heard
a fisherman's lamps are bright.
No one knows what to say about history.
I walk alone in moonlight.

Bamboo Branch Song

Willows are green, green and the river water flat.
I hear a man on the river singing me songs
and see sun on my east, rain to my west.
The sun is shying off, but I feel his shine.[1]

Black-Uniform Lane

Wild grass blossoms by the Red-Bird Bridge.
Sun sets at the open end of Black-Uniform Lane.
The old swallows who built nests under the prime minister's eaves
now fly into the households of common folk.

Looking at Dongting Lake

Lake light and autumn moonlight in harmony;
the calm lake surface is an unpolished metal mirror.
From afar the green mountain by Dongting Lake
is a green field-snail on a silver plate.

---

[1] The last line literally means: "If you say there is no sunshine, yet sunshine there is," but the word for sunshine, *qing*, and the word for love, *qing*, sound the same, creating a double entendre here. Of course, this is one of those delightful, impossible translation problems. We did our best to include a similar punning homophone with "shying" and "shine."

BAI JUYI

(772–846)

Bai Juyi was born in Henan to a poor family of scholars. He took the imperial exam at age twenty-seven and dreamed, with his friend Yuan Zhen, of being a reformer. However, his career as an official was less than illustrious, and his attempts to criticize incidents of injustice only caused him to be banished from the capital (Changan) in 815. He was the prefect of Hangzhou (822–825) and then of Suzhou (825–827) but eventually retired from political life, which he found to be a disappointment. He turned to Buddhism and fared somewhat better as a writer than as a politician. He was popular in his lifetime, both in China, where his poems were known by peasants and court ladies alike, and in Japan, where a number of his poems found their way into *The Tale of Genji* and where he was the subject of a Noh play and became a sort of Shinto deity. More than twenty-eight hundred of his poems survive, as he was careful to preserve his work; in 815 he sent his writings to Yuan Zhen, who edited and compiled them into an edition of his collected work in 824–825.

Bai Juyi's poems show an interest in recording both his times and his private life and often reveal an empathy with the poor that belies the heights of his own career. They are often written in a deliberately plain style, and some of his poetry is written in imitation of the folk songs collected by the Music Bureau (*yuefu* poems) in the second century BCE. According to a popular account, Bai Juyi used to read his poems to an old peasant woman and changed any line that she couldn't understand. There is a benevolent directed intelligence in his poems that comes through the refractions of culture and translation and makes us feel the powerful presence of this poet who died more than a thousand years ago.

Assignment Under the Title
"Departure at Ancient Grass Field"*

Green and thick, weeds in the field.
Every year they wither and bloom.
Wildfire cannot destroy them;
they come back again with spring wind.
Distant grass invades ancient roads;
its sunny green links abandoned cities.
Now I'm seeing off my friend again.
The sorrow of parting is a field of rampant weeds.

Night Rain

Chirp of an early cricket. Silence.
The lamp dies then flares up again.
Night must be raining outside the window:
plink, *plunk* on the banana leaves.

Song of an Evening River

A ray of setting sun paves the water,
half the river is emerald, half the river ruby.
I love the third night in the ninth month—
dewdrops turn into pearls, the moon into a bow.

Lament for Peony Flowers

I grieve for the red peony flowers by the steps.
By this evening two branches have withered.
Tomorrow morning wind will blow away the rest.
At night I keep sad watch, hold flame over the dying red.

---

*Written when the poet was only sixteen years old, this was an assignment
poem (with a predetermined title) to practice for the imperial exams.

Buying Flowers

Spring's dusk comes to the imperial city.
Rattle, clatter, carriages and horses pass.
Everyone is saying, "It's peony season,"
and I follow them to buy flowers.
Expensive or cheap, there is no fixed cost,
prices shift with the number of blossoms.
Though a hundred red ones are like flames, flames,
even a small bouquet is worth five rolls of silk.
Canopies are used to cover the flowers
and bamboo frames protect them.
They are sprinkled and sealed with mud
so that, transplanted, their color doesn't change.
Every household follows this craze,
and no one wakes up from the addiction.
Now an old farmer
chances by the flower market,
lowers his head and sighs alone.
No one understands his sigh.
One cluster of deep-colored flowers
would pay the taxes of ten households.

Light Fur and Fat Horses

Arrogance fills the road
and shiny saddles light up the dust.
If you ask who these men are
you'll be told, "Officials close to the emperor."
Those in red are ministers.
Those in purple are generals.
They are off to attend the army banquet
on horses like racing clouds.
Famous wine brims over the jugs.
They have countless delicacies from water and land.
Their fingers break open Tungting tangerines

and they eat fine fish filets from the Celestial Lake.
They feel so content when full
and their arrogance swells with the wine.
This year on the South bank of the Yangtze River there is drought.
In the State of Chu, people are eating people.

Watching the Reapers

Farmers have few slow months
and the fifth one is double busy.
Southern wind rises at night
and the wheat fields yellow.
Women carry food on shoulder,
kids bring water along.
They go together to feed their men
who are working at the South Hill
with feet burned by hot soil,
backs scorched by the bright and flaming sky.
But they are too exhausted to feel the heat
and don't want the long summer days to end.

There is a poor woman nearby,
carrying her son on her arm.
She gleans wheat ears with her right hand,
a broken basket hanging on her left elbow.
She looks up and tells me
a story that twists my heart:
all their harvest is gone to pay for the land rent.
She picks these ears to fill hungry stomachs.

What achievement, what virtue, have I
that I need not labor like a farmer?
I have an income of three hundred bushels,
and a surplus of food at the end of year.
I am ashamed, and these thoughts
nag at me for the rest of the day.

The Old Charcoal Seller

The old charcoal seller
chops wood and makes charcoal at South Mountain.
With a face full of dust and soot,
his hair is gray and his fingers all black.
How much can he make from selling charcoal?
Just enough to clothe his body and feed his mouth.
His clothes are very thin,
but he wishes it colder to keep charcoal prices high.
It snowed one foot outside the city during the night,
and he drove his charcoal cart through frozen ruts at dawn.
Now the sun is high, the ox is tired and the man hungry;
they take a rest in the mud outside the South Gate.
Who are those two men galloping near on horseback?
—messengers in white shirt and yellow gown.
They read a document in the name of the emperor
and turn the cart around, yell at the ox to head north.
A cartful of charcoal weighs about a ton,
but the palace messengers make the old man give it up
for just half a roll of red gauze and a piece of damask silk
they leave tied around the ox's head.

Song of Everlasting Sorrow*

The Chinese emperor longs for a beauty who could topple empires
but for many years he cannot find one in his country.
There is a girl from the Yang family just coming of age,

---

*This poem recounts the story of Yang Guifei, the famous beauty and the
concubine of the Tang emperor Xuanzong (685–762, ruled 713–756). Xuan-
zong was among China's greatest emperors, but he neglected his rule once he
met Yang Guifei and made her his concubine. Yang was close to An Lushan,
the Turkic general, and adopted him as her son. When An rebelled in 755 (in
the famed An Lushan Rebellion that devastated the empire), Yang and her
brother, the prime minister, were blamed. As the emperor and his court fled
the capital in the face of a rebel advance, the furious royal guards killed
Yang's brother and forced the emperor to have Yang strangled at Ma Wei.

hidden deep in her chamber and no one knows about her.
It's hard to waste such natural beauty in anonymity,
and one morning she is chosen to be at the emperor's service.
She returns his gaze and a hundred charms rise from her smile,
making all the painted faces in the Six Palaces seem pale.
In chilly spring she is privileged to bathe in the Imperial Huaqing
    Spa.
Her skin like cream is cleansed in the slippery hot spring water.
She seems so coyly weak when maids help her to her feet;
this is when she first receives the emperor's favor,
with her cloudlike hair, flowerlike face, her gait that sways like gold.
They spend spring nights warm in a bed with lotus nets.
Since spring nights are so short and the sun soon rises high
the emperor neglects to attend morning court.
Never at rest, she attends and serves him at banquets
and spring outings and his every night belongs to her.
There are over three thousand beauties in the palace
but his love for three thousand is focused on her alone.
When her makeup is done in the golden chamber she serves him at
    night;
after banquet in the jade towers they sleep together drunk.
All her siblings are bestowed with royal rank and land,
and she is admired for bringing honor to her family.
This changes the hearts of parents—
they want to give birth to girls instead of boys.

In a tall building rising into clouds on Li Mountain
her fairy music is carried everywhere by wind,
her unhurried songs and slow dances freezing strings and bamboo.
The emperor can never see her perform enough.
But suddenly military drums from Yuyang make the earth vibrate,
shattering her performance of "The Rainbow and Feather
    Garment."
Smoke and dust rise from the nine city gates
as thousands of horsemen march northwest.
But their flapping green-pinion banners fall still;
the imperial column has only moved thirty miles out the west gate.
The six armies of imperial guards all refuse to move on

till the beauty with long moth-eyebrows twists and dies before
    their horses.
Her jewelry is scattered on the ground and no one picks up
her hairpieces of emerald, gold, and jade.
The emperor cannot save her. He just covers his face.
When he turns to look, tears and blood streak down together
and yellow dust spills everywhere in whistling wind
as they take the narrow zigzag mountain path up to Sword Pavilion.
Travelers are rare under Emei Mountain;
the flags and banners look blanched and the sun is thin.
The river and mountains in Sichuan are so green
that the emperor is lost in emotion each day and night.
In this temporary palace he sees a moon the color of heartbreak.
Through night rain he hears bells and the sound tears his guts.

The sky swirls and the sun orbits until the emperor returns in his
    Dragon Chariot
but he lingers here where she died and cannot move on.
In the mud on the Mawei slope,
he doesn't see her jade face, just the spot where she died.
The emperor and his ministers gaze at each other, clothes wet with
    tears.
Looking east to the capital's gate, they let the horses take them
    home.
The garden and ponds all look the same after his return,
the lotus flowers in Taiye Lake and willows in Weiyang Palace.
The lotus flower and willow leaves remind him of her face and
    eyebrows.
How could he not shed tears at this sight
when spring wind comes on a peach-and-plum-blooming night,
or when it rains in autumn and the parasol tree leaves fall.
In the Western Palace and South Garden autumn weeds are rampant,
fallen leaves cover the steps and no one cleans up the dropped
    petals.
The royal drama troupe is starting to grow white hair
and the palace maids in the queen's quarters are getting old.
In the dusk palace fireflies trace his silent thoughts.
He picks at the lonely lamp till the wick's end and still cannot fall
    asleep.

Late and late come the bells and drums in these long nights.
Now the Celestial River clearly shines just before dawn.
Cold frost flakes are heavy on the mandarin-duck tiles.
The kingfisher quilt is cold and there is no one to share it with him.
Slowly so slowly a year passes since the final farewell,
but her ghost never visits in his dreams.
Yet a shaman from Linqiong, a visitor in the capital,
says absolute sincerity can reach the soul of the dead.
As the emperor is so obsessed with her,
it is arranged to let this necromancer search for her soul.

Flying in the sky, riding clouds fast like lightning,
he searches everywhere in heaven and earth,
looking everywhere in blue space and down in the Yellow Springs,[1]
but she is nowhere to be seen in these two vast places.
Suddenly he hears of a fairy mountain in the sea.
The mountain is invisible, hidden in a thin mist of nothingness,
with delicate towers and pavilions where five-colored clouds arise.
Through blurred vision one seems to see many goddesses moving
    there.
One of them is named Taizhen;
her creamy skin and flowery face resemble Yang.
A gold gate to the west chamber and a knock on the jade door,
and the word is passed from one maid to another
that a messenger from the Han's emperor is here,
interrupting her dream in her nine-flower canopied bed.
Grabbing her clothes and pushing away her cushions, she sits up.
Pearl curtains and silver screens open one after another.
Her cloud-hair tilts to one side as she has just gotten up,
and she races down the hall half undressed,
wind puffing up her long loose sleeves,
recalling her dance to "The Rainbow and Feather Garment."
Her jade face looks lonely and her tears are not yet dry.
She looks like a branch of pear flowers in spring rain.
With love in her gaze she thanks the emperor,
"After our parting we haven't seen or heard each other.

---

[1] Yellow Springs is the land of the dead.

Our love came to an end in Zhaoyang Palace.
Here in the fairy Penglai Palace, the sun and the moon are long.
I look back and look down at the human world,
unable to see the capital, just dust and mist.
The only way is to use old souvenirs to express deep feelings.
I'll send a lacquered box and gold hairpin to you
and save one prong of the hairpin and one panel of the box,
snapping the decorated panel and hairpin in two.
Just make your determination as firm as the gold,
we will have a chance to meet in the human world or in heaven."
Before the shaman departed she asked him to take a message
with vows that only the emperor and she knew.
It was said on the seventh day of the seventh month in Longevity
    Hall
they had said to each other in private at midnight:
"In the sky let's fly as birds sharing wings,[2]
and on earth let's be trees with trunks growing as one."
Though heaven and earth are long, they will cease at last,
but this regret stretches on and on forever.

Song of the Lute

In the tenth year of the Yuanhe Period [815], I was demoted
to deputy governor and exiled to Jiujiang. In autumn the next
year, I was seeing a friend off at the Penpu ferry when I heard
through the night someone playing lute in a boat. The tune,
crisp and metallic, carried the flavor of the music of the capi-
tal. I asked her who she was, and she told me she was a prosti-
tute from the capital, Changan, and had learned to play lute
from Master Mu and Master Cao. Now she was old and her
beauty had declined and therefore she had married a mer-
chant. So I ordered wine and asked her to play several tunes.
We fell silent for a while. Then she told me about the pleasure

---

[2] Sharing-wing birds are legendary birds with one eye and one wing; only by
sharing wings can they fly.

of her youth, though now she is low and withered, drifting about on rivers and lakes. I had been assigned to posts outside the capital for two years and had enjoyed myself in peace. But touched by her words, that evening I began to realize what I truly felt about being exiled. So I wrote this long poem for her with a total of 612 characters, entitled "Song of the Lute."

Seeing off a guest at night by the Xunyang River,
I felt autumn shivering on maple leaves and reed flowers.
I dismounted from my horse and my guest stepped on the boat;
we raised our cups for a drink without the music of pipes or
    strings.
We got drunk but not happy, mourning his departure.
When he embarked, the moon was half drowned in the river.
Suddenly we heard a lute sing across the water
and the host forgot to return home, and the guest stopped his
    boat.
Following the sound we softly inquired who the musician was,
the lute fell silent and the answer came after a pause.
We steered our boat close and invited her to join us,
with wine refilled and lamp relit, our banquet opened again.
It took a thousand pleases and ten thousand invitations before she
    appeared,
though with her lute she still hid half her face.
She plucked a few times to tune her strings.
Even before the melody formed one felt her emotion.
Each string sounded muted and each note meditative,
as if the music were narrating the sorrows of her life.
With eyebrows lowered she let her hands freely strum on and on,
pouring pent-up feelings out of her heart.
Softly strumming, plucking, sweeping, and twanging the strings,
she played "Rainbow Garment" then "Green Waist."
The thick strings splattered like a rain shower,
the thin strings whispered privately like lovers,
splattering and whispering back and forth,
big pearls and small pearls dropping into a jade plate.
Smooth, the notes were skylarks chirping under flowers.
Uneven, the sound flowed like a spring under ice,

the spring water cold and strained, the strings congealing silence,
freezing to silence, till the sounds couldn't pass, and were
  momentarily at rest.
Now some other hidden sorrow and dark regret arose
and at this moment silence was better than sound.
Suddenly a silver vase exploded and the water splashed out,
iron horses galloped through and swords and spears clashed.
When the tune stopped, she struck the heart of the instrument,
all four strings together, like a piece of silk tearing.
Silence then in the east boat and the west.
All I could see in the river's heart was the autumn moon, so pale.

Silently she placed the pick between the strings,
straightened her garment and stood up with a serious face.
She told us, "I was a girl from the capital,
lived close to the Tombs of the Toad.
I finished studying lute at the age of thirteen,
and was first string in the Bureau of Women Musicians.
When my tunes stopped, the most talented players were humbled,
other girls were constantly jealous when they saw me made up,
the rich young city men competed to throw me brocade head scarves,
and I was given countless red silks after playing a tune.
My listeners broke hairpins and combs when they followed my
  rhythm.
I stained my blood-colored silk skirt with wine
and laughed all year and laughed the next,
and autumn moon and spring wind passed unnoticed.
My brother was drafted and my madame died.
An evening passed, and when morning came my beauty was gone.
My door became desolate and horses seldom came,
and as I was getting old I married a merchant.
My merchant cared more about profit than being with me.
A month ago he went to Fuliang to buy tea.
I am here to watch this empty boat at the mouth of the river.
The bright moon circles around the boat and the water is very cold.
Deep into the night I suddenly dreamed about my young days
and wept in dream as tears streaked through my rouge."

I was already sighing, listening to her lute,
but her story made me even sadder.
I said, "We both are exiled to the edge of this world
and our hearts meet though we've never met before.
Since I left the capital last year,
I was exiled to Xunyang and became sick.
Xunyang is too small to have any music;
all year round I heard no strings or pipes.
My home is close to the Pen River, low and damp,
and yellow reeds and bitter bamboo surround the house.
What do you think I hear there day and night?
Cuckoos chirping blood and the sad howls of apes.
Spring river, blossoming morning and autumn moon night—
I often have my wine and drink by myself.
It is not that there are no folk songs or village flutes,
but their yawps and moans are just too noisy for my ear.
Tonight I heard your lute speak
and my ear pricked up, listening to fairy music.
Please don't decline, sit down to play another tune,
and I'll write a 'Song of the Lute' for you."
Touched by my words she stood there for a long time,
then sat down and tuned up her strings and speeded up the rhythm.
Sad and touching it was different from her last song
and everyone started to weep.
If you ask, "Who shed most tears in this group?"
The marshal of Jiangzhou's black gown was all wet.

Seeing Yuan Zhen's Poem on the Wall at Blue Bridge Inn

In spring snow at Blue Bridge you were called back to Changan.
In autumn wind I was exiled to the Qin Mountains.
Whenever I got to a horse station I would dismount
and meander around walls and pillars, hoping to find your poems.

On Laziness

When offices are open I'm too lazy to apply for office.
And though I have lands I'm too lazy to farm them.
My roof leaks but I'm too lazy to fix it
and I'm too lazy to patch my gown when it splits.
I'm too lazy to pour my wine into my cup;
it's like my cup is always empty.
I'm too lazy to play my lute;
it's as if it has no strings.
My family says the steamed rice is all eaten;
I want some but am too lazy to hull it.
I receive letters from relatives and friends
I want to read, but am too lazy to slit them open.
I heard about Qi Shuye
who spent all his life in laziness,
but he played the lute and smelted iron.
Compared with me, he isn't lazy at all!

On Laozi

"The ignorant speak, but the sage stay silent."
I heard this saying from Laozi.
But if Laozi knew the Way,
why did he write a book of five thousand characters?

Madly Singing in the Mountains

There is no one among men that has not a special failing;
And my failing consists in writing verses.
I have broken away from the thousand ties of life;
But this infirmity still remains behind.
Each time that I look at a fine landscape,
Each time that I meet a loved friend,
I raise my voice and recite a stanza of poetry
And marvel as though a god had crossed my path.

Ever since the day I was banished to Hsün-yang
Half my time I have lived among the hills.
And often, when I have finished a new poem,
Alone I climb the road to the Eastern Rock.
I lean my body on the banks of white Stone;
I pull down with my hands a green cassia branch.
My mad singing startles the valleys and hills;
The apes and birds all come to peep,
Fearing to become a laughingstock to the world,
I choose a place that is unfrequented by men.

Translated by Arthur Waley

After Getting Drunk, Becoming Sober in the Night

Our party scattered at yellow dusk and I came home to bed;
I woke at midnight and went for a walk, leaning heavily on a friend.
As I lay on my pillow my vinous complexion, soothed by sleep,
    grew sober:
In front of the tower the ocean moon, accompanying the tide, had
    risen.
The swallows, about to return to the beams, went back to roost
    again;
The candle at my window, just going out, suddenly revived its
    light.
All the time till dawn came, still my thoughts were muddled;
And in my ears something sounded like the music of flutes and
    strings.

Translated by Arthur Waley

Resignation

(Part of a Poem)

Keep off your thoughts from things that are past and done;
For thinking of the past wakes regret and pain.
Keep off your thoughts from thinking what will happen;
To think of the future fills one with dismay.
Better by day to sit like a sack in your chair;
Better by night to lie like a stone in your bed.
When food comes, then open your mouth;
When sleep comes, then close your eyes.

Translated by Arthur Waley

On His Baldness

At dawn I sighed to see my hairs fall;
At dusk I sighed to see my hairs fall.
For I dreaded the time when the last lock should go. . . .
They are all gone and I do not mind at all!
I have done with that cumbrous washing and getting dry;
My tiresome comb for ever is laid aside.
Best of all, when the weather is hot and wet,
To have no topknot weighing down on one's head!
I put aside my messy cloth wrap;
I have got rid of my dusty tasseled fringe.
In a silver jar I have stored a cold stream,
On my bald pate I trickle a ladleful.
Like one baptized with the Water of Buddha's Law,
I sit and receive this cool, cleansing joy.
Now I know why the priest who seeks repose
Frees his heart by first shaving his head.

Translated by Arthur Waley

Old Age

(Addressed to Liu Yü-hsi, who was born in the same year, 835 CE)

We are growing old together, you and I;
Let's ask ourselves, what is age like?
The dull eye is closed ere night comes;
The idle head, still uncombed at noon.
Propped on a staff, sometimes a walk abroad;
Or all day sitting with closed doors,
One dares not look in the mirror's polished face;
One cannot read small-letter books.
Deeper and deeper, one's love of old friends;
Fewer and fewer, one's dealings with young men.
One thing only, the pleasure of idle talk,
Is great as ever, when you and I meet.

Translated by Arthur Waley

Since I Lay Ill

Since I lay ill, how long has passed?
Almost a hundred heavy-hanging days.
The maids have learned to gather my medicine herbs;
The dog no longer barks when the doctor comes.

The jars in my cellar are plastered deep with mold;
My singers' mats are half crumbled to dust.
How can I bear, when the Earth renews her light,
To watch from a pillow the beauty of spring unfold?

Translated by Arthur Waley

A Dream of Mountaineering

(Written when he was seventy)

> At night, in my dream, I stoutly climbed a mountain
> Going out alone with my staff of hollywood.
> A thousand crags, a hundred hundred valleys—
> In my dream-journey none were unexplored
> And all the while my feet never grew tired
> And my step was as strong as in my young days.
> Can it be that when the mind travels backward
> The body also returns to its old state?
> And can it be, as between body and soul,
> That the body may languish, while the soul is still strong?
> Soul and body—both are vanities;
> Dreaming and waking—both alike unreal.
> In the day my feet are palsied and tottering;
> In the night my steps go striding over the hills.
> As day and night are divided in equal parts—
> Between the two, I *get* as much as I *lose*.

Translated by Arthur Waley

LIU ZONGYUAN

(773–819)

Liu Zongyuan was one of the finest prose writers of the Tang dynasty and one of only two Tang dynasty writers included among the "Eight Great Prose Masters of the Tang and Song." A friend of Han Yu, he was one of the followers of the Ancient Style Prose Movement, which emphasized clarity and utility over ornament in prose writing. As a poet he was relatively minor. He was born and raised in Changan, the capital during the Tang dynasty. After a highly successful early career in civil government, he was reassigned to a post in the provinces (in Yongzhou, Hunan province) after the abdication of Emperor Shunzong in 805. A decade later he was banished even farther away, to modern Guangxi. His works in exile are considered his finest. While he was in the capital, his writing was bureaucratic in nature, and he considered it primarily a means to advance his career; in exile, however, he wrote a number of delightful didactic pieces, showing a neo-Confucian synthesis of both Daoism and Buddhism (unlike Han Yu, Liu Zongyuan was not averse to the wave of Buddhism that was then sweeping across China). He is particularly known for his allegorical writings and for his fables, which, like Aesop's, often feature animals. His poem "River Snow" is considered a prime example of "minimum words, maximum message" and has been the subject of numerous landscape paintings.

River Snow

> A thousand mountains. Flying birds vanish.
> Ten thousand paths. Human traces erased.
> One boat, bamboo hat, bark cape—an old man
> alone, angling in the cold river. Snow.

Poem to Relatives and Friends in the Capital After Looking at Mountains with Monk Hao Chu

> Sharp-pointed cliffs by the sea are swords
> that slice my homesick guts in autumn.
> If I could split into millions of selves,
> I'd scatter them on all the peaks to gaze home.

Summer Day

Damp summer in Nanzhou intoxicates like wine;
with northern windows open I take a nap on the tea table.
I wake at noon alone and hear nothing but the sound of mountain
 boys
pounding tea leaves in stone mortars in the bamboo grove.

Fisherman

> A fisherman spends the night under West Rock,
> pails clear river water and burns bamboo.
> Smoke vanishes, sun rises, and no one is seen.
> The swishing oar turns mountains and water green.
> Floating the central current, he turns to gaze at sky
> above rock where mindless clouds chase each other.

The Caged Eagle

> Chill wind noisily sifts a hard frost
> as a black eagle soars up the dawning light.
> Clouds shatter, mist cracks, a rainbow breaks in half!
> The eagle skims a hillock like thunder and lightning.
> The sound of fierce wings cuts thorns and brush;
> he snatches foxes and hares and soars through sky again.
> Hair on claws, blood on beak, one hundred birds gone.
> He stands alone, gazing round, often excited.
> But fiery wind and damp summer suddenly come,
> now caged, his feathers droop and his wings ache.
> In the wilderness raccoons and rats are just pests,
> but now ten times a night they come to startle and to attack.
> If only wind would swell my wings again
> and I could fly in clouds, all constraints gone!

ZHANG JI

(C. 776–C. 829)

Zhang Ji should not be confused with the other Tang dynasty poet named Zhang Ji whose work is also included in this volume (although their names are different in Chinese, they read the same transliterated into English). Zhang Ji was helped along in his career by a number of powerful friends and admirers. The poet Meng Jiao, for example, arranged for Zhang Ji to work with him and Han Yu on the staff of the military governor of Xunwu. With Han Yu's help Zhang Ji passed the provincial and imperial examinations and became a tutor in the Directorate of Education, where, after a number of further postings, he eventually became the Director of Studies.

In Zhang Ji's *yuefu* (Music Bureau style) poem "A Soldier's Wife Complains," he evinces a sympathy for the poor and the ordinary and participates in a Confucian critique of social injustice. It is modeled on the work of Du Fu, whose genius Zhang Ji was among the first to recognize. Of Zhang Ji's four hundred poems, seventy are in the *yuefu* style, and many decry the effects of war and taxation on the poor. His work influenced such poets as Bai Juyi and Yuan Zhen, who also used the Music Bureau style to critique social ills and try to convince the government to change.

A Soldier's Wife Complains*

In September the barbarians killed the border general
and all our Han soldiers died by the Liao River.
No one can travel three thousand miles to pick up white bones,
so the families tried to summon the lost souls and bury them.
Women depend on their sons and husbands,
happy to live together, even in poverty,
but my husband is dead in a field and my son's in my belly
and though my body remains, my life is a candle in daylight.

Song of a Virtuous Woman

(To Governor Li Shidao at Dong Ping)

You know I'm married
yet you gave a gift of two bright pearls.
Grateful for your affection

---

*Since they didn't have the bodies, the families buried the dead soldiers' clothes and summoned their souls to lie at rest.

I tied them on my red silk skirt.
My home's tall buildings and gardens extend afar
and my husband holds his halberd in the Bright Light Palace.
I understand your intentions are honest as sun and moon,
but I've sworn to share life and death with my man.
I return two pearls to you, and two tears drop.
Why didn't we meet before I married?[1]

Arriving at a Fisherman's House at Night

The fisherman's house is near the river mouth.
Tides flow into his brushwood gate.
A traveler, I wish to spend the night here
but the host is not back yet.
The bamboo grove is deep and the village road long,
fishing boats are few when the moon rises,
but look, on the distant sand bank,
a straw cloak flapping in spring wind.

WU KE

(EIGHTH–NINTH CENTURIES)

Wu Ke's original surname was Jia. He became a monk at an early
age and was the cousin of the poet Jia Dao, whose monk name
was Wu Ben (they had the same grandfather on the father's side).
Born in Juo County, Hebei province, Wu Ke lived as a monk with
Jia Dao in the Green Dragon Temple in the capital. He was friend
to many poets. His own poetry is written mostly in five-character
lines, and he is known for his ability to describe things without
explicitly naming what he is describing. For example, in the first
of the lines "I listened to rain till the last night drum ceased /
and opened my door to find fallen leaves deep," Wu Ke is describing

---

[1] This is actually a poem written by a man to another man, declining an invi-
tation to leave his current post and work as an adviser.

not the rain but the sound of falling leaves. His poems are found in the *Complete Tang Poems (quan tangshi)*.

To Cousin Jia Dao in Autumn

> Dark insects noisy at dusk
> as I sat in meditation in the West Woods.
> I listened to rain till the last night drum ceased
> and opened my door to find fallen leaves deep.
> Because we used to suffer from the illness of ambition[1]
> we turned our minds to Dongting Lake.
> This same old business in the capital
> still keeps you far away.

JIA DAO

(778–841)

Jia Dao was a Buddhist monk who gave up the monk's life around 810 after meeting the poet Han Yu and moving to the capital, Changan. Along with Zhang Ji and Meng Jiao, Jia Dao followed the aesthetic principles advocated by Han Yu, who celebrated the didactic and moral effects of literature and presented the poet as an honest Confucian rectifier of societal wrongs. With the encouragement of Han Yu, he tried to pass the imperial examination but failed repeatedly. Although he was not a successful official, he gained a strong reputation as a poet. Here is a famous story about the first meeting of Jia Dao and Han Yu, from the compilation of poetic anecdotes titled *Notes of Xiang Su:*

---

[1] The illness of ambition refers to Jia Dao's continuous efforts to pass the national imperial exam, which he failed many times. Even after passing it he was assigned only a very minor position. Supposedly he and his cousin discussed the possibility of living a hermit's life, like that of a fisherman on Dongting Lake.

When the monk Jia Dao came to Luoyang, monks were forbidden to leave the monastery after noon. Jia Dao wrote a sad poem about this and Han Yu liked the poem so much he helped him get permission to become a layman.

When he was concentrating on his poems he would often run into important people without being aware of it. One day, riding his donkey, he was thinking about these lines: "Birds return to their nests in trees by the pond. / A monk is knocking at a door by moonlight."

He couldn't decide whether to replace the word "knocking" with "pushing," so he was making wild gestures on his donkey, acting out first a knock and then a push. While doing this he encountered the procession of the mayor, Han Yu, and neglected to give way. Arrested by the bodyguards, and brought before Han Yu, he was asked to explain his actions. He explained how he was trying to decide between these two words. Han Yu considered this for a long time, and said, at last, "knocking" is better. They became fast friends after that.

The great Song dynasty poet and statesman Ouyang Xiu admired Jia Dao's intense evocations of hardship: "Like Meng Jiao, Jia Dao was a poor poet until his death and liked to write lines reflecting his hard life. . . . He writes: 'I have white silk in my sideburns / but cannot use it to weave a warm shirt.' Even if one could weave hair, it wouldn't do him much good. Jia Dao also has a poem 'Morning Hunger' with these lines: 'I sit and hear the zither on the western bed: / two or three strings snapping in the cold.' People say that this poem shows that hunger as well as cold is unbearable."[1]

Looking for the Hermit and Not Finding Him

> Beneath a pine I question a boy.
> He says, "Master has gone to gather herbs
> somewhere on the mountain
> but who knows where? The clouds are deep."

---

[1] See *The Art of Writing: Teachings of the Chinese Masters* (Boston: Shambhala Publications, Inc., 1996), translated, edited, and with introductions by Tony Barnstone and Chou Ping, pp. 62–63, 75–76.

YUAN ZHEN

(779–831)

Known as Yuan the Genius, Yuan Zhen was among the most brilliant poets and statesmen of the Tang dynasty. He was born in Changan to a family descended from the royal house that ruled Northern China in the fifth and sixth centuries during the Northern Wei dynasty. Though his father died when he was a child, he became a brilliant scholar under his mother's tutoring. He passed the examinations in the category of "clarification of the classics" when he was fourteen, and when he was twenty-four he passed the "highly selective" examination, which landed him an appointment in the imperial library with Bai Juyi, the poet who was to be his lifelong friend. Several years later he took the final palace examination, monitored by the emperor, and gained the highest score, resulting in a position close to the emperor. Like his friend Bai, Yuan dreamed of being a reformer, a dream that was to result in a series of banishments. He did, however, help to create "The New Music Bureau Songs Movement," which attempted to recapture the formal freedoms and the simplicity of diction of the Music Bureau (*yuefu*) form of the Han dynasty and to use poetry for the serious ends of social reform.

When Told Bai Juyi Was Demoted and Sent to Jiangzhou

A dying lamp's low flame tosses the shadows.
This evening, told you've been demoted to Jiangzhou,
I am so startled I sit up in my final sickbed.
Dark wind is blowing rain into cold windows.

Late Spring

Calm day through the thin curtain, swallows talking fast.
Pairs of fighting sparrows kick up dust on the steps.
Wind at dusk, a brushwood gate swings shut.
Flowers drop their last petals. No one notices.

Petals Falling in the River

At sunset the Jialing River flows east
and thousands of pear petals chase the river wind.
What twists my stomach as I watch the river flowers?
Half have fallen in the river, half drift on the air.

from Missing Her After Separation

2

A mountain spring randomly flows over the steps:
a small house among thousands of peach flowers.
Before getting up, I leaf through a Daoist book
and watch her combing her hair under the crystal curtain.

LIU CAICHUN

(LATE EIGHTH–EARLY NINTH CENTURIES)

Liu Caichun, a native of Zhejiang, was a well-known Tang dynasty
courtesan. Though she was a singing girl, she was married to the
actor Zhou Jinan. Between 823 and 829 she visited Yuezhou and
became a friend of Yuan Zhen, the well-known Tang poet. Their
friendship was recorded in a book entitled *Cloud Brook Friend
Discussions* (*yunxi youyi*). Six of her poems are included in the
Complete Tang Poems (*quan tangshi*).

Song of Luogen

(Three Poems)

1

Don't be the wife of a merchant.
He'll use your gold hairpins as divination coins.
Every morning I look at the river mouth,
and over and over run to greet the wrong boat.

2

I don't like the Qin and Huai Rivers.
I hate the boats running on the water.
They carried away my husband.
It's already a year, and then another year.

3

That year on the day you left
I thought you went to Tonglu
but no one could find you there at Tonglu.
Today I got your letter—from Canton!

LI HE

(791–817)

Distantly related to the imperial clan and extremely talented, Li He was nevertheless an unsuccessful scholar who attained only the lowest posts in his brief life (he died at the age of twenty-six). His poetry, like that of Meng Jiao, can be bitterly sarcastic and reflects the frustration he must have felt in his career. In his fifth "Horse Poem," for example, he compares himself to a fine desert horse without an appropriate rider, which longs to be harnessed and directed by imperial (golden) reins. He also has a penchant for erotic, romantic, and even morbidly violent imagery, and his poems grate against the nerves with the shrieking of ghosts, the weeping of flowers, and the burning of sinister fires. He was something of a Chinese Edgar Allan Poe, though a much better poet than Poe was, and like Poe his reputation suffered because literary culture couldn't stomach his unclassifiable works of genius. Sponsored in his day by the prominent poet and prose writer Han Yu, Li He quickly disappeared from literary consciousness after his death, making a comeback only in the last two centuries. Two hundred forty of his poems have survived centuries of neglect, though legend states that what remains was part of a larger collection that was thrown into a toilet by his vindictive cousin.

from Twenty-three Horse Poems

4

This horse is no ordinary horse.
It is celestial like the Horse Constellation.
Walk up and tap its thin bones
and they'll sing like bronze.

5

The great desert of sand is snow
and the Yen Mountain moon is a hook.
When will I be harnessed with golden reins,
galloping clear autumn beneath my hooves?

Shown to My Younger Brother*

After three years away from you,
I'm back at last for one day, and more.
We drink green Luling wine this evening

---

*This poem was written because Li He was deprived of his candidacy for the imperial exams on the grounds that the degree "Jinshi" he was seeking sounded like the name of his father, "Jinshu." According to the Confucian tradition, it is a violation of filial piety to mention directly one's father's name. It was therefore taboo for Li He to sit in an exam for "Jinshi."

and I see yellow cloth-wrapped books, like when I left.
My sick bones still exist,
so nothing is impossible in this world!
Why bother to plead with the cows-and-horses dice,[1]
just throw and let them roll!

from Speaking My Emotions

2

All day writing, I stopped at dusk,
startled by my own frosty hair.
I laughed at myself in the mirror.
Is this the way to live as long as South Mountain?
I have no wrapping on my head
and my clothes are cheaply dyed with bitter bark.
Just look at the fish in the clear brook;
they drink and swim, pleased with themselves.

Flying Light*

Flying light, flying light—
I urge you to drink a cup of wine.
I do not know the height of blue heaven
or the extent of yellow earth.
I only sense the moon's cold,
sun's burn, sear us.
Eat bear, and you'll grow fat;

---

[1] Cows-and-horses is a gambling game.

*The allusions in "Flying Light" are extremely difficult. The speaker of the poem laments the brevity of life and wants to slay the dragon that draws the sun across the sky, to stop time and recover peace. He considers it ineffective to use elixirs (yellow gold, white jade) to become an immortal and derides Liu Che (Emperor Wu-di of the Han) and Ying Zheng (the first emperor of Qin) for their attempts to build massive, grandiose tombs and immortalize themselves.

eat frog, and you'll waste away.
Where is the Spirit Lady?
And where the Great Unity?
East of the sky is the Ruo tree:
underneath, a dragon, torch in mouth.
I will cut off the dragon's feet
and chew the dragon's flesh:
then morning will never return
and evening cannot bend.
Old men will not die
nor young men weep.
Why then swallow yellow gold
or gulp down white jade?
Who is Ren Hungzi,
riding a white ass through the clouds?
Liu Che, in Maoling tomb, is just a heap of bones.
And Ying Zheng rots in his catalpa coffin,
wasting all that abalone.

Translated by Arthur Sze

There is a story that Ying Zheng died on a journey; his followers, anxious to keep his death a secret, filled a carriage with rotting abalone to disguise the stench of his decomposing body, then smuggled his corpse back into the capital.

One commentary says that the Spirit Lady was worshiped by the Han emperor and that the Great Unity was the supreme deity of the Daoists. I think the speaker is searching for ultimate knowledge and believes the Spirit Lady has it.

The Ruo tree is a mythical tree in the far west, whose foliage is supposed to glow red at sunset. Intriguingly, Li He places the Ruo tree in the east.

Ren Hungzi appears to be an immortal; the emperors are "just a heap of bones," whereas Ren Hungzi, an utter unknown, has somehow achieved the transcendence that they sought.

from Thirteen South Garden Poems

13

Among the saplings, a path revealed at dawn,
long grass blades wet from night mist.
Like a snowy river mouth the willow catkins amaze.
A wheat season rain swells brooks and field.
Sparse bells echo from an ancient temple.
Broken moon hung over a far mountain.
On a sandbank someone strikes stones to make a fire.
Burning bamboo lights up fishing boats.

Su Xiaoxiao's Tomb*

Dew on lonely orchids
like eyes brimming tears.
I find nothing to tie her a heart-shaped knot.
I can't bear to cut the misty flowers.
Grass is her soft green cushion,
pines are her parasol.
She wears the wind,
and water tinkles her jade pendants.
In her lacquered carriage
she waits in the evening
while like a cold emerald candle
a will-o'-the-wisp sparkles
and under the Western Tomb
wind blows the rain.

---

*Su Xiaoxiao was a well-known courtesan from Qiantang who lived in the fifth century. In this poem, her ghost, manifested in the sounds and sights of nature by her tomb, is tinkling jade, lighting candles, and waiting for lovers at dusk.

Song of Goose Gate Governor

Black clouds press the city till it's almost crushed,
and our armor reflects moonlight on shifting metal fish scales.
The sound of horns fills the sky with autumn colors.
Night congeals purple on the fortress like rouge.
With half-furled scarlet banners we approach the Yi River
and in heavy frost our cold drums seem muted.
To live up to the king's expectation on Yellow Gold Tower,[1]
we will wave our jade-dragon swords and die.

Under the City Wall at Pingcheng

Hungry and cold under the Pingcheng City wall,
every night we guard the bright moon
but our parting-gift swords have lost their gloss
and sea wind breaks our hair.

This long fortress extends into white space.
We see Chinese flags red in the distance,
hear short flutes from their black tents.
Mist and smoke soak their dragon banners.

Standing on the city wall at dusk,
we see things blurred under the wall.
Wind throws withered bitter fleabane about,
and our thin horses neigh inside the city.

Please tell us, officer in charge of wall construction,
how many thousand miles are we from the pass?

---

[1] Yellow Gold Tower is located six miles northeast of the Yi River. In the
Warring States period, it was the site where King Zhao of the State of Yan
placed one thousand pieces of gold to attract talented soldiers.

Our one worry: will our bundled corpses be sent home?
We're ready to turn our halberds on ourselves.[1]

Song of an Old Man's Jade Rush

Jade rush, jade rush! A man needs to find emerald jade
to be made in vain for love of beauties into hairpins that quiver at
    each step.
The old man is so starved and cold even the water dragon is worried.
The waters and air of Blue Brook can never be clear again.
Night rain on the hills where the old man munches hazelnuts,
the cuckoo sings till its beak drips blood like an old man's tears.
The water in the Blue Brook loathes living men
and men still hate these waters a thousand years after their deaths.
Slant mountains, cypress wind, and howling rain,
and he dives to the bottom of the spring, a rope tied to his foot
    dangling in the green.
Thinking of his cold village of white huts he misses his fragile babies
by an ancient terrace where stone steps are scattered with hanging
    guts grass.[2]

A Piece for Magic Strings

(A Shamaness Exorcizes Baleful Creatures)

On the western hills the sun sets, the eastern hills darken,
Horses blown by the whirlwind tread the clouds.
From colored lute and plain pipes, crowded faint notes:
Her flowered skirt rustles as she steps in the autumn dust.

---

[1] The last line has been interpreted in various way to mean, heroically, "We're
ready to die upon the halberds," or mutinously, "We're willing to turn our
weapons against our side," or suicidally, "We're ready to turn our halberds on
ourselves."

[2] "Hanging guts grass" is also called "departure grass" or "missing children
vines."

When the wind brushes the cassia leaves and a cassia seed drops
The blue raccoon weeps blood and the cold fox dies.
Dragons painted on the ancient wall with tails of inlaid gold
The god of rain rides into the autumn pool;
And the owl a hundred years old, which changed to a goblin of
the trees,
Hears the sound of laughter as green flames start up inside its nest.

Translated by A. C. Graham

An Arrowhead from the Ancient Battlefield of Changping

Lacquer dust and powdered bone and red cinnabar grains:
From the spurt of ancient blood the bronze has flowered.
White feathers and gilt shaft have melted away in the rain,
Leaving only this triple-cornered broken wolf's tooth.

I was searching the plain, riding with two horses,
In the stony fields east of the post station, on a bank where
bamboos sprouted,
After long winds and brief daylight, beneath the dreary stars,
Damped by a black flag of cloud that hung in the empty night.

To left and right, in the air, in the earth, ghosts shrieked from
wasted flesh.
The curds drained from my upturned jar, mutton victuals were my
sacrifice.
Insects settled, the wild geese swooned, the buds were blight-
reddened on the reeds,
The whirlwind was my escort, puffing sinister fires.

In tears, seeker of ancient things, I picked up this broken barb
With snapped point and russet flaws, which once pierced through
flesh.

In the east quarter on South Street a peddler on horseback
Talked me into bartering the metal for a votive basket.

Translated by A. C. Graham

A Sky Dream

The old rabbit and the cold toad[1] are weeping sky color
and a cloud tower is half open, revealing a slant white wall.
The jade wheel rolling over dewdrops is a wet ball of light;
on a cassia-fragrant road chariots meet jade pendants.[2]
Yellow dust, clear water under the three mountains;
the change of a thousand years is rapid as a galloping horse.
In the distance China is nine wisps of smoke
and in a single cup of water the ocean churns.

HAN SHAN

(LATE EIGHTH–EARLY NINTH CENTURIES)

Han Shan, who may or may not have existed, is the name given
to the putative author of a collection of fascinating Tang dynasty
poems, more than three hundred in number. The poems tell the
story of the author's retreat to Cold Mountain to live a life of her-
metic simplicity, seeking Daoist and Chan (Zen) enlightenment in
nature. They are proselytizing poems, but in their vernacular
speech, their clarity of focus, and their celebration of simplicity,
they embody what they seek to teach, and in this they achieve
their greatest success.

Strangely enough, Han Shan is not considered a major poet in

---

[1] In Chinese mythology the old rabbit and the cold toad are creatures who live
on the moon.

[2] The jade pendants suggest the presence of fairy moon women, or perhaps
specifically of Chang E, the woman who stole the potion of longevity and was
banished to the moon in punishment.

China. The Chinese complain that his work is too vernacular, full of good ideas but lacking in elegance and polish. And yet he has become a favorite poet in English translation, in part because he has had marvelous translators, among them Red Pine, Burton Watson, and Gary Snyder. Perhaps he is a poet who, to echo Robert Frost's famous snub about Carl Sandburg, "can only be improved in translation." The politics of literary reputation aside, though, there is an undeniably remarkable voice that emerges from the poems of Han Shan, one that is quite rare in Chinese poetry. Like Meng Jiao, Han Shan was a cynic and an ironist, and the two poets' bitterness seems to have damaged their reputation among readers in China. Han Shan was also a strange mixture of dogmatist and freethinker, and one senses a personality behind the poems that is harsh and yet humorously irrepressible. Whatever the craft value of his poetry in Chinese, there is much to appreciate in its riddling Buddhist thought and in the way it captures the personality of a writer who may never have lived.

5

My heart[1] is the autumn moon
clear and white in a green pool.
No, nothing else is like it.
How can I make you understand?

72

Pigs eat dead men's flesh.
Men eat dead pigs' guts.
Pigs are not put off by men's stink.
Men say pigs really smell good.
Pigs are thrown in water when dead.
Holes are dug to bury dead men.
If the two don't eat each other,
lotus flowers will bloom from boiling soup.

---

[1] The words "heart" and "mind" are the same in Chinese, but since in China one is supposed to think with the heart, we opted to use this term.

87

Greedy men love to store wealth
like owls love their babies,
but small owls eat their mother when grown,
and the self is hurt by too much wealth.
Give away your wealth and you are blessed;
gathering it makes disasters rise.
With no wealth and no disasters,
you can glide on wings in blue clouds.

92

Heaven is endlessly high,
Earth so thick it has no poles,
and in between live creatures
supported by the Maker's strength;
fighting head-to-head for food and heat,
they scheme to eat each other,
never understanding cause or effect,
blind babies asking, "What color is milk?"

100

The life and death metaphor
can be found in ice and water.
Water solidifies into ice;
ice dissolves into water.
The dead are going to be born;
once born they'll be dead again.
Ice and water do not hurt each other.
Life and death are perfect complements.

125

New rice not yet ripe in the field,
old rice all gone,
I went to borrow a sack
and hesitated outside the door.
The husband came out, said talk to his wife,

his wife came out, said consult her husband.
So closefisted, they don't help the needy.
More wealth loads them with stupidity.

128

An elegant, poised, and handsome young man,
well versed in canons and histories,
everyone calls him a teacher,
or addresses him as a scholar,
but he fails to obtain an official position,
and he does not know how to farm.
He wears only a shabby gown in winter,
totally ruined by books.

131

During thirty years since my birth
I've hiked thousands of miles,
seen green grass converging with a river
and red dust rising at the frontiers,
searched in vain for immortals and elixirs,
studying books and histories.
Today I've returned to Cold Mountain.
I lie back in a stream, washing out my ears.

140

When Mr. Deng was in his youth
he traveled in and out of the capital
with clothes a tender yellow,
handsome as if in a painting.
He rode a horse with snow-white hooves,
stirring up waves of red dust.
Onlookers filled the roadsides
wondering: who was this young man?

141

Who was this young man?
A man hated deeply,
his idiotic mind often angry,
his vulgar eyes often drunk and blurry.
He did not show respect to Buddhas.
He did not give alms to monks.
He only knew how to eat fat slices of meat.
Otherwise, he was totally useless.

146

My way passed ancient tombs,
tears and sighs long dispersed.
Yellow intestines poked from sunken graves.
Shattered coffins showed white bones
and there were leaning urns.
I found no hairpins when I stirred the ash
but wind came swirling
and spilled a mess of dust into the air.

158

There's a tree that existed before the woods,
in age twice as old.
Its roots suffered as the valley changed,
its leaves deformed by wind and frost.
People all laugh at its withered aspect,
caring nothing about the core's beauty.
When the bark is all stripped off,
only essence remains.

165

In idleness I go to visit a prominent monk
in mountain mist and a thousand thousand peaks.
The master himself points out the road
and the moon hangs its lantern out for me.

194

A crowd of stars lines up bright in the deep night.
Lone lamp on the cliff, the moon is not yet sunk,
full and bright without being ground or polished.
Hanging in the black sky is my mind.

204

I gaze on myself in the stream's emerald flow
or sit on a boulder by a cliff.
My mind, a lonely cloud, leans on nothing,
needs nothing from the world and its endless events.

210

Talking about food won't fill your stomach.
Talk about clothing won't keep out cold.
To be full, eat rice.
To stay warm, wear clothes.
Those who don't understand
complain it's hard to get help from Buddha.
Look inside your heart. That's where Buddha is.
Don't look for him outside.

218

When people meet Han Shan,
They all say he's crazy.
His look doesn't attract the gaze,
and he is wrapped up in a cloth gown.
He speaks and they don't understand,
when they speak he keeps silent.
So he tells people,
"Come and visit me on Cold Mountain."

225

The ocean stretches endlessly
with millions of fish and dragons.

They bite and eat each other up,
such foolish slabs of meat.
If the mind is not purged,
illusions rise like mist.
Our nature is bright like the moon.
It can shine without limit.

237

This life is lost in dust.
Like bugs in a bowl
we all day circle, circle
unable to get out.
We're nothing like immortals.
Our sorrows never end,
years and months flow off like water
and in an instant we're old men.

262

In this world people live then die.
Yesterday morning I was sixteen,
healthy with a strong life force.
Now I'm over seventy,
strength gone, body withered.
A flower in spring
blossoms at dawn. At night it dies.

265

The hermit escapes the human world
and likes to sleep on mountains
among green widely spaced vines
where clear torrents sing harmonies.
He steams with joy,
swinging at ease through freedom,
not stained with worldly affairs,
heart clean as a white lotus.

266

A word to meat eaters:
you eat without pause,
but this life is planted in the past
and the future's shaped by today.
If you live for great flavors
fearless of the next life's bill,
you're like a rat in a rice steamer,
so full you can't get out.

307

Keep Han Shan's poems in your home.
They are better than sutras.
You can place the book on top of a screen
and read it through every now and then.

DU QIUNIANG

(EARLY NINTH CENTURY)

Du Qiuniang was born in Jinling in the first half of the ninth century and was married young to the poet Li Chi. After Li Chi died, Du Qiuniang served a prince as a lady-in-waiting, retiring to her hometown once the prince lost his status as heir apparent. Little is known of her after that, except that the Tang poet Du Mu wrote a poem to her in her old age. She was the only woman poet included in the famous anthology *300 Poems of the Tang Dynasty*.

The Coat of Gold Brocade

I tell you, don't adore your coat of gold brocade.
I tell you, adore the short spell of youth.
When the bloom is ready it must be plucked.
Don't wait till flowers drop and break the empty twig.

DU MU

(803–852)

Tang poet, calligrapher, painter, and essayist Du Mu was born in the Tang dynasty capital, Changan (present-day Xian), to an illustrious family. After the death of his father and grandfather when he was still young, the family fell on lean times and was forced to give up servants and sell off property to survive. Du Mu nevertheless managed to receive a classical education and passed the imperial exam at twenty-five. He had a number of minor positions, but not enough to satisfy his ambition. He made a habit of writing to those in high places, praising his own credentials and critiquing civil and military policies, but he achieved a post he was happy with only a few months before his death in 852. Five hundred twenty-four of his poems survive.

Written While Moored on the Qinhuai River

Mist touches cold water and moon embraces the sand.
I'm moored for the night near a tavern on the Qinhuai.
The singing girl doesn't know the empire is in bitter ruin.
Across the river I hear her singing "Blossom of the Inner Court."

Two Poems Improvised at Qi An County

I

Dying sun hovers two bamboo sticks high above the stream's
    bridge.
Half a wisp of mist flows in the blurry willows.
Countless green lotuses lean together and commiserate.
I can't face it, and for a moment turn my back to the west wind.

2

Autumn sounds always stir my traveler's mind.
Rain is deep in the reeds of the Yunmeng marsh in the state of Chu.
By the steps, rain keeps dripping on its own from the parasol tree's
　　big leaves.
Why does it tangle my thoughts and make me improvise sad poems?

On Purebright Day*

> Purebright Season comes with fine fast drizzle
> and travelers on the road feel their souls sliced off.
> Please tell me where I can find a wine shop?
> A cowherd boy points to distant Apricot Blooming Village.

The Han River

> White gulls fly over the broad, rippling river.
> Its pure water in deep spring can dye your clothes green.
> Navigating north and south will make a man age.
> Late sun stays a long time seeing a fishing boat home.

Visiting Leyou Park†

> Open space like an ocean where a lonely bird drowns.
> Ten thousand years are eroded and buried in this field.
> What are the achievements of the Han dynasty?
> Five Tombs, all treeless, and rising autumn wind.

---

*Purebright Day, *qingming*, is the fifth solar term (out of twenty-four divisions) of the Chinese astrological calendar, which is a combination of lunar months and solar terms. Each term starts with the particular day that gives the term its name—e.g., Purebright Day begins the Purebright Solar Term.

†Leyou Park, located in today's southern suburb of Xianan City, was originally a spring park in the Qin dynasty, named Qinyi Chunyuan. It was renamed Leyou Park by Emperor Xun in the Han dynasty. In the Tang dynasty, Princess Taiping added many pavilions to it, and it became a popular

WEN TINGYUN

(812–870)

Wen Tingyun was a native of Taiyuan, in Shanxi province. Known for his wit, intelligence, and handsome looks, he was a failure as an official (he failed the exams many times) and lived the dissolute life of a drunkard and frequenter of brothels. He was a friend of the important late Tang dynasty poet Li Shangyin, and the two of them were poetic innovators and among the first important writers in the lyric (*ci*) form, in which poetry is written to the meter of popular songs. Lyric poetry has a variable number of words per line, and so is called "long and short" poetry. It is rhymed and has a strict pattern of verse and tones and thus requires a quick imagination and exceptional skill for it to be used effectively. Like the sonnet in the European tradition, the poems were exhilaratingly complex and difficult. Although lyric poems were originally written to music that came from Western China, or from beyond, the scores have now been lost.

In contrast to the pure and deceptively simple poetry of the high Tang, Wen Tingyun's poetry is ornate, allusive, and typically concerned with love, loss, and sensuality. As Wen Tingyun was known for consorting with courtesans, his work is often set in the boudoir of a lady, in the entertainment world, or in the glamour of the court. Like the work of other important early lyric poets, his poems anticipated the overwhelming importance of the lyric form in the Song dynasty.

---

scenic spot. People often go to Leyou Park on the last day of each lunar month. The third day of the third month and the ninth day of the ninth month are the most popular times to visit.

If you look northward from Leyou Park, you can see the famous Five Tombs. Until the time of Emperor Yuan of the Han dynasty, each Han emperor had a tomb built for him, with an abutting county named for each tomb. Thus "Wuling" or "Five Tombs" refers both to the tombs themselves and to the five counties.

from To the Tune of "The Water Clock Sings at Night"

1

The willow weeps long silk,
a slender spring rain.
Past the flowers a water clock sings forever,
startling frontier geese,
crows on the city wall,
even gilded partridges on the painted screen.

A thin perfumed mist
seeps through the curtain
and grief fills the ponds and pavilions of Lady Xie.[1]
One red candle
behind the drooping embroidered curtain.
She dreams on forever of things he won't understand.

3

The jade incense burner smokes
and a red candle sheds tears,
casting slant light on the hall of paintings and an autumn sorrow.
Her painted eyebrows are fading
and her hair is tangled clouds.
The night is forever, the quilt and pillow cold.

On the parasol trees
rain falls at the time of the midnight drum
unaware of the pain of separation, this intense bitterness;
leaf by leaf,
plink, plunk,
it drips on the empty steps till dawn.

---

[1] Lady Xie was a concubine said to have been kept against her will in the luxurious mansion of Li Teyu.

To the Tune of "Dreaming of the South Side of the River"

After combing and washing,
she leans alone on the River Gazing Tower.
A thousand boats sail by, but none are his.
Slant sunlight lingers like passion on the unhurried water
passing an islet of white duckweed.[1] She is broken inside.

To the Tune of "Beautiful Barbarian"

Tiny mountains upon mountains gleam darkly gold on the folding
   screen.
Her hair is a perfumed cloud sweeping the snowfield of her cheek.
She rises late and draws winged eyebrows like moths,
washes, combs, lazily puts on her face.
Mirrors on either side reflect a flower.
Her face and the blossom illuminate each other.
On her freshly embroidered silk jacket
are golden partridges flying wing to wing.

LI SHANGYIN

(813–858)

Li Shangyin, also known as "Jade Stream Scholar," was born in
Huojia (in modern-day Henan province). His father, a magis-
trate, died when he was nine, and his early life was unsettled and
transient. Yet he was a diligent student, and in 837 he passed the
imperial examinations. An early patron was an enemy of his
father-in-law, and so he found himself attacked and held back in
his career. He remained a minor official for most of his life, work-

---

[1] "Islet of white duckweed" is a traditional Chinese coded phrase for the place
of departure and separation.

ing in the capital and for provincial military governors. About six hundred of his poems survive. His poetry is noted for its difficulty, denseness, allusiveness, symbolism, and obscurity. He wrote a number of untitled poems that are most probably erotic poems about secret love affairs (the lover in the poems could have been a concubine or the Daoist nun with whom he had an affair), but he also wrote poems about his friends and family, poems on historical and current events, and poems on objects. Despite his undistinguished official career, he was a major poet, an original voice in Chinese poetry, and a major influence on succeeding generations of writers.

The Patterned Zither

There's no reason for the patterned zither to have fifty strings;
each string and fret evokes my younger years.
Dreaming at dawn, Zhuangzi confused himself with a butterfly.[1]
King Wang's spring heart entered into the cuckoo.[2]
Dark ocean, bright moon, teardrops on a pearl.
Jade smokes on Blue Field Mountain when the sun is warm.
This emotion could mellow into memory
but in the instant it just perplexes.

Visiting Leyou Park*

Toward evening I feel upset,
driving my wagon up this ancient field.
The late sun's beauty seems boundless.
But dusk is close.

---

[1]The Daoist sage Zhuangzi dreamed one night that he was a butterfly. When he woke up he was uncertain whether he was a man who had dreamed of being a butterfly or a butterfly dreaming he was a man.

[2]In the Zhou dynasty, the emperor of the Shu, Wang Di, was supposed to have turned into a cuckoo upon his death and to have appeared every spring to sing "return" to his people, reminding them to plant their crops.

*See the note on Du Mu's poem "Visiting Leyou Park."

Untitled

So hard to reunite, so hard to part
as the east wind slackens and the flowers all wither.
A spring silkworm spits silk till the moment it dies.
A candle weeps till it's a charred nub.
In the morning mirror I worry my hair is changing color;
at night when chanting poems I feel cold moonlight.
It is not far from here to the Island of Fairies.
Bluebird, please help me find my way.

Poem Sent as a Letter to the North on a Rainy Night

You ask, "When will you return?" and I can't say.
On Ba Mountain night rain swells the autumn ponds.
When will we trim candles by the west window
and recollect tonight and the Ba Mountain rain?

WEI ZHUANG

(836–910)

Wei Zhuang came from Duling, near the Tang capital of Changan (present-day Xian, Shanxi province), and despite coming from a distinguished family, had a troubled life. His parents died when he was young, and the family declined, but despite financial hardship he found himself an education and eventually became a high official. When he was a young man, the country fell into warfare between warlords, and in these times of agitation his life was displaced and transient. He tried several times to take the highest imperial examinations but failed, succeeding only in 894. He was given a minor post in the capital, and then was posted to Sichuan, where he came to know Wang Jian. After the fall of the Tang dynasty in 907, he worked for Wang Jian, who had proclaimed himself the new emperor of Shu. He helped to form the new state and became grand councilor to the emperor. He lived in Chengdu and, being a great fan of Du Fu's poetry, bought his old home to renovate and live in. He is well known for his lyric poems (*ci*-form poems), fifty-three of which survive, and for a long narrative poem titled *The Lament of the Lady of Chin*, which depicts the fall of Changan to rebel forces in 881. He later suppressed this poem, striking it from his collected poems, and it disappeared for more than a thousand years, only to be discovered in 1899 in a cache of manuscripts in the caves of Dunhuang. With Li Yu, Wen Tingyun, and Feng Yansi, Wei Zhuang is considered one of the four early masters of lyric-form verse. He often wrote erotically charged or lovelorn boudoir-theme poems, and he compiled an important anthology of Tang dynasty poetry.

To the Tune of "Silk-Washing Brook"

Sorrow is dream's aftertaste. A slant mountain moon.
A lone lamp lights the wall and she turns her back to the window.
In this high attic of a small mansion lives Lady Xie.[1]
Imagine her white jade complexion,
frozen plum flowers on a branch of spring snow,
a body of fragrant mist against the morning glow.

To the Tune of "The River City"

He coddles her, she acts naïve, their feelings fragile.
The hour is late.
She unfastens the mandarin-duck-embroidered robe
and before her red lips move
he tastes her sweet lip paint.
Slowly she pulls up the embroidered quilt and with one white wrist
pushes off the phoenix pillow
and pillows her handsome man.

---

[1] Lady Xie is Xie Daowen, the wife of Wang Ni, who was considered a great literary talent. By referring to her, Wei Zhuang implies that the woman in the poem is learned and talented.

To the Tune of "Missing the Emperor's Hometown"

> A spring outing,
> apricot petals blown all over his head,
> who is that young man in the street?
> So handsome,
> I want to marry him
> for all my life
> and even if he leaves me
> I won't feel ashamed.

To the Tune of "Daoist Priestess"

> It was the seventeenth of April,
> this day last year
> when you were leaving,
> I lowered my head to veil my tears
> and knit my brow to hide my shyness.
>
> I didn't know I'd lose my soul
> and chase after you in dream.
> Except the moon on the sky's brink,
> no one else knows this.

SIKONG TU

(837–908)

Sikong Tu was the author of "The Twenty-four Styles of Poetry," an influential Tang dynasty *ars poetica* that categorized classical Chinese poetry into twenty-four genres while embodying the essence of each style within a poem. Despite its stated purpose—to bring clarity and definition to poetic practice—this series of poems is notoriously difficult and opaque. Much of its difficulty derives from Sikong Tu's somewhat ill-defined Daoism (blended with Buddhist and Confucian elements), which permeates these

poems and converts many lines into gnomic, mystical riddles that
tie commentators and translators into fantastic knots. Yet the
conjunction of inspiration and mysticism can be auspicious. The
imagination *is* sublimely indefinite and slippery, and it does resist
being chopped up and constrained into little boxes, so a nomen-
clature that has a spiritual cast to it may express more about the
murky sources of poetry than a rigorously precise one.

In fact, a Daoist changeability and lack of differentiation is the
point of many of these poems, as in "The Implicit Style":

> It is dust in timeless open space,
> is flowing, foaming sea spume,
> shallow or deep, cohering, dispersing.
> One out of a thousand contains all thousand.

"The Dao," writes Sikong Tu, "isn't confined by shape, / it's
round at times or square." The same goes for the inspirational
essence that gives a poem its charge. For Sikong Tu, these two
essences are not differentiated, either. Thus, poets are practition-
ers of a divine craft who must perfect themselves internally to
achieve perfection in what they write: "If you free your nature /
you'll have this style." Such perfection, like spiritual perfection,
can only be alluded to, never actually defined: "It is beyond
words / and these are clumsy metaphors." It is extraordinarily
hard to find, yet it will come to you by itself. It must be achieved
through *lack of desire* and through *lack of effort*, since in both
Daoism and Buddhism, grasping desire, effort, and attachment to
the world are precisely what chain us to our mundane state.

Sikong Tu came from Shanxi province, from a distinguished
family of government servants, but he himself had an official
career marked by banishments and political instability. Neverthe-
less he was celebrated in his time for both his poems and his criti-
cism. He was powerfully influenced by the Confucian tradition
and later turned to Daoism and Buddhism. It is said that when
the Tang dynasty was overthrown and the last Tang emperor was
murdered, Sikong Tu starved himself to death in protest.

from The Twenty-four Styles of Poetry

The Placid Style

> Dwell plainly in calm silence,
> a delicate heart sensitive to small things.
> Drink from the harmony of yin and yang,
> wing off with a solitary crane,[1]
>
> and like a soft breeze
> trembling in your gown,
> a rustle of slender bamboo,
> its beauty will stay with you.
>
> You meet it by not trying deeply.
> It thins to nothing if you approach,
> and even when its shape seems near
> it will turn all wrong inside your hand.

The Potent Style

> Green woods, a wild hut.
> Setting sun in the transparent air.
> I take off my head cloth, walk alone,
> often hearing the calls of birds.
>
> No flying swan brings me messages
> from my friend traveling so far.
> Yet the one I miss isn't far.
> In my heart we are together.

---

[1] An allusion to a number of Chinese Daoist tales in which Daoists who become immortal fly off on the back of a crane.

Ocean wind through emerald clouds.
Night islets and the moon, bright.
After one good line, stop.
A great river spreads across your path.[2]

The Natural Style

Bend over anywhere and pick it up
but you can't take it from your neighbors.
Go with the Dao
and what you write is fine as spring.

It's like meeting flowers in bloom,
like seeing the year renew.
Once given to you it can't be taken
but gain it by force and soon you're poor again.

A hermit in the empty mountain
after rain collects duckweed
and gains this calm inspiration,
moving about unhurried as heaven's potter's wheel.

The Implicit Style

Without a single word
the essence is conveyed.
Without speaking of misery
a passionate sadness comes through.

It's true, someone hidden controls the world;
with that being you sink or float.

---

[2] These last lines suggest the dangers of saying too much, of overwriting. If you go on too long, Sikong Tu warns, you walk right out of the style, whereas a good line stops you like a great river, and echoes profoundly inside of you. This effect can be described by two lines from Tang poetry: "The song is over, the musician gone, / but the river and green mountains keep singing."

This style's like straining full-bodied wine
or like a flower near bloom retreating into bud.

It is dust in timeless open space,
is flowing, foaming sea spume,
shallow or deep, cohering, dispersing.
One out of a thousand contains all thousand.

The Carefree and Wild Style

Abide by your nature,
honestly and unrestrained.
Whatever you pick up makes you rich
when candor is your friend.

Build your hut below a pine,
toss off your hat and read a poem.
You know if it's morning or evening
but have no idea what dynasty it is.

Do what fits your whim.
Why bother to achieve?
If you free your nature
you'll have this style.

The Bighearted and Expansive Style

We live no more than a hundred years,
not too long before we depart.
Happiness is bitterly short,
gloom and fretting abound.

Why not take a jar of wine
and each day visit the misty wisteria?
Let flowers cover the straw-thatched roof.
Let mountain showers pass over.

When wine is finished
take a vine stick and sing out loud.
What life doesn't end in death?
Only South Mountain can last.[3]

The Flowing Style

It takes in like a watermill
and turns like a pearl marble.
It is beyond words
and these are clumsy metaphors.

Earth spins on a hidden axis
and the universe rolls slowly around its hub.
If you search out the origin
you'll find a corresponding motion.

Climb high into spiritual light.
Then dive deep into dark nothing.
All things for thousands of years
are caught up in the flow.

YU XUANJI

(C. 843–868)

Yu Xuanji is among the finest women poets of the Tang dynasty. Only fifty of her poems are extant, but they reveal a passionate person mourning absent lovers, letting her feelings out in nature, all in exquisite and imaginative language scarcely surpassed in her time. She was born in the Tang capital of Changan (modern-day Xian) and was a sophisticated courtesan. Eventually she

---

[3] South Mountain is famous in poetry as a place of Daoist peace and quietude. It often appears in the poetry of Wang Wei and Tao Qian.

became the concubine of the poet and government official Li Yi, whom she calls Zian in her poetry, but Li Yi abandoned her after taking her to the south of China. Yu Xuanji managed to return to the capital, where her extreme poverty may explain her decision at the end of her brief life to become a Daoist nun. She lived a pious life, and yet she continued to receive her lovers (among them the important poet Wen Tingyun) in her quarters at the Convent of Gathered Blessings—a double role that may seem more unusual to Westerners than it was in her time. When she was twenty-four she was executed on a trumped-up charge of murdering her maid in jealousy over one of her callers.

Visiting Chongzhen Temple's South Tower and Looking Where the Names of Candidates Who Pass the Civil Service Exam Are Posted

Snow-topped peaks fill my eyes with new spring sun
as my fingers brush a calligraphy of clear, clear silver hooks.
I hate my silk dresses. They veil my poems' lines.
I raise my head and admire in vain the names posted on the board.

To Zian: Missing You at Jianling

Maple leaves cover a thousand, ten thousand branches.
An evening sail returns late, emerging from the river bridge.
Like water in the West River my heart aches for you,
day and night flowing east without end.

A Farewell

After these few happy nights in the Qin Tower,
immortal man, I didn't expect you to leave.
Sleep, don't speak of where the clouds have gone.
A wild moth flies into the guttering lamp.

Sent in an Orchid Fragrance Letter

Drunk from dawn to dusk, my body complains.
Now it's spring again I miss him.
A messenger runs off in the rain.
By the window I stand, broken inside.
Mountain. I roll up the pearl curtain and gaze.
My sorrow renews with the fragrance of grass.
Since I left him at the light banquet
how many times have the roof beams leaked dust?

Autumn Complaints

I sigh to myself. Too much passion brings grief.
So much wind and moon[1] in this courtyard full of autumn.
The watchman beats his drum right by my bridal chamber.
Night after night with my lamp. My hair is almost white.

QI JI

(861–935)

Qi Ji was a monk poet. He was born in Yiyang, Hunan, but was orphaned when he was seven and entered a Buddhist monastery, where he worked herding cattle. He showed an early talent for poetry (he was said as a youth to have scratched his poems with a bamboo stick on the backs of cattle). He traveled widely, eventually gaining the patronage of the king of Nanping, who gave him a position of influence in a monastery.

---

[1] "Wind and moon" can be a symbol for a love affair.

Looking at the Zhurong Peak in a Boat at Twilight

A cold dark mountain pierces the sky's edge.
In my boat I watch it coated with late sun.
For ten years I've dreamed of it.
Today I finally can approach that ghostly height.
Huge rocks look black overhead,
flying waterfalls glimmer at night.
I need to climb up that solitary peak
and sit waiting for white clouds to rise.

LI JING

(916–961)

Li Jing was the second emperor of the Southern Tang dynasty. He reigned for only nineteen years, dying at the age of forty-six. His father was a usurper who took over the state of Wu and founded the dynasty. Under Li Jing the capital became a great cultural center, but as an emperor with expansionist designs he led his people into costly wars that lost many lives and much territory. He was the father of Li Yu, the last emperor of the Tang, and like his son was an excellent poet, though only a few of his poems survive.

To the Tune of "Silk-Washing Brook"

Hands roll the pearl curtain up to a jade hook.
She locks her hatred for spring in tall towers,
but who can own flowers falling in the wind?
Thoughts swing long.

No bluebird carries a message for her through clouds.
She can't keep grief from budding like a lilac in the rain
and turns toward Sanchu at dusk, as green waves darken,
flowing up into the sky.

To the Tune of "Silk-Washing Brook"

Lotus flowers' fragrance is burned up, emerald leaves torn.
The west wind like sorrow rises from the green waves.
My best days are gone, and I am withered.
I can't bear to look.

In drizzling rain my dream returns from a far frontier pass.
A jade reed pipe pierces the small tower with cold.
So much hatred, so much weeping.
I sag against the banister.

MADAM HUARUI

(FL. C. 935)

Madam Huarui was an important female poet of the Tang
dynasty. Her husband, Meng Xu, the king of Sichuan during the
Five Dynasties Period, gave her the appellation by which she is
known—"Madam Flower Pistil." After their kingdom was con-
quered by the founder of the Song dynasty, Emperor Taizi (ruled
960–975), Madam Huarui was forced to join the harem of the
conqueror. She was said either to have been killed by the emperor's
heir apparent or to have been forced to commit suicide at the
emperor's command. Much of her poetry focuses on the life of
women in the imperial harem. The poem included here was com-
posed extemporaneously in response to the emperor, who had
questioned her as to why her husband's troops had surrendered.

On the Fall of the Kingdom, to the Tune of "Mulberry-Picking Song"

When the king raised a white flag on the battlements
how could I know deep in the palace?
One hundred and forty thousand soldiers dropped their weapons.
Was not even one of them a man?

LI YU
(936–978)

Li Yu was the last emperor of the Southern Tang dynasty. He is also known as Li Houzhu (*houzhu* means "last ruler"). He ascended to the throne in 961 and ruled from the Southern Tang capital of Nanjing. But his rule ended only fourteen years later, when the House of Song conquered his realm. He was carried north to the Song capital, Kaifeng, and imprisoned. Years later, on his birthday, he was sent a glass of poisoned wine by the Song emperor, who was upset upon hearing the court's female musicians sing Li Yu's poem "To the Tune of 'Beauty Yu.'" He died, forty-one years old.

Li Yu seems to have been much better at the business of culture than he was at running his empire. He was a noted painter, musician, and calligrapher, and under his reign the Southern Tang became an important cultural center. He is considered the first important innovator in the lyric (*ci*) form of poetry, which was to be the form in which much of the best poetry of the Song dynasty was written. In the hands of Wen Tingyun and Wei Chuang and other early *ci* poets, love of nature and romantic love were the principal subjects of the form but Li Yu expanded the form to include meditations upon great philosophical themes— the impermanence of life and the vanity of human wishes. He also made it startlingly personal. His best poems mourn the death of his first wife in 964, and bitterly lament his imprisonment.

To the Tune of "A Bushel of Pearls"

> Morning makeup is almost done—
> a few more light touches on the lips.
> Revealing the tip of a lilac tongue,
> she sings transparently clear,
> her mouth just parting, like a cherry.

Charming how her wide silk sleeve turns crimson wet
after sweeping across sweet wine in a deep goblet.
She is fragile, seductive, lying aslant an embroidered bed.
After chewing on her red hair-string,
with a laugh she spits it on her man.

To the Tune of "Bodhisattva Barbarian"

The flowers flicker. Moon in soft mist.
Just the time to go to my man,
walking in stockings on fragrant moss,
gold-threaded shoes in my hand.

South of the painted hall we meet.
I throw myself on his chest, trembling,
tell him, "It was so hard to sneak out.
So love me now with all abandon!"

To the Tune of "Clear and Even Music"

Since you left, spring is half gone
and everything I see breaks my heart:
a chaos of plum petals falling by the steps like snowflakes.
I brush them off and they cover me again.

Migrating wild geese bring me no word of you.
The road is so long that my dream cannot reach you.
The grief of departure is like spring grass
—the farther you go, the deeper it grows.

To the Tune of "Lost Battle"

My family's kingdom lasted forty years—
three thousand *li* of mountains and rivers.
In phoenix pavilions and dragon towers built up to heaven,

among jade trees and branches like spring mist and vines,
how could I know anything about wars?

But since being captured and enslaved,
my waist has shriveled,
my hair turned gray.
I was most lost the day we parted at the Temple of Ancestors:
the imperial orchestra was playing farewell songs
while I stood in tears facing my palace girls.

To the Tune of "Beauty Yu"

Will spring blooms and autumn moon never end?
These memories are too much.
Last night east wind pierced my narrow tower again,
and I saw lost kingdoms in the clean bright moon.
The carved railings and jade steps must still be there,
though lovely faces must have aged.
How much sorrow do I feel?
Like river water in spring it flows to the east.

To the Tune of "Crows Cry at Night"*

Spring red fades in falling forest blossoms
so quickly, so quickly,
no way to stop the cold rain of dawn, the wind of night.
You weep red tears
and keep me drinking here
not knowing when we'll return.
Sorrow like a river flows endlessly to the east.

---

*Sometimes called "To the Tune of 'Encountering Joy.'"

To the Tune of "Crows Cry at Night"*

Silent, alone, I ascend the west tower.
The moon is a hook.
Deserted parasol trees trap clear autumn in the inner courtyard.
Cut, it won't break,
straightened, it stays tangled
—the sorrow of parting
is a strange taste in my heart.

---

*Sometimes called "To the Tune of 'Encountering Joy.'"

SONG DYNASTY

(960–1279)

AFTER THE FALL OF THE TANG DYNASTY IN 907, CHINA DIS-
integrated into a series of smaller dynasties warring for domination
and seeking the reunification of the empire. The Song dynasty,
which alongside the Tang and the Han is generally considered one
of the three peaks of Chinese civilization, was founded by Zhao
Kuangyin, who seized power in a coup d'etat in 960 and took on
the imperial name Taizu. During the Northern Song (960–1127)
the capital of the dynasty was located in Dongjing (which is today
Kaifeng City); during the Southern Song (1127–1279) the capital
was moved to what is today Hangzhou. Much of the administrative
structure of the Tang dynasty, including the civil service and exami-
nation systems, had been maintained during the period of warfare
that followed its collapse, and so when China moved into a new
period of relative stability under the Song, the stage was set for
another renaissance.

The early Song was a time of great economic expansion and sta-
bility and of reforms in the examination system and the bureau-
cracy. Taizu created a professional army, and he and his successors
expanded the empire to the south, but the empire was always
threatened by foreign invasion, and increasingly by peasant rebel-
lions and internecine warfare. The decisive change came in 1126,
when the army of the Jurchens of the Jin dynasty invaded from the
north and took over the capital at Kaifeng. Emperor Huizong and
much of his family were captured and taken prisoner to Manchuria,
but his ninth son, Zhaogou, managed to flee to the south, where he
established the Southern Song dynasty in 1127. The Southern Song
was a prosperous time economically as well as a great period for the
arts, but it was a weak dynasty, with limited territory, incompetent

officials, the constant threat of invasion from the north, and a defensive military strategy that played into the hands of the invading Jin, and later of the invading Mongols. Zhaogou, known as Emperor Gaozong, made peace with the Jin by accepting the humiliation of having to pay tribute. Warfare in the north among three forces, the Mongols, the Jin, and the Western Xia, resolved itself with the disappearance of the Western Xia and the conquering of much of the Jin by the Mongols. When the Jin turned against the Southern Song, the Song emperor collaborated with the Mongols to defeat them. The Mongols, in turn, turned against the Song and conquered Hangzhou in 1276.

The technology of printing, invented in the Tang dynasty, spread in the Song and made it possible for books to be preserved and widely available to different classes. The civil service ranks thus swelled with talented people who would in previous dynasties have had difficulty affording and attaining an education. Many people took up writing poetry in the Song, and they were able to carefully preserve their works. The new form of lyric verse called *ci*, which developed in the late Tang, achieved its apex in the Song. Though traditional poetry in the *shi* forms continued to be written, notably by the Southern Song poet Lu You, the heart of Song poetry lies in the lyric verse. As Burton Watson comments, "it was some time before a new style of poetry developed that was in any way distinct from what had gone before. The first 70 or 80 years of Song rule saw instead a prolongation of the Late Tang style—mannered, morose, with all the faults of Li Shangyin and none of his compensations."[1] The *ci* poem is set to music and can be sung. It is characterized by erotic content (especially early on in the form's development), strict rhyme, tonal patterns, and irregular line length. *Ci* was a poetic reaction to the popularity and influence of Central Asian music and to native tunes. The 875 song patterns to which the poems were written remain, although they are known only by their song titles, since the music itself has been lost.

---

[1] Burton Watson, *Chinese Lyricism: Shih Poetry from the Second to the Twelfth Century* (New York: Columbia University Press, 1971), pp. 197–198.

Li Qingzhao (1084–c. 1151), China's greatest woman poet, flourished during the Song, as did such great poets as Su Shi (1036–1101) and Ouyang Xiu (1007–1072). Su Shi helped to develop the *ci* poem away from the erotics and the occasional crudity of its original inspiration and toward a wider range of topics. The poetry of this period tends to echo the kind of realism and social critique that characterized the great Tang poets Du Fu and Bai Juyi. It allowed the use of colloquial expressions and diction and, as Watson notes, often treated themes heretofore considered "unpoetic" and mundane, in part because of the influence of neo-Confucianism. Though *shi* poetry declined in quality after the Tang, *ci* poetry, with its formal flexibility (there were many different patterns one could write to) and its introduction of vernacular and everyday speech and events into poetry, revitalized the poetic scene.

ANONYMOUS FEMALE POET

(UNCERTAIN DATES)

Drunk Man

> The puppy barks outside
> and I know my man is here.
> I walk downstairs in my stockings.
> He's drunk tonight, my enemy.
>
> I help him into the silk mosquito net
> but he doesn't want to undress,
> he is too smashed. Well, let him be.
> It is better than sleeping alone.

SUN DAOXUAN

(UNCERTAIN DATES)

Sun Daoxuan (also known as Chongxu Jushi) was married to a man named Zhen Wen and was gifted in prose as well as poetry. She was the mother of Huang Zhu, who was taught by the same master as the well-known neo-Confucian scholar Zhu Xi.

To the Tune of "As in a Dream"

Jumbled shadows of green banana leaves,
a moon halfway up the red railing.
Wind arrives from the turquoise sky,
blowing down like a string of singing pearls.
Invisible,
invisible,
my lover is hidden by an emerald curtain.

To the Tune of "Longing for Qin e"

Autumn is solitude
and autumn wind and night rain makes this rift between us hurt.
The rift hurts
and my old feelings have no way out
as tears drop.

Lover, you are gone without a return date
and I've written you a foot-long letter to be delivered by a west
    wind crane,
a west wind crane,
but where are you, lover,
in the water villages or the mountain cities?

LIU YONG

(987–1053)

Liu Yong came from Fujian. Though he was very talented as a musician and a poet, he led an itinerant and dissipated youth, passing the imperial examination only in 1034, at the age of forty-seven. He was content with a minor post as an agricultural supervisor in Zhejiang. Liu Wu-Chi paints the following portrait of Liu Yong: "In the early years of the Song dynasty, many poets had contributed to *ci* poetry, but it was Liu Yong who set a new standard for its form and style. Unsuccessful in the literary examination, Liu Yong held only minor positions in the outlying provinces and spent most of his time in the gay and congenial world of the capital. A profligate, he was addicted to the pleasures of the 'singing towers and dancing pavilions,' where he moved amidst 'a bevy of red sleeves in the upper chamber.' Friend and patron of the singing girls, he wrote *ci* songs to the new melodies they had learned to sing. He was popular with the common people, and his *ci* songs were sung wherever they gathered to draw water from the well."[1] Liu Yong was especially popular among the courtesans for whom he wrote new songs, but despite the extraordinary popularity of his songs, he died destitute. After his death, the courtesans started a tradition of visiting his tomb each year to pay him respects.

To the Tune of "Phoenix Perched on the Parasol Tree"

On a high tower I lean long against a slender breeze.
My vision ends in spring sorrow
rising dark and dark at the sky's edge.

---

[1] Liu Wu-chi, *An Introduction to Chinese Literature* (Bloomington: Indiana University Press, 1973), p. 106. To match the usage in the rest of this book, we have converted the Wade-Giles transliteration of Chinese words and names in this passage to Pinyin transliteration.

Grass colored by misty light of the dying sun.
No words. Who can understand why I stand at this banister?

Maybe I should go wild and get drunk,
singing over my cup.
But forced joy is tasteless.
I don't regret my loosening belt and robe.
I'm fading away for you.

To the Tune of "Rain Hits a Bell"

Cold cicadas sing plaintively.
In twilight I face a long pavilion
after a brief rain.
Outside the city gate we drink farewell in a tent without joy,
lingering
while the boatman rushes us.
Hand in hand, looking at each other through tears,
we choke on words.
How far you will be, across a thousand miles of mist and waves,
past heavy evening mist hanging low on the broad horizon of Chu.

Since ancient times, separation has wounded lovers,
but it is worse
today in cold and solitary autumn.
Where will I be tonight when I sober up from the wine?
—along a willow riverbank, in morning breeze, under a leftover
    moon?
Though years spin past after we part
all sweet hours and beautiful landscapes will seem counterfeit,
and even if a thousand tender feelings rise in me,
to whom will I reveal them?

To the Tune of "New Chrysanthemum Flowers"

About to draw the fragrant curtains and make love
I knit my eyebrows—the night is so short!
"Hurry up,
you get in bed first
and warm the mandarin-duck quilt for me."

After a moment, I put away my needlework
and slip out of my silk skirt,
each movement brimming with tender lust.
"No, don't blow out the lamp by the bed.
For every second that remains
I want to see your lovely face."

To the Tune of "Poluomen Song"

Last night
I slept in my day clothes.
Tonight
I do it again
after a little drink
returning as late as the night drum's first beat,
drunk and breathing heavily.
After midnight
I am awakened, by what?
From a cold sky of frost
a fine wind blows
against my sparsely latticed window,
flickering the lamp.
Tossing in my empty bed I seek
a dream of being in you like rain and clouds,
but it dissipates as I lean against my pillow,
thousands of feelings straining in my inch-sized heart.
A few feet off feels as bad as a thousand miles.
Such wonderful times, such great days,
but we love each other uselessly.
We don't know how to be together.

FAN ZHONGYAN

(989–1052)

Fan Zhongyan's father died when he was a child, and he was raised in great poverty in a Buddhist temple. He was lucky enough to be championed by patrons, who helped support him while he studied, and in 1015 he passed the imperial examinations and began an official career. He was a Confucian reformer, which landed him in political trouble. He was demoted and sent to fight the Xi Xia in their invasion of 1040, but he did so well in disciplining and administering the military that he was able to stop the Xi Xia, negotiate peace, and make a name for himself. Although his attempts to reform the Song bureaucracy were ultimately unsuccessful, he ended up a man of wealth and respect. The financial uncertainty he faced in youth motivated him to create an estate to support the poor in his family and assure them an education. His poetry is at once direct and delicate, and his subject matter ranges from military life to romantic estrangement.

To the Tune of "Sumu Veil"

A white cloud sky,
and earth of yellow leaves
as autumn color spreads on waves
and a cold mist looks blue.
The mountain reflects a slant sun as sky links with water.
Grass is fragrant but emotionless,
staying out of the sun.

The homesick soul is darkened
chasing the thoughts of a traveler
every night sleepless
unless a good dream keeps him in sleep.
Bright moon, high tower. Don't stand there alone.
When the wine pierces to an inner sorrow,
it will rise as tears of love.

To the Tune of "Imperial Avenue Procession"

Busy leaves tumble over the fragrant steps
in quiet night,
a crisp cold sound.
The curtain of pearls is rolled up, but her jade tower is empty.
As the sky lightens the River of Stars pours down to earth.
Each year on this night
moonlight gleams like a silk ribbon
but my lover is gone a thousand miles.

My entrails feel shattered. I can't even get drunk.
The wine I drink
just turns to tears.
A guttering lamp, the pillow aslant,
I know the taste of sleeping alone,
and it seems as if
between knitted brows and my heart I'm caught
with no possible escape.

MEI YAOCHEN

(1002–1060)

Mei Yaochen was an official-scholar of the early Song dynasty whose poems helped initiate a new realism in the poetry of his age. He was a lifelong friend of the poet Ouyang Xiu, but he never attained Ouyang Xiu's career success. He was forty-nine when he finally passed the imperial examinations, and his career was marked by assignments in the provinces alternating with periods in the capital. Twenty-eight hundred of his poems survive in an edition that Ouyang Xiu edited. His early poems are marked by social criticism based on a neo-Confucianism that sought to reform the military and civil services; these poems tended to be written in the "old style" form of verse (*gushi*). Mei Yaochen was also a distinctly personal poet who wrote about the loss of his first wife and baby son in 1044 and about the death of a baby daughter a few years later. His poems are colloquial and confessional and strive for a simplicity of speech that suggests meanings beyond the words themselves; as he writes in one poem: "Today as in ancient times / it's hard to write a simple poem."

Plum Rain

For three days rain did not stop,
earthworms climbed into my hall,
wet mushrooms grew on dry fences,
and damp air brought white mold to clothes.
Frogs in the east pond,
one jumps after another endlessly.
Reeds invade my flower garden,
suddenly as tall as the banister.
No wagon and horse in front of my door.
The moss looks so dark.
Zhaoting Mountain behind the house
is blocked by clouds again
and directionless where can I go?
I just meditate on a bed
in solitude and forget outside concerns,
in a low voice read aloud the Daoist canon.[1]
My wife laughs at my leisure,
"Why not raise a cup to yourself?"
She is better than the wife of Bolun.[2]
She stays by my side when I am drunk.

---

[1] "Daoist canon," literally, "Huangting canon," a seven-character song telling how to reach Daoist longevity through self-cultivation.

[2] In the Jin dynasty, Liu Ling, who was known as Bolun, was one of the Seven Sages of the Bamboo Grove. He indulged in wine and had no respect for manners or rules. His wife, in an attempt to stop him from drinking, destroyed his set of drinking cups and utensils. Rather than stop, he instead wrote an ode to the virtue of wine.

On the Death of a Newborn Child

The flowers in bud on the trees
Are pure like this dead child.
The East wind will not let them last.
It will blow them into blossom,
And at last into the earth.
It is the same with this beautiful life
Which was so dear to me.
While his mother is weeping tears of blood,
Her breasts are still filling with milk.

Translated by Kenneth Rexroth

Sorrow

Heaven took my wife. Now it
Has also taken my son.
My eyes are not allowed a
Dry season. It is too much
For my heart. I long for death.
When the rain falls and enters
The earth, when a pearl drops into
The depth of the sea, you can
Dive in the sea and find the
Pearl, you can dig in the earth
And find the water. But no one
Has ever come back from the
Underground Springs. Once gone, life
Is over for good. My chest
Tightens against me. I have
No one to turn to. Nothing,
Not even a shadow in a mirror.

Translated by Kenneth Rexroth

A Small Village

The Huai River opens up to sandbars and suddenly—a village.
A thin, collapsed bramble fence suggests a gate.
Cold hens cluck to friends when they find food.
A shirtless old man hugs a grandchild close.
A wild boat tilts like a bird stretching over a broken mooring rope.
Water eats the roots of dead mulberry trees.
I sigh to see a life so hard.
The census taker is mistaken. Is this what it is to be a citizen?[1]

Reply to Caishu's "Ancient Temple by a River"

Old trees with tangled hanging tassels
by a deserted temple open to the river.
Rain, rain threw down the clay statues,
and wind blew down this ancient building.
Wild birds nest in dusty shrines;
fishermen hold a bamboo lottery cup.
About to play the tune "Mountain Ghost,"[2] I stop:
the Verses of Chu make me too sad.

The Potter

The potter uses all the clay before his door
yet has not one tile for his own house.
Those whose ten fingers never touched clay
live in tall houses with fish-scale tiles.

---

[1] The line literally says, "It's a mistake to register these people as the king-dom's citizens," but the implication is that the government does not take care of its people.

[2] "Mountain Ghost" is a poem by Qu Yuan from the Verses of Chu (see the Verses of Chu in this book).

OUYANG XIU

(1007–1072)

Ouyang Xiu was raised in great poverty by his widowed mother in an isolated region of what is today Hubei. He nevertheless gained access to books (facilitated by the rise of printing early in the Song dynasty) and studied for the imperial examinations. While studying he was strongly influenced by Han Yu, whose works had been largely forgotten by this time. He passed the imperial examinations in 1030 and embarked on a successful career as an official in Luoyang. He is the author of a famous history, *The New History of the Tang*, and the compiler of *The New History of the Five Dynasties*, and he wrote an influential set of commentaries on historical inscriptions titled *Postscripts to Collected Ancient Inscriptions*. He is also the author of a set of commentaries on poetics titled *Mr. One-six's Talks on Poetics*. (Mr. One-six was a pen name of his that referred to his desire to be always in the presence of his wine, chess set, library, zither, and archaeological collection; the five things he enjoyed plus himself—one old man among them—made six "ones.") This compilation was the first treatise in the aphoristic poetry talk (*shi-hua*) form. Ouyang Xiu is esteemed as a prose master whose essays are characterized by clean and simple language and fluid argumentation. He helped lead a movement away from ornamental prose styles to a simpler style of "ancient prose," a traditionalist movement that had as its aim a Confucian moral regeneration.

Ouyang Xiu's poetry is also marvelous, and he was instrumental in making the lyric (*ci*) form (poems written to fit popular songs) a widespread and important Song poetic style. His plain style and use of colloquial expressions made his poetry accessible to larger audiences and helped preserve its freshness for audiences today. Like Andrew Marvell, he was a sensualist known for his carpe diem poems. Just before his death he wrote a poem about how "Just before the frost comes, the flowers / facing the high pavilion seem so bright." He was also an individualist, both in his approach to writing and in his interpretations of the classics; sinologist J. P. Seaton sees this individualism as an outgrowth of his self-education. A man with many talents and dimensions, Ouyang Xiu is considered a prime example of the Chinese ideal of the multifaceted scholar-official, equivalent to the Western ideal of the Renaissance man.

About Myself

I'm quite a loose and free person,
and the same kind of official.
I look like a big wine pot
carried around in a wagon.
Fashion chasers won't bend their heads to look at me.
To whom can I talk? I just stay silent.
Fortunately I have talented friends from Luoyang
who keep me company each day.
We get drunk from redistilled pure wine,
and wear spring orchids for the scent.
After mulling over official documents,
poetry and wine are enough to make me happy.

To the Tune of "Spring in the Tower of Jade"

The wild geese flown, spring also goes.
I pick over the thousands of loose threads in this floating life.
They come like a spring dream, ephemeral,
then are gone like morning clouds, traceless.

Hearing my zither, she gave me her jade pendant with an
    immortal's love,
I couldn't make her stay, though I held onto her silk skirt until it tore.
Listen to me, don't be the only sober one.
The rest of us are rotten drunk among the flowers.

The Lamp-wick's Ashes, Blossoms Droop, the Moon Like Frost

The lamp-wick's ashes, blossoms droop, the moon like frost,
now light of sun and moon together through the screen.
Almost too drunk, she has a fragrance of her own.
Two hands, the dancing done, grasp blue-green sleeve.
In the sound of the song we'll drain the cup again.
Don't turn your pretty face away,
you'll break my heart.

Translated by J. P. Seaton

To the Tune of "Spring in the Tower of Jade"

You've left and I don't know if you're near or far.
Everything I see is broken and dull.
The farther you go, the fewer letters come.
Who can I ask? This river is so broad it drowns the fish.[1]

In deep night the wind beats the bamboo—it sounds like autumn,
ten thousand leaves making a thousand cries of grief.
Alone on my pillow I search for dreams of you.
No dream comes. I watch the lamp—guttering, out.

Painting Eyebrows, to the Tune of "Pouring Out Deep Emotions"

A light frost on the curtain in early morning, she rolls it up,
and blows her hands warm, begins to paint her face new.
Longing for him, she draws her eyebrows long as distant mountains.

---

[1] Your letters ("fish") can't reach me across this distance.

Thinking about the past,
she sighs over the flowing petals
and easily drops into grief.
She almost sings, but stops herself.
She almost smiles, then knits her brows.
It's enough to tear your heart.

Walking Back in Moonlight from Bohdi Trees to the Guanghua Temple

Sound of a spring waterfalling down rocks.
Silent mountain deep in night.
Bright moon washes the pine woods clean.
A thousand peaks, all one color.

Encouraging Myself

Watering flowers is always a pleasure.
I can't wait for spring color in Zhenyang.
Officials are moved around like relay messengers,
but at least for three years I've been master of this place.

To the Tune of "Butterflies Adore Flowers"

Falling petals swirl in wind against my face.
The willows are dense, the mist is deep,
and snow-white catkins shift and float.
After rain a light chill remains
like spring sorrow and this melancholy hangover.

The bed-screen mountains circle my pillow like green waves.
On my emerald quilt with ornamented lamps
I am alone night after night.
Lonely, I rise and lift the embroidered curtain
to a dazzling moon, pear blossoms glowing.

To the Tune of "Mulberry-Picking Song"

Ten years ago I used to indulge in cups of wine
under a white moon, in clear wind,
but cares have withered me,
and age has come with startling speed.

Hair at my temples has changed color, but my heart is the same.
I grasp a golden goblet
and listen again to old tunes,
familiar, that carry me into old days, drunk.

Poem in the *Jueju* Form*

Cold rain swells the Jiaopi Pool.
No one on the solitary mountain slope.
Just before the frost comes, the flowers
facing the high pavilion seem so bright.

WANG ANSHI

(1021–1086)

Wang Anshi was born to a modest family with a history of government service. Although he started out as a provincial official, under the Emperor Shenzong (reigned 1067–1085) he became the most important politician of his time, a reformer who sought to regulate many aspects of Northern Song culture, from education to the military. When the conservative forces in the government opposed his reforms, he fell from favor and resigned. He was a protégé of Ouyang Xiu, who praised his work. Like Ouyang, he saw literature in the Confucian tradition of promoting moral

---

*This poem was written in 1072, just before Ouyang Xiu's death. The *jueju* form is a four-line rhyming poem in either five or seven characters.

and social improvements. His collected poems number above one thousand five hundred, and a number of his prose pieces also survive. He is known for the simplicity and clarity of his poems, especially those written in the regulated verse form, and as one of the "Eight Masters of Song and Tang Dynasty Prose."

Plum Blossoms

Where the wall turns, several branches of plum flowers
unfold blossoms on their own against the cold.
From afar I know they are not snow
as an invisible fragrance spreads.

Late Spring, a Poem Improvised at Banshan

Spring wind took flowers away.
It paid me back with clear shade.
Dark flourishing trees quiet the road on the slope.
The garden house is deep behind waves of branches.
I take short rests when the seat is set up,
with a walking stick and sandals I look for hidden scenes
but see only Northern Mountain birds
passing by and leaving a sweet sound behind.

SU SHI (SU DONGPO)

(1036–1101)

Su Shi was born in Meishan in Sichuan province to an illustrious family of officials and distinguished scholars. He and his brother and father—the Three Su's—were considered among the finest prose masters of both the Tang and Song dynasties. Su Shi took the imperial exam in 1057 and was noticed by the powerful tastemaker, politician, poet, and chief examiner Ouyang Xiu, who became his patron. Like Ouyang, Su Shi was a Renaissance man who, in addition to having a political career, was an innovator and master of poetry, prose, calligraphy, and painting.

Among the founders of the Southern Song style of painting, Su Shi felt that poems and paintings should be as spontaneous as running water, yet rooted in an objective rendering of emotions in the world. Around 2,400 of his poems in the *shi* form survive, along with 350 *ci* form poems. Like Ouyang, Su was important in expanding the uses and possibilities of *ci* poetry. His political career, like that of his patron, was unstable and included demotions, twelve periods of exile, and even three months in prison. During an exile in Huangzhou he began calling himself Su Dongpo (Eastern Slope), which was the name of his farm. His poems are informed by a knowledge of Daoism and Chan (Zen) Buddhism, and like the earlier mystical farmer-poet Tao Qian, he was content on his farm, away from the political world.

A very personal poet, Su Shi wrote about the pain of his separations in exile, the death of his baby son, his joy in a simple walk in the countryside, and the pleasures of a good cup of wine. He is known for the exuberance he brought to his writing and is credited with founding of a school of heroic abandonment in writing.

Written on the North Tower Wall After Snow

In yellow dusk the slender rain still falls,
but the calm night comes windless and harsh.

My bedclothes feel like splashed water.
I don't know the courtyard is buried in salt.

Light dampens the study curtains before dawn.
With cold sound, half a moon falls from the painted eaves.

As I sweep the north tower I see Horse Ear Peak
buried except for two tips.

Written While Living at Dinghui Temple in Huangzhou, to the Tune of "Divination Song"

A broken moon hangs from a gaunt parasol tree.
The water clock has stopped, and people hush into sleep.
Who sees a hermit like me passing alone
like a shadow of a flying wild goose?

Startled and soaring off, I look back
with grief no one understands,
going from branch to branch, unwilling to settle,
and landing at last on a cold and desolate shoal.

Written in Response to Ziyou's Poem About Days in Mianchi*

A life touches on places
like a swan alighting on muddy snow—
accidental claw tracks left in the slush
before it soars east or west into the random air.

The old monk is dead, interred beneath the new pagoda,
and on ruined walls the poems we brushed are illegible.
Do you still remember the rugged path,
the endless road, our tired bodies, how our lame donkey brayed?

Boating at Night on West Lake

Wild rice stems endless on the vast lake.
Night-blooming lotus perfumes the wind and dew.
Gradually the light of a far temple appears.
When the moon goes black, I watch the lake gleam.

---

*In earlier years Su Shi and his brother had traveled together through this region. Their horses had died, so they were riding on donkeys. They stayed at the temple in Mianchi and wrote poems on the wall.

Brushed on the Wall of Xilin Temple

From the side it is a range; straight on, a peak.
Far, near, high, low, it never looks the same.
I can't see Mount Lu's true face
because I'm on the mountain.

from Rain on the Festival of Cold Food

2

The spring river is pushing at my door
but the rain will not let up.
My small house is like a fishing boat
surrounded by water and clouds.
In the empty kitchen cold vegetables are boiled,
wet reeds burning in the broken stove.
Who knows it is the Cold Food Festival?

Ravens carry the dead's money in their bills,[1]
the emperor sits behind nine doors,
and my ancestors' tombs are ten thousand *li* away.
I want to cry at the forked road.
Dead ashes won't blow alive again.

Because of a Typhoon I Stayed at Gold Mountain for Two Days

Up in the tower a bell is talking to itself.
The typhoon will wash out the ferry by tomorrow.
Dawn comes with white waves dashing dark rocks
and shooting through my window like deflected arrows.

---

[1] This symbolic money is made of punctured yellow paper cut in the shape of
banknotes. It is burned at the tomb of the dead, a sacrifice to give them means
on their way to the other world.

A dragon boat of a hundred tons couldn't cross this river
but a fishing boat dances there like a tossed leaf.
It makes me think, why rush to the city?
I'll laugh at such fury of snakes and dragons,
stay aimlessly till the servants start to wonder
—with this kind of storm, my family won't mind.
I look for my friend, monk Qianshan. He's alone,
meditating past midnight and listening for the breakfast drum.[1]

To the Tune of "Song of the River Town," a Record of a Dream on the Night of the First Month, Twentieth Day, in the Eighth Year of the Xining Period (1705)

For ten years we two, one live, one dead, have been lost in a vast mist.
I don't think always of you
yet cannot forget.
Your lonely tomb is a thousand miles away.
I have no one to tell my sadness.
Even if we could meet again you wouldn't know me
with my dusty face,
my temples coated with frost.

At night in a dark dream I suddenly found myself home.
By the small window
you were combing your hair.
We looked at each other without words,
just a thousand lines of tears.
I know you'll wait for me each year in that heartbreak place
through nights of bright moon
under dwarf pine by your mound.

---

[1] Literally, the "porridge drum," the wooden board that when beaten
announces that porridge breakfast is served.

To the Tune of "Prelude to the Water Song"

"When will there be a luminous moon?"
I lift my wine and ask the black sky.
I don't know which year it is tonight in the sky palace.
I wish I could ride the wind and go there,
but I'd be afraid in heaven's jade towers.
It is too cold to be that high.
So I start to dance with my own shadow.
Nothing is better than the human world!

The moon circles a red pavilion
settling to the carved doors
and shines light on my insomnia.
I don't think it feels malice,
yet why is the moon so round when lovers separate?
We have sad and happy partings and reunions.
The moon has bright and dark fullness and waning.
Since ancient times nothing has been perfect
but love may last without end
since even a thousand miles apart we can share this full moon.

To the Tune of "Butterflies Adore Flowers"

Flowers fade to scraps of red. Small green apricots.
Swallows are flying
and green water circles a house.
On branches the cotton of willow catkins dwindles in wind.
Nowhere from here to the sky's edge is without fragrant grass.

Inside the wall is a swing. Outside is a road
where someone walks past
and hears a beauty laughing inside.
The laughter gradually fades, and the voices slowly quiet.
Those who feel love are teased by those who feel none.

Recalling the Past at the Red Cliffs, to the Tune of "Charms of Niannu"

The great river flows east
and its waves have washed away
all the heroes from ancient time.
West of the old fortress
is the Red Cliffs where it is said
Master Zhou[1] won his battle in the Three Kingdoms era.
Wild boulders spear into the sky,
terrible waves beat the bank
and swirl up a thousand snow sprays
and the river and mountains seem a painted landscape
where in old times so many heroes contended.

I imagine that year
when Gongjin had just married Xiao Qiao,
his bearing radiating a gallant spirit.
With a feather fan and silk headband
his talk and laughter
turned strong enemies to ashes. Gone like smoke.
And I, taking this spirit-voyage into the past,
perhaps I am laughable
with my white hairs sprouting so young.
This life is just a dream.
I raise my cup and pour a libation to the river moon.

Returning to Lingao at Night, to the Tune of "Immortal by the River"

Drunk at night, Dongpo awoke and got drunk again
and returned late as the night drum beat for the third time.

---

[1] Master Zhou was a military counselor who oversaw a great victory for the Kingdom of Wu over the Kingdom of Wei at the Red Cliffs, where fireboats destroyed the Wei fleet. Gongjin is another name for Master Zhou, and Xiao Qiao was his bride.

My page boy's snores were thunder.
I knocked and no one answered.
Leaning against my stick, I listened to the river.

I often mourn this body that doesn't really belong to me.
When can I forget this life of contention?
The night is deep, wind quiet, ripples smoothed flat.
In a small boat I could leave here
and live out the rest of my life on this river and the sea.

QIN GUAN

(1049–1100)

Known for his erotic lyric (*ci* form) poetry, Qin Guan was said to have married the sister of his friend Su Shi, the great Song dynasty poet, though this is doubtful. He failed in the imperial examinations at first, but passed them in 1085. He was the protégé of Su Shi and was known as one of the "Four Scholars at Su Shi's Gate." His career was marked by the vicissitudes of the political winds—successful when those of his political ilk were in office, less so when not. Along with Su Shi and his other friends, he suffered exile, and his works were banned.

To the Tune of "Magpie Bridge Immortal"*

As slender clouds form clever shapes,
shooting stars convey the lovers' complaints.
They secretly ferry across the wide Celestial River.

---

*The poem refers to the mythical story "The Cowherd and the Weaver Girl."
See note to Poem 10, "Far and far is the Cowherd Star," from "Nineteen
Ancient Poems" of the Han dynasty.

In this moment gold wind and jade dew[1] meet
with more ecstasy than any human world encounter.

Their tender feelings are like soft water,
but the reunion is short as a dream.
Unbearable to go back across this bridge built by magpies.
If love lasts long between a couple
they don't need to be together morning and night.

MADAM WEI

(FL. C. 1050)

Wei Wan, known as Madam Wei (and also as Yunu), lived in the
Northern Song dynasty and held a high reputation as a poet.
Some critics ranked her poems with those of Li Qingzhao,
though others dissented. She was married to the important politi-
cian Zeng Bu (1036–1107) and given the title Madam of Lu
State. Though we know her poems were collected under the title
Madam Wei's Works, the compilation has now been lost.

To the Tune of "Bodhisattva Barbarian"

A mountain stream in the setting sun where
a reflected tower shakes as mandarin ducks take flight.
Two or three cottages on the far bank with
red apricot flowers overhanging their walls.

On this path under green poplars by the stream bank
I walk at dawn and in dusk.

---

[1] "Gold wind and jade dew": "gold wind" is a symbol for the man and "jade
dew" a symbol for the woman (they are also symbols for autumn).

Since he left I've seen willow catkins fly three times
but my man is still gone.

To the Tune of "Bodhisattva Barbarian"

A wind from the east greens the grass in Yingzhou.
In a painted tower I roll up the curtain in morning frost
and see plum trees by the lake, so pure,
scattered flowers on their branches.

The long sky has cut off all word of you.
Again I see wild geese flying home.
This grief of separation is
bright moon over a tower in Changan.

To the Tune of "Attached to Her Skirt"

The lamp flickers bright, bright, and the water clock drips and drips.
Now that my lover has left
the night is so cold.
A frenzied west wind blows and fetches me back from dream.
Does anyone miss me
as I lean alone on my pillow
with knitted brows?

My brocade screen and embroidered drapes show in autumn dawn.
This pain breaks me inside
and I shed secret tears.
I still see a bright moon in my small west window.
I hate you,
I adore you,
but what would you know of that?

NIE SHENQIONG

(UNCERTAIN DATES)

Nie Shenqiong was a courtesan known for her sweetness and intelligence. She lived in the capital of the Northern Song dynasty. Legend has it that an affair took place between Nie Shenqiong and Li Zhiweng, who stayed in the capital with her for quite a few months. When Li was urged by his wife to return home, Nie gave him the first poem presented here, "To the Tune of 'Partridge Sky.'" Li's wife found this poem in Li's luggage and asked him to explain. In the end she decided to help her husband marry Nie. After Nie became a member of the family, she dressed down and gave up her makeup and treated Li's wife with utter respect. It is said that they lived a very harmonious life together.

To the Tune of "Partridge Sky"

The jade feels tragic, the flowers grieve, because you've left
    Phoenix City.
Willow twigs are tender green under Lotus Tower.
When you raised a cup of wine I sang the "Song of Farewell at
    Yangguan"
then walked how many miles in seeing you off.

I'm looking for a good dream
but a dream is hard to find.
Does anyone know my feelings now?
My tears fall on the pillow as the eaves drip on the steps.
Separated by my window, we both drip until the dawn.

ANONYMOUS
("THE GIRL WHO TOOK THE GOLD CUP")
(EARLY TWELFTH CENTURY)

The following poem was written by a young woman known only as "The Girl Who Took the Gold Cup." Under Emperor Huizong (reigned 1101–1125), women were allowed to go out at night and enjoy a cup of wine during the capital's Lantern Festival. When one young woman was seen walking off with a gold cup, she was arrested by the guards. Brought before the emperor, she recited this poem, arguing that after drinking wine she needed to take the royal cup to prove to her in-laws that the emperor himself had given the women permission to drink. The emperor was so impressed with her poem that he gave her the cup as a gift and ordered the guards to walk her home.

To the Tune of "Partridge Sky"

Moon fills the sky while lanterns burn like stars.
Hand in hand I walked with my man to the Duan Gate
but drawn in by songs and goose-formation dances
I didn't realize I'd become a mandarin duck without my mate.
In the slow dawning,
I was grateful for your imperial largesse
when the royal gift of wine was announced,
but afraid my parents-in-law would scold me for drinking
I took this cup to prove my innocence.

ZHOU BANGYAN

(1056–1121)

Zhou Bangyan came from Qiantang (present-day Hangzhou) in Zhejiang province. He was a musician and a poet who extended the lyric song (*ci* form) tradition with original compositions and poems.

According to Zhang Duanyi's *Guier Lu* (*Records of Aristo-cratic Ears*) and a collection titled *Anecdotes of Ci Poets*, one day Emperor Huizong of the Song dynasty visited courtesan Li Shishi. The poet Zhou Bangyan happened to be there and had no way to exit, so he hid under the bed and observed their tryst. It was based on this experience that he wrote "To the Tune of 'Rambling Young Man,'" which critics praised for the way he presented the woman, who delicately manipulates the emperor into staying without overstepping her bounds. On his visit the emperor had brought with him a fresh orange from south of the Yangtze River as part of a tribute. The poet turned this event into a song, which the courtesan some time later sang before the emperor. The emperor was so enraged that he had Zhou Bangyan expelled from the Forbidden City. The emperor then went to see Li Shishi and found her in tears, distraught at Zhou Bangyan's expulsion. He asked whether Zhou had written any new songs, and she replied that he had written "Willows, to the Tune of 'King of Lanling,'" which she proceeded to sing for him. The emperor was so pleased with the song that he restored Zhou to his post as chief musician of the Da Cheng Imperial Conservatory.

To the Tune of "Rambling Young Man"

A knife from Bing State like a wave,
salt from Wu State like snow.
Her slender hands cut the orange.
The curtained room is warming up.
Endless smoke from the animal-head incense burner.
A couple sits close necking.

She asks low,
"Where are you going to stay?
The midnight drum has sounded
and your horse may slip with the frost so heavy.
Better not to leave.
Few people go home at such an hour."

To the Tune of "Butterflies Adore Flowers"

Moon so bright that crows can't settle for the night.
The water clock is about to run out.
Someone is fetching water from a well with a windlass.
He wakes to two eyes, clear and focused,
dropping tears on his pillow, staining the cold red cotton.

He holds her hand as frost winds tug at her hair
and his resolution to go wavers.
So hard to hear *good-bye*.
The Great Dipper rolls into line with the upstairs banister.
Cold dew, the man is gone, and the cocks are calling to each other.

Willows, to the Tune of "King of Lanling"

Willow shadows hang in straight lines,
misty threads of emerald silk.
On the Sui bank how many times did I see
the twigs touching water and catkins floating in air, the color of
    departure?
I climb here to gaze at my hometown
but who could know me, a tired traveler from the capital
on this road by the Long Pavilion
who as old years died and new years came
must have broken over a thousand feet of willow twigs?
In the time I have I seek old memories
but now with a sad music
lanterns light my farewell banquet

and pear flowers and elm torch fire hasten the day of the Cold
    Food Festival.
I am plagued by this wind, fast as an arrow,
see the boatman with half a pole in warm waves,
the piers retreating from me one by one when I look back.
My friend you are gone, north of heaven.

Heartsick,
my pain piles up.
The boat sails off but the water circles back
to the silent pier
as a slant sun extends through endless spring.
I remember holding your hands in a moonlit pavilion,
listening to a flute on a dew-soaked bridge.
I think of the past,
all just a dream,
and drop secret tears.

ZHU SHUZHEN

(1063–1106)

Zhu Shuzhen was born in Hangzhou, Zhengjiang, to a scholar-
official's family. Her unharmonious relationship with her hus-
band was revealed in her poetry. Although she was very prolific,
her parents burned most of her poems. Wei Zhonggong collected
what survived of her writings and wrote in his preface to the
1182 volume: "I have heard that writing beautiful phrases is not
women's business. Yet there are occasionally cases [of women]
with great natural talents and exceptional character and intelli-
gence who come up with words and lines no man can match."
Though the poet had been dead for decades, the compiler praised
her poems for their evocations of sorrow and womanhood.[1] In

---

[1] Patricia Buckley Ebrey, *The Inner Quarters: Marriage and the Lives of
Chinese Women in the Sung Period* (Berkeley: University of California Press,
1993), p. 123.

addition to being a wonderful poet, Zhu Shuzhen was also said
to have been a painter.

To the Tune of "Mountain Hawthorn"

Every year at the jade mirror stand,
it's harder to paint myself into a plum flower.
You didn't return home this year,
and each letter from across the Yangtze fills me with fear.

I drink less since our separation,
my tears exhausted in sorrow.
I see deep Chu clouds when I think of him in distance.
My man is far and the world's edge is near.

To the Tune of "Mountain Hawthorn"

When the Cold Food Day has just ended
the east wind becomes cruelly strong.
I'm in no mood to hunt flowers in the wilds
and even when idle I don't spend my time on swing sets.

My jade body is so thin my skirt can be folded at the waist.
Silk clothes feel so sheer when I feel this sick.
I don't have the heart to roll up my curtain and look.
Just let the pear flowers fall in solitude.

To the Tune of "Washing Creek Sands"

Spring night,
my jade body is soft as a gold hairpin
as, back to the lamp, I unfasten my silk skirt.
But the quilt and pillow are cold. The night's fragrance is gone.

Spring is a deep courtyard of many locked doors.
Petals falling in falling rain make the night seem forever.
Regret comes to me in dream. There is no escape.

Spring Complaint, to the Tune of "Magnolia Blossoms"

(Short Version)

I walk alone, sit alone,
sing alone, drink alone, and sleep alone.
Standing lone, my spirit hurts.
A light cold caresses me.

Who can see how
tears have washed off half my makeup,
sorrow and sickness have joined hands,
how I trim the lamp's wick till it's gone and dream still does not
    come?

The Song of A-na

Returning from dream, sobering up, I fear spring sorrow.
Smoke dies in the duck-shaped incense burner, but the fragrance
    lingers.
My thin quilt can't stop the dawn chill.
Cuckoos sing and sing till from the west tower the moon drops.

ZHU XIZHEN

(UNCERTAIN DATES)

Zhu Xizhen, the daughter of Zhu Jiangshi, came from Jiangan.
According to *Talks in the Garden of Lyric Songs (ciyuan cong-
tan)*, she is also known as Zhu Qiuniang and was the wife of Xu

Biyong. Her husband was a merchant who traveled often, sometimes not returning for years. Zhu Xizhen wrote poetry that expressed her longing for him. This is essentially all that we know about her. Her poems are found in *Complete Song Lyric Songs* (*quan songci*), where she is put in the category of figures that appeared in *Vernacular Fiction of the Song Dynasty.* People who appeared in *Vernacular Fiction* could be real or fictional; the works attributed to them could be their own or could have been composed by other people under their names.

from Fisherman, to the Tune of "A Happy Event Draws Near"

(Five of Six Poems)

1

Shaking his head, he walks out on the dusty world.
Awake or drunk, he is outside of time.
Wearing green cape and bamboo hat to make his living,
he is used to wearing frost and charging into snowflakes.

The wind ceases toward evening and his fishing line idles.
The new moon is above and below.
For a thousand miles water and sky are the same color.
He watches a lonely swan goose brightening up and fading out.

2

In my sight are a few idlers.
Of them the fisherman is most relaxed.
Wearing the seal of the palace of underwater immortals
he fears no bad wind or waves.

His heart can't be fathomed by common folk
since names are only empty counterfeits.
His one oar crosses five lakes and three islands.
He just lets the tip of his boat play.

3

The fisherman arrives standing up.
I know it's him by the fishing rod.
He spins his boat around at will,
traceless like a bird across sky.

Blooming or fading, reed flowers have their own floating lives
so the best strategy is get drunk all the time.
Last night, a riverful of wind and rain.
No one heard anything.

4

Steering the fishing boat around.
All rivers and seas are my home.
I'm going to Dongting Lake to buy wine,
Leaving Qiantang River behind, a bamboo hat on my back.

My drunk face turns redder in the cold.
The tide goes down the moraine.
Passing Ziling shoal
I see in bloom one plum flower.

5

Short oars and a light fishing boat.
Evening mist veils water along the river.
Fortress wild geese and sea gulls take separate flights,
highlight the autumn scene between the river and heaven.

Metallic fish scales clash in the crowded fish basket.
Just enough to buy some wine.
A sail returns in smooth wind.
No one can hold it.

LI QINGZHAO

(1084–C. 1151)

Li Qingzhao is China's finest woman poet, a master of the *ci* form. She was born in what is today Qinan, Shandung province, to a gifted literary family; her talent was recognized in her teens. In 1101 she married Zhao Mingzheng, the son of a powerful politician, who shared her tastes for literature, painting, and calligraphy and who soon embarked on a career as an official. When China went through the tumultuous transition from the Northern to the Southern Song dynasties, Li Qingzhao's husband's career was cut short, and they devoted themselves to art collecting and cataloging. An invasion of the Qin Tatars in 1127 sent Li Qingzhao fleeing from the capital with just a few belongings; her husband was away from Nanjing at the time, attending his mother's funeral. Li Qingzhao traveled across China for months, finally joining her husband in Nanjing, where he had become mayor. Just two years later her husband died en route to a new posting, and Li Qingzhao drifted across China, settling at last in Linan (modern Hangzhou), where in 1132 she entered into a brief marriage with a minor military official. Her poems are the best evidence of her life, capturing the sorrow she endured over separations from her husband and over his death and sketching her life as a society woman. From her voluminous writings (six volumes of poetry, seven volumes of essays) only about fifty poems have survived, but what does remain is powerful and masterful enough to have cemented her reputation as a major world poet.

To the Tune of "Intoxicated in the Shade of Flowers"

Slight mist, fat clouds. This endless day is torture.
Lucky Dragon incense dissolves in the gold animal.
It's Autumn Festival, a good season,
but by midnight the chill will pierce
my jade pillow and thin silk curtains.

I drink wine by the east fence in yellow dusk
and a secret fragrance fills my sleeves.
Do not say my spirit isn't frayed.
The west wind tangles in the curtains.
I am thinner than a yellow flower.

To the Tune of "One Blossoming Sprig of Plum"

The scent of red lotus fades and my jade mat is cold as autumn.
Gently I loosen my silk robe
and enter the magnolia boat alone.
Who has sent an embroidered letter via clouds?
Wild geese form a character in the sky: *return*.
The west tower fills with moon.

Blossoms drift and water flows where it will,
but my heart is still sick,
split between this place and where you are.
I can't kill this desire.
Even when my eyebrows relax,
my heart flares up again.

To the Tune of "Spring at Wu Ling"*

The wind fades. Dropped blossoms perfume the earth.
At the end of the day, I'm too lazy to comb my hair.
His things remain, but he is gone, and the world is dead.
I try to speak but choke in tears.
I hear that spring is lovely at Twin Brook.
I'd row there in a light craft
but fear my grasshopper boat
is too small to carry this grief.

---

*Written after her husband's death.

To the Tune of "Silk-Washing Brook"

I don't need deep cups of thick amber wine.
My feelings will warm before I drown in drink.
Already sparse bells are answering the night wind.

Lucky Dragon incense fades as my soul-dream breaks.
From my loose hair drops a soft gold hairpin;
I wake alone and watch the red candle die.

To the Tune of "Dream Song"

I'll never forget sunset at Brook Pavilion—
drunk with beauty, we lost our way.
When the ecstasy faded, we turned our boat home,
but it was late and we strayed into a place deep
       with lotus flowers
and rowed hard, so hard
the whole shore erupted with herons and gulls.

To the Tune of "Immortal by the River"

My courtyard is deep, deep, how deep is it,
with cloudy windows and misty tower always shut?
Willow leaf tips and plum blossoms take shape
as spring returns to trees at Moling Tombs.
In the City of Good Health, I am aging.

Once I felt the moon and chanted poems of wind,
but now I am old and have done nothing.
Who could care for this withered self?
I haven't the will to light the lantern
or even to walk in the snow.

*Translated by Willis Barnstone and
Sun Chu-chin*

To the Tune of "Lone Wild Goose"

> Rattan bed, paper netting. I wake from morning sleep.
> I can't reach the end of saying: I've no happy thoughts.
> Incense flickers on, off. The jade burner is cold,
> a companion to my feelings, which are water.
>
> I play three times with the flute,
> astonishing a plum's heart.
> How I feel spring's ache!
> Slender wind and thin rain, tapping, tapping.
> Down come a thousand lines of tears.
>
> The pipe-playing jade man is gone. Empty tower.
> My chest is broken. On whom can I lean?
> I break off a blossoming twig.
> On the earth and in heaven,
> there's no one to send it to.

*Translated by Willis Barnstone and
Sun Chu-chin*

To the Tune of "The Fisherman's Song"

> Sky links cloud ways, links dawn fog.
> A star river is about to turn. One thousand sails dance.
> As if in dream my soul returns to a god's home,
> hearing heaven's voice,
> eagerly asking: Where are we going back to?
>
> I say: The road is long, the day near dusk;
> in writing poems startling words come invisibly.
> Ninety thousand miles of wind, the huge *peng* bird takes off.
> Wind, don't stop.
> The frail boat is to reach the three holy mountains.

*Translated by Willis Barnstone and
Sun Chu-chin*

To the Tune of "Butterflies Adore Blossoms"

Warm rain and sunny wind start to break the chill.
Willows like eyes, plums like cheeks.
I already feel spring's heart throbbing.
Wine and poems.
Whom can I share them with?
Tears dissolve my makeup. My gold hairpin is heavy.

I try on a light spring robe threaded with gold
and lean against a hill of pillows.
The hill damages the gold phoenix pin.
Alone I hug dense pain with no good dreams.
Late at night, I am still playing
as I trim the wick.

*Translated by Willis Barnstone and
Sun Chu-chin*

LU YOU

(1125–1210)

Lu You was the most prolific poet of the Southern Song dynasty. He wrote approximately ten thousand poems. He is known as the Patriotic Poet for his fervor in exhorting the government in his poems to go to war and reunify China. In 1153 he was successful in passing the examinations necessary for a government position, but as the prime minister was his enemy, he found himself without a post until the prime minister's death in 1160. His military service on the border of Sichuan and Shaanxi deeply affected his outlook and his writing. After some years in the capital, he was dismissed from office for his outspokenness and went through a series of provincial posts until his retirement in 1190. His poetry is noted for its criticism of Song bureaucracy, its celebration of wine and Daoist individualism, and its sympathy for the poor.

On the Fourth Day of the Eleventh
Month During a Windy Rainstorm

Lying stiff in a lonely village I don't feel sorry for myself;
I still think of defending Luntai for my country.
Deep in night in bed I hear wind blowing rain,
and iron horses on an ice river enter my dream.

Record of Dream, Sent to Shi Bohun,
to the Tune of "Night Roaming in the Palace"

A chaos of clear horns rings in the snow dawn
of a place I visit in dream,
I don't know where.
As iron cavalry silently rivers past
and I think of frontier waters
west of Goose Gate,
or of the Blue Sea of Qinghai.

I awaken in cold lamplight.
The water clock has stopped dripping.
Slant moonlight through the paper window.
I still wish to be knighted ten thousand miles from home.
Hear this:
though the hair on my temples is snow
my heart is not yet old.

Thinking of Going Outside on a Rainy Day

As the east wind gusts rain, travelers struggle
on a road of thin dust now paved with mud.
The flowers are napping, willows nod, even spring is lazy.
And I, I am even lazier than spring.

To the Tune of "Phoenix Hairpin"*

Her pink and creamy hands,
some yellow-label sealed wine,
a city full of spring and willows by palace walls.
The east wind[1] is evil,
our happiness short.
A cup of sorrow,
many years apart.
Wrong! Wrong! Wrong!

The spring is the same,
someone wastes away in vain,
her handkerchief of mermaid silk[2] is soaked with tears and rouge.
Peach blossoms fall on
an abandoned pool and pavilion.
Our vows are still mountain strong
yet it's hard to send even cryptic messages.
No! No! No!

---

*Lu You married a cousin with whom he grew up and was so in love with
her that his mother grew jealous and wanted him to divorce her. Lu You
bought another house for his wife and would often visit her there. When his
mother found out about this, she was furious. She closed up the new house
and forced him to divorce his wife. This poem was written on a wall in a
garden on a day when Lu You met with his ex-wife and her new husband. His
ex-wife asked her new husband to send over dishes and wine to Lu You, after
which Lu You wrote the poem. See also "Tang Wan's Reply, to the Tune of
'Phoenix Hairpin'" and "The Sheng Garden," both below.

[1] The east wind symbolizes his mother.

[2] Mermaids were said to spin silk.

The Sheng Garden*

(Two Poems)

1

A military horn sounds sad on the city wall in the setting sun.
The old landscape of the Sheng Garden doesn't seem the same.
The green spring waves under the bridge hurt my heart—
they once reflected her shadow coming like a startled swan goose.

2

For forty years a dream and fragrance—interrupted.
Willows in the Sheng Garden are too old to blow catkins.
My body is going to turn into Qi Mountain soil soon,
and yet mourning over the old traces I'm all tears.

To My Sons

(His Deathbed Poem)†

I know the world's ten thousand things end in emptiness after
    death,
and yet I still grieve the splintering of the Nine States of China.
When the royal troops regain the heartland in the north,
don't forget to tell your old man when you perform rituals for the
    dead.

---

*In the spring of 1155, Lu You met his ex-wife, Tang Wan, in the Sheng
Garden and exchanged well-known lyric poems (see "To the Tune of 'Phoenix
Hairpin,'" above). After that encounter, Tang Wan died in depression. In the
spring of 1199, Lu You revisited the Sheng Garden and wrote the above
poems.

†Lu You's last poem, written on his deathbed at the age of eighty-five.

TANG WAN

(UNCERTAIN DATES)

Tang Wan was the wife of Lu You (1125–1210). For the origin of this poem, see the note to Lu You's poem "To the Tune of 'Phoenix Hairpin.'"

Tang Wan's Reply, to the Tune of "Phoenix Hairpin"*

Human relationships are short.
Human intentions are evil.
When rain accompanies evening, flowers fall easily,
but morning wind is dry.
Tearstains remain.
I want to write you my feelings
but I only whisper to myself, leaning against banister.
Hard! Hard! Hard!

We are separate.
Today is not yesterday.
My sick soul moves like a swing between us.
A cold blast from a horn.
The night is late.
Afraid of questions,
I swallow my tears and smile.
Hide! Hide! Hide!

---

*Tang Wan was said to have written this poem in reply to Lu You's poem "To the Tune of 'Phoenix Hairpin'" (earlier in this volume), but only the first two lines were recorded and someone else probably finished the poem. Some critics say that she wrote the entire poem.

YANG WANLI

(1127–1206)

Yang Wanli was governor of Changzhou in Jiangsu province and director of the Imperial Library. He burned more than a thousand of his poems, but this didn't seem to have stopped his writing. Like his friend Lu You, he was an extraordinarily prolific poet, the author of thousands of later poems in many collections. Though his early work was written in imitation of such poets as Chen Shitao and Wang Anshi, he wrote that in 1178, when he was fifty-two, he underwent a poetic catharsis, an enlightenment that allowed him to discard all masters and write in his own style. He is a poet of the vernacular who had an influence on later poets, among them Yuan Mei. Despite his distinguished official career, his work evinces an affection for ordinary people. He was known as one of the "Four Masters of Southern Song Poetry."

Cold Sparrows

Hundreds of cold sparrows dive into the empty courtyard,
cluster on plum branches and speak of sun after rain at dusk.
They choose to gather en masse and kill me with noise.
Suddenly startled, they disperse. Then, soundlessness.

XIN QIJI

(1140–1207)

Xin Qiji was born in Jinan, Shandong province, in 1140, a time when the north of China was occupied by Tartar invaders. When Xin grew up, he joined an uprising and fought the Tartars. Like his friend Lu You, he was a poet of idealism, patriotism, and militarism. Although he was a military hero and served in a series of government posts, he was not successful in translating his patriotic and militaristic fervor into government policy. He held a series of minor positions and was ultimately forced into retirement. While retired he took comfort in the Daoist tradition, which—like Buddhism—has often provided Chinese poets an alternative to the Confucian ideals of service and reform, especially when their careers have gone astray. Xin Qiji also wrote love songs, nature poems, and poems of a more learned and academic nature. He loved the lyric form, writing 626 *ci* poems to the patterns of 101 tunes. Like Su Shi, he is admired as a poet of unrestrained force, bold and free.

Written on a Wall in the Boshan Temple, to the Tune of "Ugly Servant"

When young I never knew the taste of sorrow
yet loved to climb up towers,
to climb up towers,
and just to write poems I pretended to be miserable.

Now I've exhausted all of sorrow's flavors
but stop before I say it,
stop before I say it,
and finally just say, "What a cool autumn day."

The Night of the Lantern Festival, to the Tune of "Green Jade Table"*

In east wind and night fireworks are thousands of trees blooming,
shooting stars blow down like a shower
over steeds and carved wagons on fragrance-filled roads,

---

*The Lantern Festival marks the main Chinese holiday season. Boiled sweet dumplings are served, and there are hanging lanterns, lion and dragon dances, and a great fireworks and light show. Today it lasts from Chinese New Year's Day until the fifteenth of the first month of the Chinese calendar.

phoenix flutes singing with energy
and the moon turns like a jade pot
as fish-dragons dance through the night.

Moth Hair and Snow Willow are dressed up in gold thread,
laughing and talking, then gone with their fragrance.
I search for my girl one thousand times in the crowd,
turn my head and suddenly
she is there
where the light and fires are almost snuffed out.

Village Life, to the Tune of
"Clear Peaceful Happiness"

A low and small thatched roof
by a stream's green grass
and two drunk voices talking sweet in a Wu dialect.
Who is this old lady with white hair?

Her eldest son is hoeing beans on the east side of the stream.
The middle son is making a bamboo chicken cage.
The youngest son is a lovely rogue—
he lies on his back by the stream, tearing open a lotus seed pod.

JIANG KUI

(1155–1221)

Jiang Kui, also known as the White Stone Daoist, came from
Boyang, Jiangxi province, though his father, a scholar-official,
moved the family to Hebei when Jiang Kui was a boy. His father
died young, so he was raised by his sister and her husband. As a
youth, Jiang Kui was a famous prodigy. A musician, a critic, and
a poet, he lived in the areas of Suzhou, Hangzhou, Nanjing, and
Huzhou in the lower Yangtze River area. Jiang Kui was not suc-
cessful in finding a career in officialdom, and so he lived by sell-

ing his calligraphy and relying on patrons. He wrote extremely important works of poetics and notes on *ci* music, and he invented seventeen lyric form (*ci*) tune patterns. His poems "Hidden Fragrance" and "Sparse Shadows" are two of the best-known and loved Chinese poems about plum blossoms.

Preface to "Hidden Fragrance" and "Sparse Shadows"

In the winter of 1191, I visited Mr. Stone Lake (Fan Chengda)[1] when it was snowing. After being back about a month, he wrote me a letter asking for new lines and new tunes. I composed the following two lyric songs. Mr. Stone Lake loved them so much that he asked the singing girls and musicians to practice them. They sounded very harmonious and nice and thus the songs were named "Hidden Fragrance" and "Sparse Shadows."

Hidden Fragrance

> The moon has an old color.
> How many times has it shined on me
> while I play a flute by the plum flowers?
> I recall a woman of jade
> even though it was chill
> breaking off a plum twig at departure.
> Now I am like He Sun,[2] getting old,
> losing my touch
> for writing songs with a spring-wind brush.
> Why
> do sparse plum blossoms outside the bamboo grove
> spread cold fragrance to my jade banquet seat?

---

[1] Fan Chengda (1126–1193) was one of the finest poets of the Southern Song dynasty (1127–1279), well known as a master of the *ci* lyric poem.

[2] He Sun, a poet in the Liang dynasty, wrote a poem on early plum flowers. Here Jiang Kui uses He Sun to refer to himself.

The river country
is all at once quiet.
I sigh, too far away to send a blossoming twig.
Night snow starts piling up.
An emerald cup easily weeps
and these silent red buds are bright with memory.
I always remember the place we held hands:
flowers pressed on thousands of trees
by cold and green West Lake.
Petal by petal,
they all blow away.
When can I see you again?

Sparse Shadows

A mossy branch decorated with pieces of jade.
A small green bird
spends the night with flowers on this branch.
As a guest I met you
by the corner of a fence in the evening.
I was speechless, leaning back on slender bamboo.
Zhaojun[1] was not used to the faraway desert
and secretly recalled her life north and south of the river.
I imagine her jade rings
on a moonlit night returning[2]
and turning into these plum flowers in solitude.

I recall an anecdote: deep in the palace
a princess[3] was asleep

---

[1] Lines 7–11 refer to Ming Fei (Wang Zhaojun). For more about her, see the note to Du Fu's "Five Poems About Historical Sites" (Poem Three) in this volume.

[2] "I imagine her jade rings / on a moonlit night returning" alludes to a line from Du Fu's poem "Five Poems About Historical Sites" (Poem Three).

[3] The *Taiping Yulan* (*Imperial Readings of Peace*) tells the story of princess Shouyang, the daughter of Song emperor Wu, who took a nap outside the Hanzhang Hall. A plum flower landed on her forehead and left a five-petal print, which could not be wiped off.

when a plum flower landed on her brow.
Don't behave like spring wind
which does not care for silvery winter plum blossoms.
Make early arrangements for a gold wedding chamber[4]
or you'll let your petal go with the waves
and then complain
like a sad tune from a jade-dragon flute.[5]
I'll wait for that time
and look again for her hidden fragrance
coming through a small window into a scroll painting.

YAN RUI

(FL. C. 1160)

Yan Rui, also known as You Fang, was registered as an official courtesan at Tiantai. She was known for her calligraphy, singing, dancing, painting, and her skill at playing Go. Attracted by her beauty and talent, gentlemen would travel a thousand miles to meet her. Well versed in literature and history, she wrote good lyric songs; three poems are attributed to her. When Tang Zhongyou was the governor at Tiantai, he once asked her to improvise a poem about white and pink peach flowers. She did it without hesitation, and they became lovers. The poem below was said to have been written after Yan Rui had been jailed and repeatedly beaten for refusing to inform on her lover. An inspector, wanting to frame Tang Zhongyou, accused him of favoring Yan Rui. He had her thrown into prison and tortured for two months, and yet she still refused to say a word about Tang Zhongyou. The poem below, in which she states her case, won her

---

[4] The *hanwu gushi* (*Story of Emperor Wu in the Han Dynasty*) tells how Han emperor Wu said to his aunt, "If I can marry Ah Jiao, I will build a gold chamber to keep her."

[5] This refers to Li Bai's two lines "Playing a jade flute in the Yellow Crane Tower, / while plum petals fall in May in a river city," from his poem "Listening to a Flute in Yellow Crane Tower."

release from prison and from registration as an official courtesan. She later got married as a concubine to someone close to her clan. Her poetry is considered to be natural and free of affectation.

To the Tune of "Song of Divination"

I don't love the dust storm of love play,
but my past life karma has made me a courtesan.
Flowers fall, flowers bloom, and the time
is chosen for them by the god of the East.

I must leave in the end,
there is no way for me to stay.
If only my hair were filled with mountain flowers!
Don't ask me where I'd like to go.

YUAN HAOWEN

(1190–1257)

Yuan Haowen is considered one of the finest poets China has produced, and certainly the finest poet of the Jin dynasty. He was born in Xinzhou, near Taiyuan in Northern China, and raised by his uncle, a provincial official. The straightforward nature of some of his poetry may have something to do with his Northern Chinese origin. He is a profound poet, and a poet of polished and considered expression. His work details with great insight and empathy the hardships of the Jin dynasty, as the Mongols under Genghis Khan swept through Northern China. His brother was killed during the Mongol invasion of his homeland in 1214, and Yuan Haowen fled with his family to Henan the following year. He passed the imperial exam in 1221 and was deeply influenced by the trend of his time, which was to imitate the poetry of Li Shangyin, though he also deeply respected other models—Su Shi and especially Tao Qian and Du Fu. His career as an official included several governorships in Henan and a posting at the capital in 1231, at a time when the Jin dynasty was undergoing further attacks by the Mongols. The capital fell in 1233, and Yuan Haowen was forced to undergo house arrest for two years in Liaocheng in Shandong. During this time he began to compile an anthology of Jin dynasty poetry, feeling a deep desire to make a record of his culture for posterity. He spent the rest of his life traveling through Northern China, gathering materials for his excellent history of the Jin dynasty, which served as a kind of tombstone for the civilization that nourished him. Although he received patronage from Yuan dynasty officials, he did not serve the new dynasty. More than thirteen hundred of his poems survive.

Living in the Mountains

Slant vines hang on thin bamboo.
Chaotic grass grows around a flower bush.

Wind is visible in a tall wood.
Water remains silent over slippery moss.

Maple trees scatter when the river turns.
A bamboo stream is serene when mountains are deep.

In thin mist leaving birds sink,
while the setting sun walks an ox home.

Dreaming of Home

A withered Chu prisoner with a southern hat,[1]
my homesick mind flows east each day.
Green mountains glow when my dream nears home
and yellow leaves rustle in autumn wind and rain.
In poverty, my poems become uncannily refined.
In turbulence, I have no tears left for grief.
Just let me see my brothers in the years I have left,
and I won't worry about the world, happy with chopped pickles.

from In May of 1233, I Ferried Across to the North

1

Countless captives are lying stiff by the roadside
as Mongol wagons pass and pass like flowing water.
You rouged women walking weeping behind Mongolian horses,
for whom are you still looking back at each step?

2

White bones lie in a tangled mess like hemp fiber.
In a few years mulberry trees have withered to a dragon's desert.
It seems to me life in Heshu has utterly ceased.
But look! Smoke rises from those broken houses.

---

[1] In 1232 Mongols besieged Bianjing twice while Yuan Haowen worked as an
official in the city. The next spring the defending general Cui Li surrendered to
the Mongols, and Yuan Haowen was detained. In the first line of this poem he
compares himself with Zhong Yi, a man seen wearing a southern hat who
turns out to be a prisoner from Chu. The passage comes from the famous
Chinese history *zuozhuan*, a commentary on *The Spring and Autumn Annals*,
one of the Confucian classics.

WU WENYING

(C. 1200–C. 1260)

Wu Wenying came from Siming (today's Yinxian, Zhejiang province) but lived mainly in the cities of Suzhou and Hangzhou, in each of which he kept a concubine. He worked in the Grain Transport Office as a private secretary and received royal patronage from Prince Rong. He was a prolific poet; 350 of his *ci* form lyric poems survive. His poetry was very personal, and he wrote extensively about his two concubines.

Departure, to the Tune of "The Song of *Tangduo*"

What is sorrow composed of?
Autumn on the heart[1] of a traveling man.
Even without rain, the rustle of banana leaves sounds sad.
They all say it is a nice cool evening,
there is a bright moon,
but I don't want to climb up the tower.

Love's season ends in dreams.
The flowers are gone, rivers flow off,
even swallows have migrated,
yet I'm still away from home.
O weeping willow, why didn't you tether her skirt
instead of for so long
tying my returning boat up here?

---

[1] The character *chou* (sorrow) consists of two radicals: "autumn" on top of "heart."

To the Tune of "Washing Creek Sands"*

In my dream I revisit your door behind deep flowers.
The setting sun is speechless, returning swallows sad.
Small jade fingers, spreading a fragrance, once touched this
    curtain hook.

The falling catkins are mute as spring dribbles tears.
Shifting clouds cast shadows and in shyness the moon hides.
It is a spring night but I feel colder than in autumn.

To the Tune of "Prelude to Oriole Song"†

A leftover coldness tortures me when I have a hangover.
I close my carved sandalwood window.
The swallows are late,
flying into the west city,
murmuring about the end of spring.
A painted boat carries me
after the Clear Brightness Day,
and a sunny mist rises slowly out of the Wu Palace trees.
My feelings as a traveler,
roaming with wind,
transform into light catkins.

For ten years by the West Lake
I tied my horse to a willow,
and chased your delicate dust and soft mist.
I traced up a valley lined with red trees,
and entered a fairy stream.
Your maid, Jiner, helped us exchange secret notes.

---

*This is a lyric song Wu Wenying wrote in memory of his dead concubine.

† This tune, a total of 240 characters, is the longest of the lyric songs. The form was created by Wu Wenying himself. It is a poem in memory of his concubine who lived at the West Lake.

Leaning against a silver screen,
you felt spring was broad and dream narrow,
interrupted, with red tears,
and you sang a song of gold-thread garments.
The evening bank was empty,
so the slanting sun was easily
handed over to the gulls and egrets.

Orchids age fast
and then grass returns again.
I travel in this country of waters,
asking for you again by the six bridges, but no one knows you.
The past is past, flowers faded, buried with jade and fragrance
after a few attacks of wind and rain.
Long river waves should be jealous of your watery glances,
and silhouetted distant mountains can't match your eyebrows' arcs.
Fishing lights divided our reflection when we slept on the river
    that spring.
I remember
with short oars we came to the Peach Roots ferry.
It seemed in a green tower
on a shabby wall
I wrote a poem at departure,
with tears mixed in the ink,
sorrow in the dust.

On a high pavilion I stretch my vision
to where grass and sky meet.
I sigh that my temples have half turned to white
and look for your things in secret.
I find tearstains and lip marks
still there in the silk handkerchief.
You're a phoenix with wings hanging low, and lost.
Facing a broken mirror, I feel too lazy to dance.
I should eagerly write you
a long letter of regret,
but the blue clouds and ocean are so broad
that wild geese will sink in them,

so I pour all my feelings
into the sad strings of my zither.
It hurts me to look at the one thousand miles of the Yangtze
    River's south bank.
I play my complaining tune to summon you again.
Is your lost soul still there?

LIU YIN

(1249–1293)

Liu Yin was also called Meng Ji; his personal name was Jingxiu.
He came from Hebei. In 1282 he accepted a position from the
Yuan court but soon resigned to take care of his sick mother.

Reading History

Records are manifold and confused, already losing reality.
Light or weighty, what they mean depends on imperial record
    keepers.

If every word were scrutinized for the author's intention,
countless people would be persecuted.

Mountain Cottage

In the water, horse hooves trample the evening glow
as my drunken sleeves catch wind and falling flowers.

River kids peek out their door. How did they know?
I guess the magpies' song reached the mountain cottage before me.

YUAN DYNASTY

(1280–1367)

DURING THE YUAN DYNASTY, CHINA WAS INVADED BY THE Mongols, a nomadic set of tribes from central Asia who had become unified under Genghis Khan (his name was an epithet meaning "universal leader"). They were fearsome warriors who fought on horseback with powerful bows. As rulers they were known for their brutal repression of dissent. Although the Mongols decimated their enemies in open combat, to conquer China they needed to develop techniques for assaulting fortified cities. It took decades of warfare and the leadership of Genghis Khan's grandson, Qubilai Khan, before they could decisively conquer the remnants of the Song dynasty in 1279. As emperor, Qubilai took on the dynastic title of Zhiyuan (meaning "the greatest of the Yuan"). The capital was moved to Dadu (the name means "great capital"), also called Khanbalik (present-day Beijing). It was here that the great Venetian traveler Marco Polo visited the court of the Yuan emperor.

The Mongols adopted Chinese ways, including the Chinese tax and administration systems, and they adopted Confucianism and other Chinese traditions. In the Tang and Song dynasties, the ability to compose poetry was an essential part of the examination system, but the Mongols abolished the examination system for scholars, breaking the continuity of teaching that had lent Chinese literature such a commonality of reference over the centuries. This was disastrous for the production of traditional poetry, but it fostered a stylistic break in the production of literature, especially noticeable in the infusion of vernacular in literary works. The Yuan was a great period for vernacular Chinese drama, though less so for poetry, but there were some fine poems written for and included in plays, known as *qu* poems. These lyric songs, or arias, were related to the *ci* form of lyric songs but often included vernacular diction, which lent the form spontaneity and naturalness. The *qu* songs developed from popular roots—tavern, theater, marketplace, and teahouse songs—and were developed to a high form by the literati. The poems were performed and set according to some 350 song patterns and were a blend of Northern Chinese and barbarian music. The most important *qu* poet was the playwright Ma Zhiyuan (c. 1260–1334).

The Yuan dynasty fell into disarray after the death of Qubilai and was weakened by rebellions and infighting among the Mongol nobles. The dynasty was overthrown by a popular uprising in the fourteenth century. The rebellion started in 1352 and grew powerful under the leadership of a former monk, Zhu Yuanzhang, who joined the Red Turban rebel group and became a general. By 1368 Zhu had conquered all of Southern China. He had been fighting for over thirty years, and he continued to fight until 1387, when he finally succeeded in driving the Mongols out of China. He established his own dynasty, the Ming, taking on the dynastic name Hong Wu.

ZHENG YUNNIANG

(UNCERTAIN DATES)

Zheng Yunniang's poems were directed to Zhang Sheng, the main character in the play *The Story of the West Wing*. Like Zhu Xizhen, Zheng Yunniang is classified in the *Complete Song Lyric Songs* (*quan songci*) under the category of figures who appeared in *Vernacular Fiction of the Song Dynasty*. Such figures might have been actual people or they might have been fictional—it is difficult to say, as the stories often spoke of real events and real people. It is thus uncertain whether she ever existed; she might have been a persona created by a male poet. The poem below, "The Song of Shoes," is also attributed to Lian Jingnu of Nanping, Fujian, who was married to the Confucian scholar Chen Yanchen.

The Song of Shoes

(To Zhang Sheng)

Vague shadows from the moon,
light shade among the flowers;
I've stood here waiting so long!
Enemy of mine! Will you not keep your word?
Everyone will see me waiting for you.
My mind fills with a thousand ideas,
ten thousand scenarios,
all kinds of doubts and guesses,
then all at once I see you!
My voice shakes in wind, though I speak very low.

Gently I move my lotus steps,
secretly slip from my silk robe.
Hand in hand we walk past the West Wing.
It is midnight and everyone is quiet.
At first I hold myself back,
then burst with you in clouds and rain.
So much joy and love,
but now we have to part.
I say, "Hold, my sweet,
just let me put on my shoes."

To the Tune of "West River Moon"

(To Zhang Sheng)

O crystal clear ice wheel,
dancing soul of the osmanthus,
why not make things easier for me?
Chang Er[1] must be jealous of me!

---

[1] The first stanza refers to the moon, where the goddess Chang Er lives in
exile and where a man is seen chopping down an osmanthus tree.

Though moonlight is lovely,
it makes our tryst difficult.
Who can pass me a cloud
I can use to eclipse the moon?

ZHAO MENGFU

(1254–1322)

Zhao Mengfu came from Wuxing in Zhejiang. Unlike many Chinese officials, he infamously accepted Qubilai Khan's invitation to serve in the Mongol government. He was fiercely criticized for this, and his reputation has never recovered. He was a master calligrapher, and as a poet he believed that poetry should imitate the heights of Tang dynasty poetry.

Guilt at Leaving the Hermit's Life

To stay in the mountains is called great ambition;
leaving the mountains you become a small weed.[1]
It was already stated in ancient times.
Why didn't I foresee all this happening?
All my life I longed to go my own way
and to give my ambition to hills and valleys.
I paint and write for my own entertainment,

---

[1] These first two lines are from *Newly Told Stories* (*shishuoxinyu*). Xie An lived during the Jin dynasty as a hermit in Shangdong province. He turned down many invitations from the court to work for the emperor. He eventually had to come out of his hermitage and began work as an official. Someone asked Xie An why a Chinese herb medicine had two different names, one being "Great Ambition" and the other "Small Weed." Another official, Hao Long, took advantage of the situation and satirized Xie An by saying, "This is easy to understand: when it stays in the mountains it is called 'Great Ambition' but when it goes out of the mountains it is a 'small weed.'"

hoping to keep my nature wild.
Unfortunately I am trapped in a net of dust,[2]
I turn and get tangled up.
I was a gull over the waters,
now a bird in cage.
Who cares about my sad singing?
Day by day my feathers turn to dry ruin.
Without relatives and friends' help,
vegetables and fruit were often scarce.
My sick wife carried my weak son,
and they left for a place ten thousand miles away.
We are separated, flesh and bones,
and our family tombs have no one to tend them.
When sorrow is deep, words all gone,
I gaze at clouds riding south till my vision fails.
A sad wind comes and I cry,
"How can I tell heaven my story?"

Poem in the *Jueju* Form*

The doors are all shut but spring cold still hurts.
The gold-duck incense burner has leftover warmth.
The swallows don't come anymore. Flowers are falling again.
In wind and rain the courtyard slips into its own twilight.

---

[2] "Net of dust": a traditional Daoist phrase for the human world, as distinguished from the world of enlightenment in nature.

*The *jueju* form is a four-line rhyming poem in either five or seven characters. Perhaps the poem is a portrait of the self as abandoned and withered, as Zhao, a former official with the Song dynasty, later worked in the Yuan dynasty, and was looked down upon for this. Though he was a great calligrapher, critics even argued that his brushstrokes indicated a feminine, malleable, and subservient personality.

MA ZHIYUAN

(C. 1260–1334)

Yuan dynasty playwright and poet Ma Zhiyuan is best known for his masterly play *Autumn in the Han Palace*, in which prose passages alternate with *qu* poems (arias). He wrote between twelve and fourteen plays; eight survive today. He also wrote *san qu* poems, *qu* poems written independent of a play. Like *ci* poems, *qu* and *san qu* poems are written in set patterns of rhyme and tonal sequence and characterized by lines of varying length, but they tend to be even more colloquial in their language. From Ma Zhiyuan's poems we know that he was a government official for some time and that in middle age he resigned his position to spend the remainder of his life writing. The poems presented here show his dual attitude toward nature: like Tao Qian, he desires to retire from public life and to be at peace in the wilderness, chasing a butterfly through his dreams; but he also knows that the law of nature is change, and his poem "Autumn Thoughts, to the Tune of 'Sailing at Night'" evokes the pathos of mutability and nature's indiscriminate devouring of human work and, in "Autumn Thoughts, to the Tune of 'Sky-Clear Sand,'" of humanity itself.

To the Tune of "Thinking About Nature"

A day is forever in the slow village to the west.
In the tedium, the first cicada buzzes,
sunflowers are poised
to open, and bees invade the morning.
Unconscious on my pillow, I chase a butterfly through my dream.

Autumn Thoughts, to the Tune of "Sky-Clear Sand"

Withered vines, old trees, ravens at dusk.
A small bridge, a flowing brook, a cottage.

Ancient roads, west wind, and a lean horse.
The evening sun dies west.
A broken man at the sky's edge.

Autumn Thoughts, to the Tune of "Sailing at Night"

(Six Poems)

1

One hundred years of light and dark is like a butterfly dream.
Looking back at the past, I can't help sighing.
Today spring comes,
tomorrow blossoms fade.
Hurry up and drink—the night is old, the lamp is going out.

2

Think of the Qin palace and the Han tombs
turned to withered weeds, cow pastures.
Otherwise, fishermen and woodcutters wouldn't chatter here.
Even if broken tombstones still lie across tangled graves,
it's hard to tell a snake from a dragon in the worn inscriptions.

3

After the "fox trace" and "hare hole" battle strategies,
how many heroes survive?
The kingdoms of Wei or Jin are like the waist of a tripod,
snapped in half.

4

Before my eyes the red sun slants west,
fast as a cart racing downhill.
When dawn comes in the clear mirror my hair has turned white.
I might as well say good-bye to my shoes when climbing into bed!
Don't laugh at a turtledove's clumsy nest—
sometimes the fool just plays the fool.

5

Now that fame and money are spent,
I have no worries about right and wrong.
Red dust no longer gathers at my front gate.
Green shade of trees is nice on the cornices.
Blue mountains patch gaps in the wall
of my thatched cottage, my bamboo fence.

6

When crickets chant I sleep well, as if ironed to the bed.
When roosters crow, all things start swirling endlessly.
Will the fight for money and fame ever end?
Packed ants circling and circling in battle formations,
a chaos of swarming, spinning bees making honey,
pushing and buzzing like flies fighting for blood.

Duke Fei of Green Wilderness Hall,[1]
County Prefect Tao of the White Lotus Society,
we all loved the coming of autumn:[2]
when dew forms, I pick yellow daylilies;
with frost, I cook purple crabs.
I mull wine over a fire of red leaves.
The life of a man is over after a few cups.
There will only be so many Festivals of the Double Ninth.[3]

---

[1] Duke Fei refers to Fei Du (765–839), an official and a man of letters in the Tang dynasty. He gave up his efforts at promotion when eunuchs became too powerful in the court. At Dongdu he built a villa called Green Wilderness Hall, where he would often gather with Bai Juyi and Liu Yuxi to drink and compose poems.

[2] County Prefect Tao refers to Tao Qian, who was not actually a member of the White Lotus Society (a religious society formed by Huiyuan, a monk from Donglin Temple on Lu Mountain in the Jin dynasty). The references to Tao and Fei evoke images of a lifestyle in which one frees oneself from worldly concerns and appreciates aspects of nature, such as the autumn season.

[3] The Festival of the Double Ninth takes place on the ninth day in the ninth month.

I'm going to tell my wily houseboy:
if anyone sends for me, even Beihai himself,
say that my name is East Fence, and I'm too drunk to come.[4]

GUAN DAOSHENG

(1262–1319)

Guan Daosheng (her style name is Guan Zhongji) was the wife of
the painter, poet, and official Zhao Mengfu (1254–1322). They
were married in 1289 and lived in the capital, Dadu (today's Bei-
jing), and in Wuxing, where she was born and where her husband
was later posted. Like Zhao Mengfu, Guan Daosheng was a
painter, calligrapher, and poet. Her work was held in high esteem
in her time by Emperor Renzong and by critics.

Love Poem*

> You and I
> have too much passion.
> Where the passion is, is hot like fire
> I knead a piece of clay into a you
> and a me
> then smash them
> and mix them with water.
> Again I knead it into a you

---

[4]Beihai refers to Kong Rong (153–208), who was once the governor of Beihai.
Kong Rong was well known for his hospitality and for having said, "With
guests filling up all my seats, and wine in all my cups, I have nothing to worry
about." Declining to meet Kong Rong when he comes to visit can be under-
stood as a gesture of living spontaneously without being bound by social
etiquette.

*It is said that Guan Daosheng's husband, Zhao Mengfu, was considering
taking a concubine and that he wrote the following lyrical poem to Guan
Daosheng to test her reaction:

then a me.
There is you in my clay,
and me in your clay.
I'll share your quilt while we live
and your coffin after death.

Fisherman's Song

(Two Poems)

1

I recall several plum trees by my distant Mountain Hall.
Despite the cold, jade flowers open on southern branches
the mountain moon shines
the morning wind blows
and I'm bitterly intent on returning to that clear fragrance again.

2

The great ranks are princes and dukes,
but floating reputation and wealth take away one's freedom.
How can that compare with
a flat boat
and chanting poems about moon and wind without return?

I'm a scholar-official
and you are the official wife.
Haven't you ever heard that scholar-official Wang had Peach Leaf and
    Peach Root,
Scholar-official Su had Morning Clouds and Evening Clouds?
Even if I marry a few beauties from Wu and Yue—it wouldn't be too
    much
since you're already over forty.
You'll still control Spring in the Jade Hall.

Guan wrote "Love Poem" in reply. It is said that upon reading it Zhao
Mengfu changed his mind and decided not to take a concubine after all.

JIE XISI

(1274–1344)

Jie Xisi, also known as Manshuo, was a native of Fengcheng, Jiangxi. He was a famous calligrapher and was also known as one of the "Four Great Yuan Dynasty Poets." He came from a poor family and studied hard to pass the imperial exam, establishing a reputation early on as a man of letters. He worked as a scholar for the court as both an instructor and a historian, and he was in charge of writing the histories for Song, Liao, and Jin. His essays are coherent and laconic, while his poems were compared to "a three-day-old bride" by another poet, his contemporary Yu Ji. Jie Xisi was not happy about the comment and personally interrogated Yu Ji about it. But it is widely acknowledged that his essays are so different from his poems that they seem to have been written by two different people. He has a collection of works entitled *Complete Works of Jie Xisi*.

Written on a Cold Night

Sparse stars are frozen in frosty sky.
A flowing moon soaks the forest.

I cannot fall asleep in this empty house,
listening to an occasional leaf drop.

Fishing Folk

The man casts a net forth like a flying wheel.
The woman in black rows the oars in the back.
All the family is trusted to waves and mist.
The boat is their house, their neighbors are gulls.
The boys are born to accept poverty,

the girls are born to cook.
Their nets are their fields to plow,
no need to look to others for clothes and food.
The boys will grow up to marry fishermen's daughters.
The girls will be fishermen's wives.
All the blood ties are near each morning.
Each year this broad river gives them all their lives need.
All that's lacking is lower taxes
so they can have enough coins to sleep drunk.
With no surplus but also no debt,
who needs an income of thousands of bushels of crops?

A Portrait of Ducks

Spring grass is very fine yet flourishing.
In spring, baby ducks gradually hatch and are raised,
their velvet hair starting to show color.
They really know how to quack out their names!

SA DUCI

(C. 1300–C. 1355)

Sa Duci was a Hui minority poet of the Yuan dynasty. His grandfather and father were military officers who served with merit. But as the family declined, Sa Duci was forced to make a living by traveling as a businessman. In 1327 he passed the national imperial examination, but by this time, some scholars maintain, he was already fifty-five years old. He worked in different positions as a low-ranking official and was very bold in writing a poem satirizing the royal family's bloody rivalry for the throne. His extant works are few, but it is known that he admired and counted as influences the three Li's in the Tang dynasty: Li Bai, Li He, and Li Shangying.

from Shangjing Instant Poems

I

A purple fortress, high wind, powerful bows,
—kings and princes out hunting on horseback.
Summoning eagles and quivering arrows they come back late.
Two white wolves hang facedown from a saddle.

Autumn Day by a Pond

I come to this serene pond in the forest
to kill the endlessness of an idle day.
Gushes of wind mess up duckweed traces.
Falling leaves disperse fish shadows.
Dewdrops are cool on a clear dawn.
Lotus flowers look cold in deep autumn.
I have no one to reveal my thoughts to.
I stand alone, my heart reflecting itself.

To a *Zheng* Player

Silver nails pluck fifty icy strings;
wind hurries through Sea Gate, stretching goose formations.

How many complaints are there from old lovers?
Like moonlight filling my boat by the Yangtze River.

MING DYNASTY

(1368–1644)

AFTER THE EXPULSION OF THE MONGOLS, CHINA WAS RULED by the Chinese again in the Ming dynasty, though it was to fall to outsiders yet again with the invasion of the Manchus and the founding of the Qing dynasty. Zhu Yuanzhang, a former monk who had led a rebellion against the Mongols, became the first Ming emperor, taking on the name Hong Wu. He reinstated the imperial examination system, but as the writing of poetry was no longer required, Chinese poetry continued its decline from its height in the Tang and Song dynasties.

Hong Wu was one of three emperors of China with peasant roots. Sympathetic to the plight of the lowly, he instituted low land taxes and shifted the economy's focus from trade to agriculture. Hong Wu reigned from the capital in Nanjing, but under the third Ming emperor the capital was moved to Beijing, and the Forbidden City (so named because it was forbidden to the common folk) was built there as an imperial palace. It was also during the Ming that the Great Wall was reconstructed and expanded into the massive structure we know today.

Hong Wu had come to power by rebellion. As he feared losing power in the same fashion, he violently suppressed those he suspected of fomenting conspiracy and revolt. Hong Wu and his successors micromanaged their empire, delegating little except to the trusted eunuchs, who became exceedingly powerful during the Ming. The eunuchs vied for power with the scholar elites and even formed a secret police to spy upon the rival scholars, the Mandarins. They utilized torture and execution and in the 1620s executed more than seven hundred scholars.

The Ming was a prosperous dynasty, reaching its peak in the

early fifteenth century, as new crops were cultivated, the empire spread and collected tribute from neighboring countries, and the population rose to around 100 million people. Seeking to maintain China's cultural purity, the government forbade the Chinese to travel beyond the empire's borders and prohibited trade with foreigners. But in the sixteenth and seventeenth centuries, Dutch, Portuguese, Spanish, and English traders smuggled and forced their way into the lucrative Chinese market. Christian missionaries came in tandem and achieved recognition in the Ming court, where some Jesuits found employment as astronomers.

Despite the isolationist policies of the Ming, the empire was porous and surrounded by enemies. In the sixteenth century Japanese pirates and Mongol invaders from the north began to erode the empire. War with Japan over Korea in the late sixteenth century and widespread peasant uprisings to protest high taxation in the early years of the seventeenth century culminated in the fall of the dynasty. In 1644 the last emperor of the Ming committed suicide, and the capital at Beijing fell to the rebel leader Li Zicheng. The rebels were driven out, however, when the commander of the Ming army collaborated with the leader of the Manchu army. The Manchus, who had been encroaching upon Ming territory since the 1580s, then seized power and founded a new dynasty, the Qing.

The Ming was famous for its porcelain, and it was also a time of great work in theater and fiction. Printing techniques advanced, fostering the dissemination of literature, the popularization of vernacular short stories of many sorts, and the development of massive and extraordinary novels, most notably *The Journey to the West*, a rollicking, hilarious account of how a stone monkey traveled to India and brought the Buddhist scriptures back to China; *The Plum in the Golden Vase*, an intricate, sexually explicit masterpiece; and *Three Kingdoms* and *Water Margin*.

In poetry, the Ming's difficult political climate worked to suppress innovation. In fact the Ming is generally regarded as a period of mediocrity in Chinese poetry, despite the prodigious quantity of poems it produced. As one critic observes, "Ming literature is striking in many ways for its routine nature and lack of imagination. The Confucian scholarly class, who seem to have been little more than a decadent middle class, upheld and aggravated an absurd sys-

tem of examinations that favored their own inertia."[1] The dominance in the Ming of the Old Phraseology School (an antiquarian
movement) led to self-conscious imitation of the forms, lines, and
themes of great poetry of the past at the expense of originality and
creativity. While many Ming poets were content with imitating the
height of Chinese poetry in the High Tang, there was also an individualist practice among Ming poets, particularly among such painter-
poets as Zhang Yu, Gao Qi, Tang Yin, Shen Zhou, and Yuan
Hongdao, who were open to influence from the Song dynasty poets
and usually more at home with self-expression than the poets of the
Old Phraseology School. As Jonathan Chaves points out, "The
sheer quantity of Ming poetry, the quality of so much of it, and its
stylistic richness and diversity all cry out for serious attention."[2]

ZHANG YU

(1333–1385)

With his friend Gao Qi (also included in this volume) and two
others, Zhang Yu was known as one of the "Four Distinguished
Men of Wu." Like many high-profile literary men of the early
Ming dynasty, a time of purges and political repression, he suffered an unhappy fate. Faced with arrest, he chose instead to
commit suicide.

Song of the Relay Boats*

Relay boats come, sounding like thunder.
One is just leaving, another demands to be rushed in.
How dare we delay any of them?

---

[1] Odile Kaltenmark, *Chinese Literature* (New York: Walker and Company,
1964), p. 111.

[2] Jonathan Chaves, *The Columbia Book of Later Chinese Poetry* (New York:
Columbia University Press, 1986), p. 6.

*The relay boats, like the Pony Express in the United States, were a system for
sending missives, messengers, and officials throughout the empire.

The officials are furious when we don't furnish them right
with painted screens, embroidered quilts, and red carpets,
but spring dreams are short and the boats are soon gone.
A captain kneels on the floor, persuading an imperial envoy:
"Please don't be too happy or too offended,
since ancient times heaven and earth have been like a relay station
with countless people rushing past."

GAO QI

(1336–1374)

Gao Qi came from Suzhou, in Jiangsu province, and is thought of
as the premier poet of the Ming dynasty. He was a precocious
youth, and as a teen formed a poetry group called the "Ten Friends
on the North Outskirts," or the "Ten Talented Ones." Along
with three literary friends (including the poet Zhang Yu, also rep-
resented in this volume), he was known as one of the "Four Dis-
tinguished Men of Wu." His reputation is that of a townsman
poet, a poet of humble origins, and he was part of a tradition of
townsman poetry in the region of Suzhou that included the
painter-poet Shen Zhou. He gravitated toward the poets of the
High Tang and of the Han and Wei dynasties, anticipating the Old
Phraseology School that was to emerge in another two centuries.
His extraordinary facility as a poet allowed him to imitate con-
vincingly the styles of past poets. He might have been associated
with the government of Zhang Shicheng, whose regime was con-
quered by the first emperor of the Ming dynasty. Only seven years
after the founding of the Ming, Gao Qi was executed on slight
pretext, only thirty-eight years old.

Where Is My Sorrow From?

Where is my sorrow from?
I suddenly see it when autumn comes.
It's hard to name it when I try to speak.

In confusion I just know it.
Is it that I'm afraid of aging?
Or complaining about my busy humbleness?
It is not the sigh of poor scholars;
can it be the sadness of being exiled?
If you say I'm counting days till my return—
I have never left my hometown!
If you say I'm sad over separation—
I have never lost sight of my beloved.
I compared my sorrow to autumn grass,
and yet cold dews could not make them wilt.
I liken it to smoke and mist,
yet even autumn wind could not drive it off.
Just let me ask since the arrival of this sorrow
how many days have passed?
When I lived by the west brook,
I enjoyed the spectacular mountains and rivers there.
But when I returned to the east garden,
I sighed over the grass and trees' withering.
Who ever comes to see me when I live here, a nobody?
Only sorrow is my companion.
Most people find ways to entertain themselves,
never tired of outings and banquets.
But I alone have this sorrow,
walking to and fro, for what?

Passing by a Mountain Cottage

In the sound of this flowing stream I hear a spinning wheel.
A stone bridge. A dark springtime of flowerless trees.
From what place does the wind carry this sweet smell?
Tea baking at noon in a cottage over the hill.

Lying Idle While It Rains

By a slant bamboo table behind a screen the bed hides.
I lie watching new swallows visiting a poor house.

Nothing on my mind, I live an idle life,
worrying whether this rain will hurt apricot blossoms.

SHEN ZHOU

(1427–1509)

Shen Zhou was the foremost Ming dynasty painter as well as a distinguished poet and calligrapher. His father was a landowner in the village of Xiangcheng (north of Suzhou), where Shen Zhou lived his entire life despite his extraordinary talent. He lived in the ancestral estate on which he was born until 1471, when he built his own home in the area. He worked as a village head and tax collector and took on painting pupils, many of whom (such as Tang Yin) went on to achieve fame themselves. As a poet Shen Zhou was influenced by Bai Juyi, Su Shi, and Lu You. His subject matter (as in his painting) often dealt with farming life in the villages of his area.

Inscription for a Painting

In green water a red mountain leans on my vine walking stick.
The setting sun lingers west of the small bridge.
I chant poems low, and from the brook a bird startles up
and is lost in a swirl of deep clouds, singing.

Thoughts Sent to a Monk

A hollow wall where a dim lamp-wick glows;
by the unused steps, insects sing chaos.
The River of Stars is shadowed by a thin edge of cloud.
Clear dewdrops are silent among thousands of trees.
In lake country, autumn water brims;
people drift off as wild smoke spills into the sky.
Who knows how to forget worries?
I face green mountains alone and think of old monk Zan.

ZHU YUNMING

(1461–1527)

Zhu Yunming came from a literary family in Changzhou prefecture, Suzhou. Born with six fingers on one hand, he took on the literary name Zhishan ("extra knob"). He was known as one of the "Four Gentlemen of Wu." A talented and intelligent youth who was able to compose poems by the age of eight, Zhu passed regional exams and became an official. He was the magistrate of Xingning, Guangdong, and earned a reputation for just governance and for moral leadership in education. He was not a proponent of neo-Confucianism or of Daoist rituals and beliefs and was critical of scholar-officials for what he saw as their puffery, hypocrisy, and even outright betrayal (he was very critical of Zhao Mengfu, for example, for agreeing to serve the government of the Mongol invaders). He became the assistant prefect of Yingtien (Nanjing), and after retiring devoted himself to scholarship and to writing.

In addition to poetry, Zhu Yunming wrote random meditations, stories, histories, and anecdotes. He was also a painter and a master calligrapher who specialized in the "mad grass" style. As Yoshikawa Kojiro notes, "His actions were as free and uninhibited as his calligraphic style. In return for his services as a calligrapher he most welcomed being recompensed with female companionship. If the payment happened to be in cash, he would squander it drinking with his cohorts, which may account for why he was pursued by creditors whenever he stepped out the door."[1] A nonconformist and a freethinker, he became the subject of a number of stories, and ultimately of a novel, *The Romance of Zhu Yunming*.

---

[1] Yoshikawa Kojiro, *Five Hundred Years of Chinese Poetry, 1150–1650*, translated by John Timothy Wixted (Princeton, NJ: Princeton University Press, 1989), pp. 126–27.

Taking a Nap by a Mountain Window

Resting my body in a monk's cloud chamber,[1] my dreams relax.
Pine trees and cranes rise between screen and pillow.
A beautiful pheasant makes a long song.
My hand pushes the window, and mountains fill my eyes.

TANG YIN

(1470–1524)

A famous landscape painter and calligrapher, Tang Yin was grouped with three other poet-painters as one of the "Four Gentlemen of Wu." In 1489 he passed the provincial exam and was listed as the top candidate. The next year he took the national exam and was involved in a case in which other candidates cheated. After a full investigation he was demoted to government clerk, ending his hopes for an official career. He worked as a painter and met with great success (along with Shen Zhou, Wen Zhengming, and Qiu Ying, he was considered one of the "Four Masters of the Ming"). He was called upon to work for a prince, Qu Chenhao (died 1521), but when he learned that the prince was planning a rebellion, Tang Yin pretended to be insane, drinking wildly, acting stupid, and stripping naked, which enabled him to resign his position. After that he was very much given to carnal pleasures and wine, and yet at the same time he tried to seek comfort in Buddhism. His amorous exploits were the source of countless anecdotes, short stories, and even a play. On his deathbed his final words were that the generations to come would misunderstand him just as his own had.

---

[1] "Cloud chamber" is a term for a monk's bedroom.

In Reply to Shen Zhou's Poems on Falling Petals

From the truth in the mirror, Cui Hui[1] painted a self-portrait,
but who can convey the beauty of the Goddess of Luo River?[2]
Seasons move faster than a finger snap
and fallen flowers are wreckage when spring is gone.
A pink-faced immortal needs to slough off three lives' bones
along a purple road where fragrance disappears in ten feet of dust.
I walk a hundred times around a tree and my heart speaks to my
    mouth:
next year who is going to be x-ed out of this world?

Boating on Tai Lake

Tai Lake is broad, with wave on wave to infinity.
The sky is frozen in ten thousand acres of lake light.
Green mountains are tiny dots in the distance.
The cold sky inverted in the lake blends into white air.
Diyi[3] is gone for a thousand years
but his high manner is still admired today.
Wu and Yue rose and fell with the flowing water.
All that's left from then is a moon to light the fishing boats.

---

[1] Cui Hui was a singing girl of the Tang dynasty who was in love with a man named Fei Jingzhong. When they were forced to separate, she asked a painter to paint her portrait and send it to Fei. Tang dynasty poet Yuan Zhen wrote a poem about this titled "Song of Cui Hui (with a Preface)."

[2] "The Goddess of Luo River" is the subject and title of a long rhyme prose (*fu*) poem by Cao Zhi (192–232). In it the poet describes a river goddess's beauty and how he (or the narrator) falls into doomed love with her.

[3] Diyi is the epithet by which Fan Li referred to himself. He helped the King of Yue destroy the Wu State and boated on Tai Lake with the beauty Xi Shi.

Thoughts

I don't pursue the pill of immortality, don't meditate,
eat when hungry, sleep when tired,
and to make a living, I've a painter's brush that also writes poetry.
My footprints can always be found by flowers and willows.
In the mirror I am aging with the spring.
By a lamp my wife and I share the full moon.
Ten thousand occasions of pleasure, a thousand times drunk,
I am a lazy person in the human world, an immortal on earth.

XU ZHENQING

(1479–1511)

Xu Zhenqing was known as one of the "Four Gentlemen of Wu,"
and later as one of the "Earlier Seven Masters of the Old Phrase-
ology School," an archaistic movement in which poets chose to
imitate the diction, imagery, and style of High Tang poetry, espe-
cially that of Du Fu. They also imitated the poetry of the Han and
Wei dynasties and disdained all other earlier periods, feeling
especially that the Song dynasty was a debased era for literature.
Xu Zhenqing was a brilliant scholar from a military family. His
poetry was well known even when he was just a youth. He came
from Suzhou to the capital in Beijing and passed the highest
imperial exam, becoming a judge in the Grand Court of Revision.
In 1509 he began working in the National University. He wrote
poetry, fiction, and prose (including biographies, anecdotes of
strange events, and meditations on Tai Lake) and was deeply
interested in Daoist religion, with its promises of longevity and
immortality. He died at the age of thirty-two, survived by a son,
who was also a poet.

Written at Wuchang

The leaves are not falling yet into Dongting Lake.
Autumn is poised to rise along Xiaoxiang River.
In this tall house I hear rain tonight,
sleeping alone in Wuchang City.
Burdened with a homesickness,
I grieve here where the Han and Yangtze Rivers merge
and can't understand why those geese outside the sky
are so happy about long migration.

YANG SHEN

(1488–1599)

Yang Shen was a brilliant scholar who came from a distinguished family in Xindu, Sichuan. He took first place in the imperial examination in 1511 and held a series of offices. When he opposed Emperor Zhu Houcong's wish to offer imperial rituals to his deceased father, who had not himself been emperor, Yang Shen, along with 133 other men, was beaten in prison, bastinadoed in the imperial courtyard. He was sentenced to exile in Yunnan as a convict in permanent military service. In his thirty-five years in exile, he became a popular, extremely prolific scholar, writing poetry, scholarly works on the classics and etymology, and collections of miscellaneous jottings, compiling anthologies, and editing editions of other authors' works. A political failure, Yang Shen was an extraordinary success as a writer and a scholar, traveling widely in his mind even as his body remained in exile in Yunnan. His second wife, Huang E (1498–1569), was a talented poet.

On Spring

> Ocean wind blows ocean trees
> and for ten days I shut my doors,
> sitting here, grieving the loss of spring blooming
> and counting red petals falling over the wall.

WANG SHIZHEN

(1526–1590)

Wang Shizhen came from Taicang, near Suzhou, and was descended from a family of scholars and officials who traced their lineage back to an important Six Dynasties Period family. Like Xu Zhenqing (1479–1511), Wang was associated with the Old Phraseology School, in which poets imitated the style of older work, especially that of the High Tang, and to some extent that of the Han and Wei dynasties. Those who followed the Old Phraseology School were told that "One should not read anything after the Tang dynasty," but Wang, especially later in life, was happy to learn from Song dynasty poets Su Shi and Lu You and Tang dynasty poet Bai Juyi, whom the Old Phraseology writers tended to disdain. Wang is closely associated with Li Panlong (1514–1570), a leader of the movement, who was his great friend; many letters and poems they wrote to each other survive. Together they were part of a group of Old Phraseology writers known as the "Later Seven Masters."

Wang passed the highest imperial exams, but in 1559 he gave up his provincial post to return to the capital in an unsuccessful attempt to save his father, a famous military man who had been ordered executed by the prime minister, an enemy of Wang Shizhen's. He found himself unable to sustain regular postings after this. He became the leading literary light of his day, revered for his passion and his scholarship (he was a poet, historian, and scholar of the arts). Scores of acolytes flocked to him for instruction and advice. The Old Phraseology School that he was a part of fell into disrepute after his death, but his reputation helped to cement it as the principal movement of the sixteenth century.

Saying Good-bye to My Young Brother

We walk to the riverbank hand in hand.
Looking back from the far bank, I'm already gone.
You stand alone in the dark and ride home late.
Now in springtime, moonlight is twice as white as frost.

Climbing Up the Taibai Tower

It is said in the past Li Bai
gave a long howl and climbed up this tower.
Once he paid a visit here,
and his high reputation remains for a hundred generations.
Behind the white clouds the sea dawns
with a bright moon, a celestial gate, and autumn.
As if to greet Li Bai's return,
the Ji River water flows with music.

GAO PANLONG

(1562–1626)

Gao Panlong came from a wealthy family of landowners in Wuxi. His father gave him away to a granduncle who was unable to have his own children. Gao passed the provincial exams in 1582 and the imperial exams in 1588. A neo-Confucianist, a stoic, and a fatalist, he became a serious scholar associated with the philosophical and political movements of the Donglin Academy and was said to spend half of each day sitting in meditation and the other half devoted to scholarship (see his poem, "Idle in Summer," below). Following a political schism in 1593, he was demoted and sentenced to live far from the capital (Beijing), becoming a jail warden in Guangdong province. In 1595 he returned home after the death of both of his birth parents. He spent years without a position, simply attending to scholarly pursuits and helping to reestablish the decrepit Donglin Academy as a meeting place for local scholars. He used his wealth and land to help widows, orphans, and the poor.

With the Manchu invasion and the death of the emperor, Gao's friends, who had lost their positions in the purge of 1593, began to come back to power between 1618 and 1620, and Gao was appointed to a series of important positions. Wei Zhongxian, a powerful eunuch, became his enemy and managed to purge him and many of his friends starting around 1624. Some were tortured to death, others sent to serve as common soldiers on the frontiers; Gao was allowed to return home to Wuxi but was made into a commoner. The Donglin Academy and others were denounced as subversive and ordered to be destroyed. When he learned that the imperial bodyguards were coming for him, he drowned himself in a pond on his family's estate. His name and those of the other Donglin victims were officially restored after the emperor's death.

Idle in Summer

> I sit in meditation in the long summer,
> not a single word all day.
> You ask me how can I do that?
> My heart is at ease when I have nothing to do.
> Fishing boats are returning in fine drizzle,
> children are noisy in woods.
> Northern wind suddenly turns south,
> the sun sets behind a distant mountain.
> I feel happy at this scene
> and pour a drink to go with this great mood.
> Gulls fly away from the pond.
> In twos they keep coming back.

XIE ZHAOZHE

(1567–1624)

Xie Zhaozhe was a poet, scholar, official, collector, and traveler who was descended from a military family from Jiangdian, Changlo, Fujian province, a coastal town facing the Straits of Taiwan, although Xie himself was born in Hangzhou, Zhejiang province, where his father was employed as a teacher. Xie took and passed the regional and imperial examinations and became a judge in Huzhou, Zhejiang. He held a number of other positions in Nanjing and Beijing with the ministries of Justice, War, and Works, and was a prolific writer who was known to compose meditations on the practices and customs of the areas in which he worked. He wrote prose, essays, collections of anecdotes, and poetry, but his most important contribution is an encyclopedia titled *Five Assorted Offerings*, a famous portrait of his times that was very popular in Japan (it was banned in China by the Manchus in the eighteenth century). He was a freethinker and a skeptic and was critical of superstitions, footbinding, greed, and sexual excess.

Spring Complaints

> Spring grass is rampant in the Changxin Palace[1]
> and sorrow slowly grows and grows
> since the emperor never comes here
> until it's high as the jade steps.

---

[1] The Changxin Palace is where the emperor's mother lived in the Han dynasty. This poem is written from the point of view of a palace maid, mourning the fact that the emperor leaves the women in his mother's palace untouched.

YUAN HONGDAO

(1568–1610)

Descended from a military and scholarly family, Yuan Hongdao was one of three famous brothers who comprised what was known as the Gongan School, after the port town of Gongan (in present-day Hunan province) where they grew up. They celebrated the poetry of Bai Juyi and Su Shi and rejected the imitative poetry of their day. All three of the brothers passed the highest imperial exams. Yuan Hongdao was a magistrate known for his travel writings and poetry. In his correspondence and criticism he celebrated spontaneity and clarity in poetry. After his older brother died in 1600, he and his younger brother retired to an island in Willow Lake to study Zen with Buddhist monks, but in 1606 he returned to his official career at the Ministry of Rites and other departments. In addition to his poetry he wrote a play, a monograph on flower arrangement, a historical romance, two prose works on Buddhism, and a set of miscellaneous essays, observations, and meditations. He died at the age of forty-two.

At Hengtang Ferry

By the Hengtang Ferry, walking close to the water,
you come from the west, and I'm going east.
I'm not a singing girl
but from big red houses with big names.
I spit on you by accident when blowing away flowers.
Thank you for returning my gaze.
I live by the rainbow bridge,
the red door at the crossroad.
Just find the lily magnolia,
but don't pass the poplars and plum trees.

ANONYMOUS EROTIC POETRY, COLLECTED BY FENG MENGLONG

(1574–1646)

With the exception of "A Nun in Her Orchid Chamber Solitude Feels Lust Like a Monster" and "We're Only Happy About Tonight," all of the anonymous erotic poems presented here were collected by Ming dynasty scholar Feng Menglong, who compiled them in a small collection of erotic folk verse called *Mountain Songs* (earlier he compiled a similar collection titled *Hanging on Branches*). Feng was a prolific writer, well known for his short stories. He was also one of the scholars of his time who showed a deep interest in folklore. He collected not only folk poems but also practical cultural artifacts and practices, such as different forms of letters, proper ways to address people, and strategies for winning in certain gambling games. In his preface to *Mountain Songs* he writes: "Folk songs are indeed very vulgar; however, aren't they the descendants of Zheng and Wei songs from the *Book of Songs*? Now we are in a deteriorated dynasty, there are phony poetry and essays, but no phony folk songs—this is because folk songs do not compete with poems and essays for a reputation, so there is no need to fake anything. Since they do not bother to be pretentious, I collect them to preserve authenticity. Isn't that something reasonable?"

Untitled

I open the door and see snowflakes flying night and day.
Three layers of embroidered quilt cannot keep me warm.
What I need is my man's hot belly.

A Dragging Cotton Skirt

> The girl came back from the lane
> where her man had torn her sash,
> so she told her mom, "I have a pain in my stomach,"
> and walked bent over, hands held to her belly.

Clever

> The mother is clever
> but the girl is clever, too.
> Mom used a sieve to spread lime on the floor,
> but the girl heaved her man up and carried him to bed
> and back again, the two sharing one pair of shoes.

Lantern

> Having an affair is like a lantern;
> don't punch holes or rumors will blow it out.
> The woman tells the man,
> "You come in secret without a light
> but you ignite me inside
> and make all my body burn red."

The Bento Box*

> Having an affair is like a bento box;
> you can carry it with you like a wine warmer,
> but just enjoy the taste of one or two dishes.
> Don't work your chopsticks too much.

---

*Bento box: a tray for presenting small dishes and appetizers, common in Japanese cuisine but originating in China.

Shooting Star

Having an affair is like a shooting star.
It penetrates the sky.
The woman tells the man,
"Whenever I see your fire I lust for you,
but you go too soon, like smoke."

The Boat

Having an affair is like a boat.
You raise the sail and toss in the waves.
The woman tells him,
"I know how to handle these wind-and-water storms;
keep a firm grip on the rudder and don't fall asleep."

A Boat Trip

The man poles the boat.
The woman rocks the boat.
Playing with wind and tide, they make a choppy ride.
She is an oar
that depends on the rower to hit water.
The more he uses his pole, the happier she is.

A Nun in Her Orchid Chamber Solitude
Feels Lust Like a Monster

In her orchid chamber solitude
her lust is a monster.
She is too lazy to beat her wooden fish.[1]

---

[1] "Wooden fish" is a hollow drum used by Buddhist monks when chanting the canon.

Her book of prayers is closed.
She's in no mood to chant mantras.
As a nun she's suffered a thousand bitternesses,
but when she gets old there's no guarantee of nirvana.
"Sigh, I should find a handsome man while I'm still young."

We're Only Happy About Tonight

We're happy, only happy about tonight.
We're worried, only worried about parting tomorrow.
Tonight two mandarin ducks grind against each other
till all the plum flowers are gone.
Now the drum tower beats midnight.
Shadows on the window-gauze show the moon falling west.
If only we could hold the moon up in our hands!

ZHANG DAI

(1597–1684)

Zhang Dai was a historian and essayist from Shanyin (Shaoxing), Zhejiang, born into a family of scholars and officials who lived lives of wealth and sensual pleasure. He was a tea connoisseur and like his family lived extravagantly, surrounded by elegant arts and fine antiques. After the 1644 Manchu invasion, however, things began to go badly for him. In 1646 his son was kidnapped by a military general who later pillaged Zhang's house and destroyed his property. In July of that year the Manchu invasion forced Zhang to flee to the mountains, where he lived like a hermit, penniless except for some books, and suffered hunger, cold, and poverty until his death. It was here, however, that he wrote two distinguished prose collections (a history of the Ming dynasty and a memoir of Ming society and practices) as well as other prose pieces.

from Ten Scenes of the West Lake: Broken Bridge in Melting Snow

A long bank and shade of a tall willow.
Sparse moonlight sifts through.
My feet step in the loose sand
as if walking in snow.

QING DYNASTY

(1644-1911)

DURING THE QING DYNASTY, CHINA WAS RULED BY THE Manchus, one of five Jurchen tribes that had conquered the other Jurchens and invaded China from Manchuria. A remarkable dynasty in many ways, the Qing lasted for 267 years and was very prosperous. It saw China expand to an immense size, annexing Taiwan, Chinese Turkestan (Xinjiang province), Mongolia, Tibet, and Manchuria. Tribute was exacted from neighboring nations, and progressive tax policies encouraged land cultivation and agriculture. The nation's population swelled to 300 million by the end of the eighteenth century, and to 400 million by 1850.

Weakened by corruption, rebellions, and warfare, the empire fell into economic trouble and had difficulty ruling and feeding its burgeoning population. Like their predecessors in the Ming dynasty, the Qing rulers maintained an isolationist foreign policy. But in a series of military actions, the imperialist powers of the West forced them to sign what came to be known as the "unequal treaties," under which China became a semicolonized region, forced to cede territories, pay crippling tributes to the British, and open ports to Western traders. Notoriously, the British twice invaded China to force the Qing to allow them to continue their lucrative business importing Indian opium to China. Furthermore, Westerners were granted special status, immune from prosecution under Chinese law and with their own police and courts and system of taxation. These humiliating treaties diminished the moral authority of the government. The tributes drained Qing coffers, leading to an increase in taxes, which in turn led to dissent. In the second half of the nineteenth century, a series of rebellions by Muslims, fundamentalist Christians, martial artists (known in the West as the Boxers), and others were put down, but only after tens of millions of people were slaughtered. Local taxes to finance armies to suppress the rebellions led to a decentralization of power that further weakened the empire. The Manchu rule came to an end in 1911, when the last emperor of China, Pu I, was overthrown by Dr. Sun Yat-sen, and the Republic of China was founded. The poetry of the anti-Manchu revolutionary and feminist Qiu Jin—though not of the highest literary quality—is particularly interesting in this context.

During this period the novel made advances as a major Chinese genre, especially with the writing in the eighteenth century of *The Dream of the Red Chamber* (also called *The Story of the Stone*), a great and immensely long work that incorporated poetry. On the whole the Qing dynasty is not generally regarded as a period of great achievement in poetry. Like the Ming, the Qing was a difficult time for intellectuals. As in the beginning of the Yuan dynasty, many intellectuals refused to work for the new and foreign imperial order, choosing instead to find other employment. Intellectuals were often persecuted by the autocratic Manchus, and their works were sometimes banned or destroyed. It should come as no surprise, then, that much of Qing poetry tends to be imitative, like that of the Ming, safely emulating the literary achievements of the great Tang poets. As Zhao Yi writes in his poem "On Poetry," "Li Bai's and Du Fu's poems have passed through ten thousand mouths / and now they are no longer fresh." However, there are some wonderfully fresh and talented voices that emerged from the Qing, notably the romantic poetry of Wu Weiye, the gorgeous *ci* lyrics of Nalanxinde, the spiritual, witty verses of Yuan Mei, and the sad, bitter, but beautiful boudoir lyrics of Wu Zao, one of China's finest female poets.

JI YINHUAI

(SEVENTEENTH CENTURY)

Ji Yinhuai, also known as Mao Lu, was born in Jiangnin, Jiangsu province. She was the sister of Ji Yingzhong (1609–1681), another Qing dynasty poet, and learned how to write poetry from her brother. She wrote a collection entitled *Deeply Cold Hall Poetry*, but she stopped writing when her husband, Du Ji, was killed during the Manchu invasion of the city. She lived in poverty with her children for over thirty years. Her line "Nesting ravens and flowing waters highlight autumn" was highly praised by Wang Shizhen.

Improvised Scene Poem

> Plum blossoms, a lonely village,
> water flowing past a few cottages.
> Against the setting sun no one is seen,
> just an ox lying in the wheat field.

WANG WEI

(C. 1600–C. 1647)

Wang Wei, also known as Xiuwei, was an orphan from Yangzhou who made her living as a courtesan at the end of the Ming dynasty. Among China's most accomplished women poets, she was deeply involved in the literary life of her time. After years as a courtesan she married a man named Xu Yuqing. Later she converted to Daoism and became a nun, taking the name "the Straw Cape Daoist." Well known as a traveler who wrote accounts and poems about her travels, she edited an anthology of travelogues titled *Records of Eminent Mountains*.

To the Tune of "Drunk in the Spring Wind"

Lover, who coaxed you to get drunk before me?
The window is cold beyond the lamp
and instead of holding me you lean the lute against the fragrant
  drapes

and sleep, sleep, sleep!
You forget how to be tender.
All you want
is the taste of being drunk.

I'm sorry I asked you that riddle about shoes.
It delayed our tryst in the mandarin duck quilt,
so when I asked if you'd taken off your clothes, you said
"No, no, no!"
Even a goddess
parting from her lover
wouldn't be able to let go of your sleeve.

FENG BAN

(1602–1671)

Feng Ban was born in Jiangsu province. Out of loyalty to the
Ming dynasty, he pretended to be insane when it fell to avoid
having to work for the new administration. He set himself in
opposition to his contemporaries, disdaining the Jiangxi School
of Poetry and the poetics of Yan Yu (1180–1235), who had cele-
brated poetic revelation and sudden enlightenment and viewed
the poetry of the Tang and earlier dynasties through the lens of
Chan (Zen) Buddhism. Feng Ban preferred a realistic, educational,
didactic application of poetry.

A Poem in Jest

In this world the rich and powerful are hooligans,
everywhere locking up good flowers behind red doors.
But women's dreams are difficult to control.
They can travel at will to the far edge of the sky.

WU WEIYE

(1609–1672)

Landscape painter, scholar, poet, and official, Wu Weiye, also known as Wu Meicun, was from Taicang and was a tutor in the Imperial Academy in Nanjing. He passed the imperial exam in 1631. Though he originally considered committing suicide upon the fall of the Ming dynasty (he decided not to after his family interceded), he eventually went to work for the Manchus of the Qing dynasty. He wrote a history of the rebellions that led to the fall of the Ming, a work that was banned, along with the rest of his writings. He lost his official rank in a tax scandal in 1661.

Among the principal poets of his time, Wu Weiye was best known for his long poem "The Song of Yuan Yuan." The question of whether to consider him a poet of the Ming dynasty or of the Qing dynasty is complicated by the fact that, while he considered himself a Ming loyalist and wrote movingly of his regret at having lived to serve a new master after the last Ming emperor committed suicide, his best work was written during the Qing. His son, Wu Jing, was also a well-known poet.

On Meeting an Old Flame, to the Tune of "Immortal by the River"

> Drifting debauched and drunk on rivers and lakes,
> after ten years I see again a fairy beauty
> still gorgeous and light enough to dance in my palm.[1]
> In front of the lamp with a smile
> she secretly unfastens her silk skirt.

---

[1] Literally the line says, "still beautiful, in palm light," referring to the beauty Zhao Feiyen (d. 1 BCE), courtesan to the Han emperor, who was said to be light enough to dance in the palm of a man's hand. Because she was so light, she was given the name Feiyen ("Flying Swallow").

But I am a withered and loveless man
and in this life cannot live up to her passion.
Outside Gusu City the moon is yellow and hazy.
Behind a green window she lives with her love gone,
tears crisscrossing her powder rouge.

HUANG ZONGXI

(1610–1695)

Huang Zongxi, also known as Tai Chong, Nan Lei, and Mr.
Lizhou, was from Yuyao, Zhejiang province, and was a well-
known philosopher and historian during the period of transition
from the Ming dynasty to the Qing dynasty. He had a wide-ranging
career, both intellectual and worldly. He spent years fighting the
Manchu invasion of China, and as a scholar he studied mathe-
matics and wrote works of philosophy on Mencius and the *Clas-
sic of Changes*, as well as a history of the Ming dynasty and a
biographical history of Ming philosophical systems and schools.
About writing poetry he said: "Poetry, linked with all that we
have between heaven and earth, is used to facilitate the free flow
of our spirit and willpower. The vulgar simply copy and imitate,
unrelated to ten thousand things between heaven and earth. How
can one write poems like that?" He declined many invitations to
serve the Qing emperor after the Ming dynasty collapsed.

A Stray Poem Written While Living in the Mountains

Knives, arrows, and imprisonment, let them come,
nothing can stop my strings and songs.
I face death with a calm heart
so what can poverty do to me?
With twenty-two ounces of cotton stuffing my broken comforter,
and three pine logs to cook my empty wok,
this winter I still feel lavishly supplied.
I can't imagine anyone doing better than me.

QIAN CHENGZHI

(1612–1693)

Qian Chengzhi, also known as Tianjian, was a writer and scholar born in Anhui. In 1649 he passed a special examination and became a member of the Royal Academy (the *hanlinyuan*). He was assigned the job of composing imperial edicts, which made him such a target of jealousy that he soon asked for leave and returned home. He was a prominent scholar on the *Book of Changes*, the *Book of Songs*, Qu Yuan, and Zhuangzi. Like others in the Old Phraseology School, he was influenced by Han and Wei poetry as well as by the Tang dynasty poetry of Du Fu. He had little respect for poetry after the Tang. His works include *Collection of Tianjian's Poetry and Prose* and *Works in Zangshan Pavilion*.

A Stray Poem Written in the Fields

So long without a sunny spring day,
and today is a washing day.
What am I to wear?
A gown that reaches my calves.
My family worries I'll catch a chill
and pours me a full cup of wine.
I can't often have a full cup
because I can't delay my farming.
I thrash hard in the fields
till strings and buttons suddenly give.
If only I move my limbs enough
I can keep myself warm naked.
Look at those fur coats:
they make people lazy in their waist and limbs.

NALANXINDE

(1654–1685)

Nalanxinde (original name Chengde) was also known as Rong-
ruo and The Man from Lengjia Mountain. He was born to a
Manchu aristocratic family in Beijing, where he lived in wealth in
a great manor and was given an education by distinguished
tutors. He excelled at cavalry, calligraphy, and lyric poetry. After
passing the national imperial exam, he worked as Emperor
Kangxi's bodyguard. He was a talented writer of lyric (*ci*) poetry,
which his work helped to revive. At the age of thirty-one, he
caught a cold and died.

To the Tune of "Endless Longing"

A journey through the mountains,
a journey on the waters,
my body moves toward Elm Pass
and sees a thousand lamps moving in tents at midnight.

Drums beating through wind,
drums beating through snow,
shatter my homesick heart and dream.
Back home I never heard such a sound.

To the Tune of "Washing Creek Sands"

This May, wheat is already sparse south of the Yangtze
and it drizzles like dream in plum-ripening season.
Idly I watch swallows teach their babies to fly.

The river in deep shade is like a colored ink painting.
Many peaks emerge after rain, shiny with reflected sun.
I wonder who that woman is, going alone to wash at the fishing rock.

To the Tune of "Bodhisattva Barbarian"

Staggering whirlwinds sweep the earth in midwinter
as I remove the saddle below a chaos of noisy evening crows.
Ice flows with the river.
My sorrow is as broad

as this scorched wasteland, exhausting my vision.
Drums and horns resound from high city walls.
Tomorrow I will near Changan,
but my homesickness travels forever.

To the Tune of "Mulberry-Picking Song"

Who first wrote the ancient "Song of Melancholy"?
Wind mourns and mourns,
rain grieves and grieves,
and the thin wick wears away another night.

I don't know what is lingering in my heart.
I feel bored when I'm sober,
I feel bored when I'm drunk.
Even my dreams can't reach my love at the Bridge of Xie.

WANG JIULING

(D. 1710)

Wang Jiuling came from a family of high officials and scholars.
He passed the imperial exam in 1683 and was an official in the
Qing dynasty, a member of the Hanlin Academy, vice president
of the Board of Civil Office, and president of the Censorate. He
wrote a book of poetry titled *Zunxiang Manuscripts*.

Inscription for an Inn

I wake at dawn. A piece of low moon in the thatched eaves.
My home country is vaguely lost in dream.
In this world what makes a man age?
Partly the crowing rooster, partly the horse's hooves.

ZHENG XIE

(1693–1765)

Zheng Xie came from Xinghua. Commonly known as Pan Qiao ("plank bridge"), he was one of the "Eight Eccentrics of Yangzhou" who painted in eccentric and individualistic styles. A brilliant youth, he displayed his talent early on as a painter, poet, and calligrapher. His mother died when he was a child, and his father died when he was a young man, so forced to seek a living despite his privileged upbringing, he supported himself by selling paintings. He took the provincial and imperial exams in 1732 and 1736, respectively, and in this time traveled to Beijing, where he cultivated friendships with Buddhist priests and the nobility. He became the magistrate of Fanxian around 1742, and apparently was an extremely good official, working to ease the plight of the people. In 1746 he was transferred to Weixian, and in 1753 he retired. Not long after, he found himself again in poverty and was forced to sell his paintings and writing for income. His own experience with poverty, as well as his wide travels across China and his interest in Chan (Zen) Buddhism, help to explain the sympathy for the poor evident in his work. Bamboo also often figures in both his paintings and his poetry, as in his poem included here, "On Painting Bamboo for Governor Bao in My Office in Wei County."

On Painting Bamboo for Governor Bao
in My Office in Wei County

> In my office I lie listening to rustling bamboo,
> wondering if I'm hearing the people moaning.
> I may be humble as a small county clerk,
> but I worry over every leaf and stem.

Homecoming Song

> After the dead were buried in the desert,
> we survivors traveled homeward.
> We heard from far away that in the outskirts
> of Qi and Lu the crops were as tall as men.
> My eyes fixed on the clouds over Mount Tai,
> my feet bid farewell to the northern coastal frost.
> I kowtowed to the tombs of the dead and cried—
> "Farewell, we will never see each other again!"
> Swallows and wild geese migrate in spring and autumn
> carrying letters with tears enclosed.
> But now what do I see when I finally come back?
> Nothing but four empty walls.
> Frogs jump upon my stove,
> foxes curl up in my bed.
> I drive out the foxes, block up rat holes,
> sweep clean the paths and throw open my glorious home,
> fresh-painting the walls with wet mud
> as tender grass grows new and yellow.
> Peach flowers must know I've returned;
> they unfold red blooms near the corner of the house.
> Old swallows are happy about my homecoming.
> They murmur above the open roof beams.
> Spring water is warming in the rush pond
> where I see a pair of mandarin ducks fly up
> and recall my wife,
> pawned to a man in a village in the southeast.

With sage-like kindness he lets me buy her back.
I carry my stringed coins in a bag.

When I hear my husband is coming
I am happy but perplexed.
It is right to go back to the old husband,
but my new husband is not bad.
Trying to remove the baby I am wet-nursing
I feel a knife stabbing my guts.
Our son knows I am not going to return,
he grabs my neck and demands, *Mama!*
My son is rolling on the ground,
dirt all over his face messed up with tears.
I go to the hall to say good-bye to his aunts and uncles,
all of them weeping.
They give me a bronze mirror as a gift
and a gilded box.
They let me take with me my jewelry
and wrap up my silk clothes.
"Just go home nice and neat,
but never forget us please!"

Her new husband is young
and he cannot bear the departure.
He silently goes away to the neighbor's
and leans back against a tree and the setting sun.
His wife is gone,
traveling around the fields, through ponds and woods.
The new husband brings home his son,
and stays alone in an empty bedroom.
The son cries and the father cannot sleep.
The lamp-wick is short, but the night is forever.

YUAN MEI

(1716–1798)

Qing dynasty writer Yuan Mei was born to a wealthy family near Hangzhou. He took the civil service examinations at an early age and was appointed to office at twenty-four. While in office at Jiangnan he developed a plot of land into an estate that became famous for its architecture and landscaping. He directed a school of women poets and was condemned by some of his contemporaries for encouraging young women writers. He retired at forty and spent his remaining years in literary and artistic pursuits. In addition to poems he wrote a collection of ghost stories titled *What the Sage Didn't Discuss* (a reference to Confucius's avoidance of the supernatural in his discourses) and a number of essays. His *Comments on Poetry from the Sui Garden* is a major compilation of poetry criticism. Though he often strikes a philosophical note in his work, he is certainly one of the most personable of Chinese poets—not averse to humor, sympathetic with the poor, and bearing a strong resemblance to the Tang poet Bai Juyi. His poems are direct, simple, often strikingly autobiographical.

from Improvisations

I

I chance on a half-blossoming plum,
lean lazily against bamboo.

Children don't understand spring.
They ask, "Why is grass now green?"

A Scene

A cowherd riding on an ox,
his songs vibrating through woods.
He has an idea: *I'll catch a cicada.*
Suddenly he shuts his mouth and stands very still.

On the Twelfth Day of the Second Month

Red peach flowers have just unfurled and willow leaves are tender.
This March[1] it's a cold spring and snow still swirls down.
Who else except my daughter remembers,
"Today is the birthday of all flowers."

An Improvisation

Three blooming plums in pots fill the whole room.
The master sits in front of them in oblivion.
My daughter was surprised when I entered the inner chambers:
"Daddy, why do your clothes smell so sweet?"

Meeting a Visitor

Watching the mountain all day, I stand on clouds.
Suddenly I hear outside my bamboo grove an urgent knock.
Arranging my clothes and hat to meet my guest,
I see my shoes pasted with yellow leaves.

---

[1] The Chinese calendar does not map exactly onto the Western one, but this
date is probably in either February or March.

Sitting Still

By West Brook I sit still
as the white sun slants and spring wind
blows me mingled fragrances
from who knows what flowers?

Inscription for a Painting

Late on a sunny day by a village.
Fresh peach blossoms by the water.
Where is the cowherd going?
On the ox's back a gull is sleeping.

A Poem Sent to Fish Gate

So far between the river south and river north
yet it is the same river in front of the doors there.
The water can pass two doors in the same day.
Why can't people be like spring tide?

from Twenty-two Miscellaneous Poems on the Lake

1

The moon like bright water soaks the sands.
I carry my walking stick, sauntering along the bank.
There is no way my servant can find me—
I sit alone west of a broken bridge deep in night.

2

The Lotus Flowers Study in Mr. Fan's Temple
—I was a pupil here forty years ago.
No one knows me when I come today.
I walk alone, lingering on each step.

Temple in the Wild

In these few rooms next to a brook
the monks are long gone, Buddha's fallen from his pedestal.
Incense ash all over the ground swirls into wind.
Squirrels gnaw prayer flags and shake their tails wildly.
I stumble over flowers on the wild vines
and in surprise clusters of butterflies swarm up.

Mocking Myself for Planting Trees

At seventy I still plant trees,
but don't take me for an idiot.
Though death has always been inevitable,
I don't know the date!

JIANG SHIQUAN

(1725–1785)

Jiang Shiquan was the finest playwright of his day and one of the finest poets from Southern China in this period, along with Zhao Yi and Jiang Shiquan's good friend Yuan Mei. They were referred to as the "Three Masters of Jiangzuo." Jiang was known as a realist, working from history and current events in his plays and poems, and yet he was also a very internal poet, celebrating intuition and inspiration. He came from Nanzhang and was tutored in the classics by his talented and educated mother. His father worked as a minor government official. As a young man Jiang was referred to as one of the "Two Luminaries of Jiangxi." From 1750–1751 he helped the magistrate of Nanzhang edit a local history, and in 1757 he took the imperial exams in Beijing, after which he worked in Shuntien in the Imperial Printing Establishment and Bookbindery and as an associate examiner of a provincial examination. He and Yuan Mei were regular correspondents—

literary pen pals. They met in person in 1764, when Jiang moved near Yuan Mei in Nanjing, and the two of them met often thereafter. Beginning in 1766 Jiang became an educator in charge of several academies and then worked in the National Historiographic Bureau. He retired in 1781, suffering from partial paralysis.

A Comment on Wang Shigu's Painting Portfolio

He doesn't paint sunny mountains, but rainy mountains,
like breathing on a bright mirror to show misty hair.
Better to obscure the ten thousand images of the human world
so wind horses and cloud wagons can come and go at will.

ZHAO YI

(1727–1814)

Zhao Yi was an important poet and historian from Yanghu. He was born poor and supported himself at first as a private tutor. In 1761 he passed the imperial examination and in a long career served in many official capacities. Upon being appointed the prefect of Zhenan, Guanxi province, in 1766, he showed himself to be a reformer, dedicated to helping the common people. From 1784 to 1786 he became the director of the Anting Academy in Yangzhou. In addition to writing a collection of "poetry talk" (critical notes on poetry), he wrote a dynastic history, histories of military campaigns, and other important works. He was a friend of Yuan Mei (1716–1798) and was considered along with Yuan Mei and the poet and playwright Jiang Shiquan (1725–1785) one of the three greatest poets of Southern China. As noted in the *Indiana Companion to Traditional Chinese Literature*, at the age of eighty-three he gave himself the nickname "The Old Man with Three Halves"—"that is to say, with eyes that could only half see, with ears that could only half hear, and with a voice that could only be half heard."

from Reading at Leisure

(Poem Six of Six)

6

When people read classics,
they read themselves.
This is like in a plaza
where an audience rings the high stage.
The short man stands on the floor,
he stretches his neck and stands on his toes.
But there are people in high towers on balconies
who watch the performance at eye level.
The show is the same
but the impressions all different.
The short man returns from the theater
bragging about having a close look.
The people upstairs
cannot help cracking up.

In a Boat

She serves two jobs at once—
who says the woman from Wu is unwise?
Carrying a baby on her back,
she rocks the oar and her baby at the same time.

On Poetry

Li Bai's and Du Fu's poems have passed through ten thousand mouths
and now they are no longer fresh.
From the rivers and mountains of each dynasty new talents emerge
to dominate poetry for a few hundred years.

from Poem Composed While Living at Houyuan Garden

1

A guest suddenly appeared knocking at my door
coming to give me a commission for my brush.
He asked me, "Write an epitaph
that will be elegantly written and flattering.
Compare his administration to Long and Huang,[1]
his scholarship to the Cheng brothers and Zhu Xi."[2]
I did it as a joke
and gave him just what he wanted
in a patchwork composition.
I made the man sound like quite a gentleman.
Check his epitaph against his deeds
and you'll find not one ounce of truth in a hundred pounds.
If this epitaph is passed on
who can know who's really a paragon and who is not?
Maybe people will quote my epitaph
so it ends up in the history books.
Now it's clear to me: at least half
of history is pure lies.

WU ZAO

(1799–1863)

Wu Zao, also known as Wu Pingxiang, came from Renhe, Zhejiang province (modern-day Hangzhou). She demonstrated exceptional literary talent at an early age. A productive poet who wrote in the *ci* and *sanqu* forms, she was a celebrated songwriter ("Qiaoyin,"

---

[1] Long and Huang: famous Han dynasty ministers.

[2] Cheng brothers and Zhu Xi: well-known scholars and philosophers of the Song dynasty.

a *yuefu* tune she composed, was very popular and widely circulated) and was the author of a play titled *Drinking Wine and Studying* Encountering Sorrow. The daughter of a merchant, her arranged marriage to another merchant was not very successful, which explains the search for a spiritual companion as one of her major themes. Late in life she moved into solitude to study Buddhism. She has two collections of lyric songs: *Flower Curtain* (*hualian ci*), which was composed before she was thirty, and *Fragrant South Snowy North* (*xiangnan xuebei ji*), a collection of her later works. Her reputation was very high in her day, and her poems have been widely anthologized, translated, and studied.

To the Tune of "Song of Flirtation"

> On the flower path,
> flower path,
> a sad person's lone shadow appears.

> Deep night, chill moon, ice wind,
> where is that broken flute from a tower?

> Broken flute,
> broken flute,
> you sing the news of early plum flowers.

To the Tune of "Beautiful Lady Yu"

Dawn window. I rise and roll up the curtain
and cold slices my fingers like scissor blades.
Last night in sparse rain and wind
countless crab apple flowers
turned wretchedly thin and red.

Maybe it's the flowers that have made me sick.
I am too sluggish to look in the mirror.
The sun is tall but I don't even comb out my hair.
I just listen to swallows murmuring about spring sorrow.

Feelings Recollected on Returning from Fahua Mountain on a Wintry Day, to the Tune of "Waves Scour the Sands"

All my way home I gaze on mountains
as in the mountains my road turns.
A thin cloud and pavilion rain darkens the setting sun.
Here and there are white flowering reeds.
The wind is caterwauling.

Since ancient times, graves have crowded other graves,
and not just broken tombstones.
How many people are burying bones and how many in grief?
In snow a red stove starts and goes cold again,
fated to become ash.

To the Tune of "A Song of the Cave Immortals"

Old moonlight
shining in the old window.
I'm too lazy to find the old *sheng* music scores by the window.
Let spring be long or short,
flowers fall or bloom.
I have never seen
long-gone flowing light regained.

For no good reason I woke from a new dream
and saw clear in my mind
how each year is exactly the same,
the same autumn chill,
the same sadness,
same separation.
Why do we need elixirs to make our pink faces stay
if butterflies can fly in pairs
oblivious of how soon spring will die?

To the Tune of "Clear and Even Music"

A courtyardful of bitter rain
has sent autumn home;
only the poetic impulse has no place to land,
disappearing into white clouds and red trees.

At dusk comes a cold moon and a misty grief.
The Xiang curtain will not release from its silver hook
but tonight my dream will travel on the wind,
carrying a chill and flying out from the jade tower.

To the Tune of "Washing Creek Sands"

Here is a volume of *Enduring Sorrow* and a book of Buddhist sutras.
For ten years I hid desires, for ten years read by lamplight
listening to autumn on the banana leaves.

I tried to weep but couldn't, so I forced a smile.
I couldn't escape from sorrow, so I learned to forget
and to mislead people with clever talk.

QIU JIN

(1879–1907)

Qiu Jin was from Zhejiang province, where from a young age she
studied martial arts and wrote poetry. In 1896 she married Wang
Zifang, with whom she had two children, but the marriage was
unhappy, and her poetry reflects her disappointment in her
domestic life. She moved with her family to Beijing but fled the
city during the 1900 Boxer Uprising. In 1904 Qiu Jin left her
family and went to study in Japan, where she participated in anti-
Manchu radicalism (she blamed the Manchu government for
China's weakness and poverty) and joined feminist groups as

well as the Restoration Society and Sun Yat-sen's United League. Returning to China, she worked as a teacher in several schools and ran the newspaper *Chinese Women*, which sought to promote equality between the sexes. She wrote essays promoting feminism and nationalism and was involved in planning an uprising against the Qing court, for which on July 15, 1907, in Shaoxing, Zhejiang province, she was arrested and decapitated.

A Poem Written at Mr. Ishii's Request and Using the Same Rhymes as His Poem

Don't tell me that women can't make heroes,
I rode ocean wind alone eastward for ten thousand *li*.
My poetic thoughts chased sails between sea and heaven.
My dreaming soul lingered with a crystal moon in the three
    islands of Japan.
I grieve to think of China's brass guardian camels sunk in thorns.
I'm ashamed—I have no real victories. I've just made my horses
    sweat.
So much national enmity hurts my heart.
How can I spend my days as a traveler here enjoying spring wind?

Letter to Xu Jichen*

Who talked passionately with me about fighting common enemies?
Who idolized the traveling swordsman Guo Jie?[1]
Now things have gotten so dangerous,
please change your girl's garments for a Wu sword.

---

*Qiu Jin sent this poem as a letter to her close friend Xu Jichen. After Qiu Jin's death, Xu Jichen and Wu Zhiyin risked their lives and had a tomb built for her by the Xileng Bridge at West Lake in Hangzhou province.

[1] Guo Jie was a well-known Han dynasty traveling swordsman who devoted his life to fighting for justice and helping those in need.

SU MANSHU (THE HALF MONK)

(1884–1918)

Novelist, poet, Buddhist monk, and revolutionary Su Manshu was born Su Jian in 1884 in Yokohama, Japan. His father was a Chinese merchant, and his mother his father's Japanese maid. As a youth he attended school in China, then returned to Japan where he studied in Tokyo and became involved in student revolutionary groups seeking to overthrow the Manchu rulers of the Qing dynasty. He traveled widely across Asia, getting involved in revolutionary activities, working as a radical journalist, and writing poems and fiction. He translated into Chinese the poems of Byron, whom he saw as his poetic master. Eventually he converted to Buddhism, taking the name "Manshu" and coming to be known as "the half monk" of the Southern School of Poets. He wrote many love poems and despite his vows was known for having affairs.

from Ten Narrative Poems

3

Dante and Byron are my masters.
My talent is like rivers and oceans, but my fate's thin as a silk
    thread.
Don't let my red string break for a beauty.
Who will listen to my lone fury, my sour emotion?

8

Green Jade, don't brood over your coarse background.
You are a fairy from my hometown; only you can erode my soul.
My robe is flecked with dots and dots like cherry petals,
half from your lipstick, and half from tears.

9

From a tall tower a flute plays spring drizzle.[1]
When will I return to watch the Zhejiang tide?
With straw sandals and a broken bowl no one recognizes me.
Which cherry blossom bridge am I stepping over?

10

Facing the wall for nine years, I was enlightened about emptiness
    and appearance.
Returning home with my monk's staff[2] I regretted having met you.
I'm sorry that I have disappointed you so much.
I can only let others be the zither under your fingers.[3]

To the Zither Player

(Three Poems)

1

Let moth eyebrows covet my Zen heart;
to a Buddha, love and loathing are the same.
In my bamboo hat and palm-bark rain cape I'm gone;
I do not love and I do not hate anyone.

2

I detest blossoms and willows in mist.
After drifting in the East Sea for twenty years,
having purged all love, all empty forms and colors,
by Pipa Lake I sleep with a sutra for a pillow.

---

[1] "Spring Drizzle" is a famous sad song for the vertical flute.

[2] The monk's staff is called the "khakkhara" and is known as an "alarm staff" because it is covered with metal rings that jingle. In this way Buddhist monks can scare off predators when they travel and warn small creatures of their approach so that they won't be stepped on. The khakkhara is often depicted in the hands of Buddhas and bodhisattvas in Buddhist art.

[3] The last line is from Huang Jun's lyric song *"yijiangnan"*: "my wish in life, to be a zither producing music—I can get close to the slender fingers of a beauty, and sing in the lap of her silk skirt—even if I have to die it will be great."

3

I stole a taste of dew from a celestial beauty's lips.
Now I keep wiping my eyes against wind.
Each day missing you makes me age faster.
What can I do? My lonely window holds twilight.

FROM MODERN TO CONTEMPORARY

(1911–Present)

CHINESE LITERATURE IN THE MODERN ERA HAD TO CONTEND with the reality of a century of political upheaval and regular warfare, the humiliating influence of Western colonial powers and an expansionist Japan, and the end of the imperial order with the overthrow of the Qing dynasty in 1911. Under the leadership of Dr. Sun Yat-sen's United League, rebel groups enlisted the aid of army officers and put an end to Manchu rule. A settlement was negotiated with the head general of the Manchus, Yuan Shikai, in which Yuan would become president and arrange for the abdication of the Qing emperor. Yuan was elected president in 1912 by a revolutionary council in Nanjing, and thus the Republic of China was born.

Yuan Shikai was not at heart a democratic leader. After a series of power struggles, Sun Yat-sen fled to Japan, and Yuan dissolved parliament and became a dictator. During World War I he attempted to restore the monarchy and crown himself king. Revolts spread around the country. Yuan, having lost control of much of his empire, died in 1916 of natural causes, and China fractured into many small powers, entering an era of competing warlords. Sun Yat-sen established a base in the south and vied for power with warlords to the north. He had founded the Nationalist Party (the Guomindang) in 1912 from the remains of his old United League, but it had been suppressed by Yuan Shikai. It resurfaced after Yuan Shikai's death and became the most important player in the struggle to unite China and expel foreign invaders. It was joined in this effort by another young party, the Chinese Communist Party (CCP), which grew out of the radical May Fourth Movement and began to spread in the 1920s.

In 1923 Sun Yat-sen allowed CCP members to join his Nationalist Party. The Communists did so but maintained a separate identity within the party. Sun Yat-sen died of cancer in 1925, before he could achieve his dream of a unified China. A split developed between the conservative and radical factions of his party, culminating in the expulsion of the Communists by Chiang Kai-shek, the leader of the Nationalist army and the head of state as of 1928. Chiang Kai-shek focused on battling the Communists, but when war broke out with the Japanese in 1937 he made an alliance with the Communists against the foreign invaders. Following the war with the Japanese, a civil war broke out between the Nationalists and Communists, resulting in the establishment of a Communist state in 1949. Chiang and his followers fled to Taiwan, where they established a rival state.

There were parallel developments in Chinese literature and education. The elimination of the civil service examination system in 1905 led to a new educational movement, with thousands of Chinese pursuing a modern education in Japan, the United States, and Europe. In 1911 an educational system based on the American model was instituted. Modern schools spread across China, as did modern ideas promulgated by the new intellectuals, whose radical rethinking of Chinese culture came together in the New Culture Movement. Inspired by Enlightenment principles of equality, liberty, and dispassionate scientific inquiry, as well as by socialism and anarchism, they sought ways of making China strong in the face of Western imperialism. Important intellectual journals of the time included *New Youth* and *New Tide*, which celebrated literature written in the vernacular. In a key essay ("Some Modest Proposals," 1917), Hu Shi called for the elimination of allusion, parallelism, imitation of the ancients, and clichéd and formal language and advocated writing in "vulgar diction," arguing that "It is preferable to use the living words of the twentieth century than the dead words of three millennia past." This literary revolution freed Chinese writers from the restrictions of classical Chinese forms and produced a literature in what was called "plain speech" writing that was readily comprehensible to Chinese readers. Chinese intellectuals devoured translations of Western literature and attempted to adapt Western themes, forms, and techniques to writing in Chinese.

The literary reform movement was part of a larger movement named for an incident on May 4, 1919, in which thousands of Beijing students protested the Versailles Peace Conference, which gave the German concessions in Shandong province to Japan. A crackdown led to deaths and mass arrests, and protests and strikes spread across the country, forcing the government to decide against signing the treaty. The May Fourth Movement spawned countless publications and created an intellectual ferment that helped to spread the new vernacular literature. The vernacular literature movement was also embraced by the Communists, among them Guo Moruo of the Creation Society, who attacked the elitism of classical Chinese literature and championed a literature of the people: "The literature we need is a socialistic and realistic literature that sympathizes with the proletarian classes." Other new writers sought to imitate such Western movements and forms as French Symbolism, Imagism, the prose poem, and even the sonnet. As exciting as this was for the development of Chinese poetry, these radical breaks from tradition signaled the end of poetry's central place in Chinese culture. As Michelle Yeh notes, "The abolition of the civil service examination in 1904—for which a command of the poetic art was desirable, if not required—closed the most important avenue of upward mobility; and extensive implementation of Westernized education shifted the emphasis from the humanities to science and technology. Consequently, poetry lost its privileged position as the cornerstone of moral cultivation, a tool for political efficacy, and the most refined form of social liaison. It came to be viewed instead as a highly specialized, private, and socially peripheral pursuit."[1]

As with pre-Revolution Chinese poetry, post-1949 Chinese poetry is closely tied to politics. According to the Confucian tradition, literature served a didactic and moral purpose, an understanding that was affirmed in the People's Republic of China. The call by early radical writers for a proletarian literature that served the revolutionary cause became state doctrine after the Revolution succeeded in 1949. Under the Communists, literature that did not preach revolution was useless and, worse, counterrevolutionary. As Mao wrote, those who refused to praise "the proletariat, the Com-

---

[1]Michelle Yeh, *Anthology of Modern Chinese Poetry* (New Haven: Yale University Press, 1992), pp. xxiii–xxiv.

munist Party, New Democracy, and socialism" were "mere termites in the revolutionary ranks." Authors and intellectuals found themselves the victims of a series of purges, from the Anti-Rightist Campaign of 1957 through the Great Proletarian Cultural Revolution of 1966–1976. It is no surprise, then, that much of the poetry produced in China after 1949 is unmitigated propaganda of a relatively low quality. Even well-known authors with some talent, such as Guo Moruo, wrote terrible verse, with howlingly bad lines like

> The people are industrious and courageous:
> Enforce national defense, revolutionize traditions.
> Strong is the leadership of our Communist government,
> Herald of the proletariat.

After the death of Mao Zedong in 1976, China moved into a new phase, seeking to find ways of incorporating the economic power of capitalism into the social egalitarianism of Communism. With economic change came at least a few gestures toward cultural openness. A new literature in China began to emerge, tentatively at first, in underground publications, along with a Democracy Movement with which many writers were associated. The most important school of poets to come out of this time was the Misty Poets, who had begun to gather privately during the Cultural Revolution to talk about and share poems and who published an underground journal called *Today*. These poets began writing an obscure (that is, "misty") poetry that went carefully—or headlong—into the forbidden territory of critique of totalitarian repression. As Bei Dao writes, "no way will I kneel / to state assassins / who lock up the winds of freedom." Instead, he writes, "in times with no heroes / I'll just be a man." In this context, even a simple love poem was revolutionary (or counterrevolutionary, depending on one's perspective), because it celebrated a personal, rather than a social, identity.

As had happened so many times in the past with the People's Republic of China, the movement toward cultural openness was but one swing of the pendulum. Challenged by student dissent and calls for democracy, the government imposed a series of repressive campaigns in the 1980s that culminated in the Tiananmen Square massacre of 1989. The People's Army was called in to disperse Democracy Movement protesters who had camped out in the square, and hundreds, perhaps thousands, were massacred. Many contemporary Chinese poets (including a number of the Misties, such as Bei Dao, Yang Lian, and Duo Duo) have since gone into exile.

The literature of China in the late twentieth century has thus become a literature of diaspora. In many ways this is part of an ongoing diaspora from China that began with Chinese immigration to the United States in the nineteenth century (and the writing of poems on the walls of the immigration detention center on Angel Island) and continued with the literature produced in Taiwan and Hong Kong. Though this larger Pacific Rim literature falls outside the scope of this book, we have included the work of Luo Fu, among the finest of Taiwanese poets, and of Ha Jin, a contemporary Chinese writer who lives in the United States and writes in English, to give a taste of this larger field of inspiration and accomplishment.

MAO ZEDONG

(1893–1976)

To Westerners, whose association of poetry with government belongs to the long-distant era of the literate and literary courtier, the fact that the most powerful politician and revolutionary of twentieth century China is also among its finest modern poets may seem stranger than it does to the Chinese. Mao Zedong was born in Shaoshan, Hunan province, in 1893 to a family of well-off peasants. He worked on his father's farm, attended schools, and was educated in Changsha at the First Provincial Normal School, where he encountered revolutionary writings. In the winter of 1918–1919 he worked in a Beijing library, where he was strongly influenced by future Communist leaders Li Dazhao and Chen Duxiu. Mao was present in Shanghai in 1921 at the founding of the Chinese Communist Party, and he participated in the 1927 peasant uprisings in Hunan. He spent several years with the Communist guerrillas in Jiangxi and other border areas, and after Nationalist armies forced the Communists to flee on the disastrous Long March of 1934, he became the supreme leader of the party. He eventually led the Communists to victory, and after the founding of the People's Republic of China in 1949, he became its chairman. Despite challenges from inside and outside the party, Mao remained China's most important politician until his death in 1976, after which party moderates, under the leadership of Deng Xiaoping, took over from the Gang of Four, Mao's political coterie.

In his 1942 "Talks at the Yenan Forum on Literature and Art," Mao stated that literature is always political, that its true purpose should be to fire up the masses with revolutionary fervor, to celebrate revolution and the people (not the subjective consciousness of the author), and that it should be judged on utilitarian grounds. This was the basis for the development of Social Realist literature and was the authority upon which writers who didn't fit the revolutionary model were criticized, censored, or worse. Mao's own poetry was written in classical forms, though he advised his readership not to emulate him in this. Its content is heroic, visionary, and revolutionary, and it dramatizes the historical events that led to the new republic.

> *The following poems by Mao Zedong were translated by Willis Barnstone and Ko Ching-po.*

Changsha*

I stand alone in cold autumn.
The River Xiang goes north
around the promontory of Orange Island.
I see the thousand mountains gone red
and rows of stained forests.
The great river is glassy jade
swarming with one hundred boats.
Eagles flash over clouds
and fish float near the clear bottom.

---

*Changsha is the capital of Hunan, Mao Zedong's native province. The city is on the east bank of the Xiang River, which flows north into the Yangtze. Mao studied in Changsha at the First Provincial Normal School of Hunan from 1913 to 1918.

In the freezing air a million creatures compete for freedom.
In this immensity
I ask the huge green-blue earth,
who is master of nature?

I came here with many friends
and remember those fabled months and years of study.
We were young,
sharp as flower wind, ripe,
candid with a scholar's bright blade, and unafraid.
We pointed our finger at China
and praised or damned through the papers[1] we wrote.
The warlords of the past were cow dung.
Do you remember
how in the middle of the river
we hit the water, splashed, and how our waves
        slowed down the swift junks?

Tower of the Yellow Crane*

China is vague and immense where the nine rivers[1] pour.
The horizon is a deep line threading north and south.
Blue haze and rain.
Hills like a snake or tortoise guard the river.[2]

---

[1] In September 1915 Yuan Shikai wanted to become emperor of China. Dang Xiangming, the warlord then controlling Hunan, supported Yuan and banned all opposition to him. Nevertheless, Mao published a pamphlet ("the papers") opposing the restoration of the monarchy.

*The Tower of the Yellow Crane sits atop a cliff west of Wuchang in the province of Hubei. There is a legend that the saint Zian once rode past the area on a yellow crane, thought to be an immortal bird. Another legend holds that Fen Wenwei attained immortality at this spot and regularly flew past on a yellow or golden crane. The tower commemorates these events and has become a pilgrimage site for scholars and poets.

[1] The many tributaries of the Yangtze that flow nearby.

[2] Literally, "snake or tortoise *grip* the river." The allusion is to Snake Hill and Tortoise Hill, which face each other on either bank of the Yangtze. The Tower of the Yellow Crane is located atop Snake Hill.

The yellow crane is gone.
> Where?
Now this tower and region are for the wanderer.
I drink wine to the bubbling water[3]—the heroes
> are gone.
Like a tidal wave a wonder rises in my heart

Warlords*

Wind and clouds suddenly rip the sky
and warlords clash.
War again.
Rancor rains down on men who dream of a Pillow
of Yellow Barley.[1]

Yet our red banners leap over the calm Ding River
> on our way
to Shanghang and to Longyan dragon cliff.

---

[3] The Song dynasty poet Su Shi wrote a poem in which he drank to the moon's reflection in the river while recalling old heroes (see "Recalling the Past at the Red Cliffs, to the Tune of 'Charms of Niannu,'" in this volume). The implication is that, like the yellow crane, the old heroes are gone.

*The full title is "War Between Jiang and the Jieshi Group." While Chiang Kai-shek was fighting with other military leaders of Guangxi, Mao and Zhu De accomplished their plan of setting up a base in north Fujian province. In the same area the Red Army took Shanghang at dawn on September 21, 1929. Longyan—Dragon Cliff—was taken earlier in the year.

[1] Yellow Barley or Golden Millet. There is a Tang dynasty story of a poor scholar, Lu Sheng, who meets an immortal, Lu Weng, in an inn in Handan. Lu Sheng complains of his harsh life, and Lu Weng lends him a pillow on which he can sleep and dream of good fortune. In his sleep all his ambitions appear to come true: honor, wealth, power, marriage to a beautiful girl, and old age. When he wakes up, the innkeeper, a Daoist friend, is cooking a meal of golden millet for him. The Pillow of Yellow Barley suggests the ambitious dreams of men.

The golden vase of China[2] is shattered.
   We mend it,
happy as we give away its meadows.

Kunlun Mountain

Over the earth
the green-blue monster Kunlun who has seen
all spring color and passion of men.
Three million dragons of white jade
      soar
and freeze the whole sky with snow.
When a summer sun heats the globe
rivers flood
and men turn into fish and turtles.
Who can judge
a thousand years of accomplishments or failures?
Kunlun,
you don't need all that height or snow.
If I could lean on heaven, grab my sword,
      and cut you in three parts,
I would send one to Europe, one to America,
      and keep one part here
      in China
that the world have peace
and the globe share the same heat and ice.

[2] Mao compares China to a golden vase shattered by the warlords. He is speaking of land reform and redistribution.

Loushan Pass*

A hard west wind,
in the vast frozen air wild geese shriek to the morning
     moon,
frozen morning moon.
Horse hooves shatter the air
and the bugle sobs.

The grim pass is like iron
yet today we will cross the summit in one step,
cross the summit.
Before us green-blue mountains are like the sea,
the dying sun like blood.

Snow

The scene is the north lands.
Thousand of *li* sealed in ice,
ten thousand *li* in blowing snow.
From the Long Wall I gaze inside and beyond
and see only vast tundra.
Up and down the Yellow River
the gurgling water is frozen.
Mountains dance like silver snakes,
hills gallop like wax-bright elephants
trying to climb over the sky.
On days of sunlight
the planet teases us in her white dress and rouge.
Rivers and mountains are beautiful
and make heroes bow and compete to catch the girl—
     lovely earth.

---

* The Loushan (Lou Mountain) Pass is in the north of Zungi county in
Guizhou province. It was a strategic position between Guizhoun and Sichuan.
The winding road makes for an arduous climb up the highest peak of the
Loushan range. The Red Army took the pass twice in 1935. The occasion of
this poem was the second storming of the pass during the Long March.

Yet the emperors Shi Huang and Wu Di[1]
were barely able to write.
The first emperors of the Tang and Song dynasties
      were crude.
Genghis Khan,[2] man of his epoch
and favored by heaven,
knew only how to hunt the great eagle.
They are all gone.

Only today are we men of feeling.

from Saying Good-bye to the God of Disease*

1

Mauve waters and green mountains are nothing
when the great ancient doctor Hua Duo[1] could not defeat
      a tiny worm.
A thousand villages collapsed, were choked with weeds,
      men were lost arrows.
Ghosts sang in the doorway of a few desolate houses.
Yet now in a day we leap around the earth
or explore a thousand Milky Ways.

---

[1] Shi Huang, first emperor of the Jin dynasty, ruled from 247/6 to 210 BCE. Wu Di, emperor of the Han dynasty, ruled from 140 to 87 BCE.

[2] Genghis Khan was the famous Mongol conqueror who ruled from 1206 to 1227.

*Mao Zedong's Note: "After reading in the *People's Daily* of June 30, 1958, that in Yujiang county the parasitic leech called the schistosome had been eliminated, my head was so filled with thoughts that I could not sleep. As a slight breeze came and blew in the dawn, and early morning sun came and knocked at the window, I looked at the distant southern skies and happily guided my pen into composing a poem."

[1] A great doctor of the Three Kingdoms Period (220–264), equivalent to Asclepius or Hippocrates.

And if the cowherd[2] who lives on a star
asks about the god of plagues,
tell him, happy or sad, the god is gone,
    washed away in the waters.

To Guo Moruo

On our small planet
a few houseflies bang on the walls.
They buzz, moan, moon,
and ants climb the locust tree and brag about
    their vast dominion.
It is easy for a flea to say
it topples a huge tree.
In Changan leaves spill in the west wind,
the arrowhead groans in the air.
We had much to do
and quickly.
The sky-earth spins
and time is short.
Ten thousand years is long
and so a morning and an evening count.
The four oceans boil and clouds fume with rain.
The five continents shake in the wind of lightning.
We wash away insects
and are strong.

---

[2] Here the cowherd, being the name of a constellation, is symbolic of a god who was originally from earth and who continues to watch over his homeland (based on the traditional legend of "The Cowherd and the Weaver Girl").

XU ZHIMO

(1895–1931)

Xu Zhimo, also known as Xu Zhangxu, was a poet and essayist born into a family of bankers and industrialists from Haining, Zhejiang province. He studied at Shanghai's Huijiang University, Tianjin's Beiyang University, and at Beijing University from 1915 to 1918. He left Beijing University before completing his undergraduate degree and went to the United States, where he studied at Clark (BA in history) and Columbia Universities (MA in economics) and was introduced to modern Western poetry. In 1920 he studied political economics in England at King's College, University of Cambridge, where he began to read the British romantic poets and write a new form of vernacular poetry. On this and subsequent trips to England, he came to know such important literary figures as E. M. Forster, I. A. Richards, and Thomas Hardy.

Xu Zhimo fell in love with a friend's daughter and abandoned his pregnant wife, Zhang Youyi, eventually divorcing her. When he returned to China in 1922, he taught at Beijing University and Qinghua University. In 1923 he founded the Crescent Moon Society, and in 1924 he was the translator and guide for Nobel laureate Rabindranath Tagore on his visit to China and Japan. With Wen Yiduo and Rao Mengkan he founded the Crescent Bookstore as well as the *Crescent Monthly*, an essential organ for the Crescent Moon Society School of poetry. He is the author of *Zhimo's Poems* (1925), *A Night in Florence* (1927), and *The Tiger* (1931), and his collection *Wandering in Clouds* was published posthumously in 1932. He is well known for his love affairs (he had to leave China in 1925 because of an affair with a married woman, whom he later married); in 2000 *The April of Humanity*, a popular Taiwanese television drama series focusing on Xu's love life, aired for the first time. He loved to fly and wrote an essay on the joys of flight, but on November 19, 1931, he flew a small plane in heavy fog from Shanghai to Beijing and crashed into a mountainside near Jinan, Shandong.

You Deserve It

It serves you right! Why didn't you come earlier?
Now my passion has become dead ash.

Don't even mention the past—
will-o'-the-wisp on a skeleton!

Future? Let's take separate paths—
Venus does not care for an evening dawn.

Love is silly, hatred is stupid,
who can count grains of sands in a river?

No matter how perfect your dream is,
it is surrounded by boundless dark.

It's like a moment of poetry dissolving.
Just bury your memory, fast!

Don't make that bitter face,
I'll always forget in the end!

Okay. Let me give you another kiss.
Hot! Now go! No more loitering here.

Farewell Again to Cambridge

Gently, I am leaving,
just as I came gently.
I wave my hand gently
to bid farewell to the clouds in the western sky.

The golden willow by the river
is a bride to the setting sun,

her beautiful reflection in the sparkling waves
ripples in my heart.

Green waterweeds in the soft mud
freely waver underwater.
In the soft waves of the Cambridge River
I wish I were a waterweed blade.

In elm shade the pool
is not clear but an iridescence
refracted among duckweeds,
distilling a rainbowlike dream.

Looking for dream? Use a long pole
and move to where grass is even greener
with a boatful of clear moonlight
and sing loud in the light of stars.

But I can't sing loud.
Silence is the *sheng* and *xiao* music of departure.
Even summer insects remain silent for me.
Silent is tonight's Cambridge.

Silently I am leaving,
just as I came silently,
waving my sleeve
and taking away not even a wisp of cloud.

WEN YIDUO

(1899–1946)

Wen Yiduo (pen name of Wen Jiahua) was born in 1899 in Xishui,
Hubei province, to a wealthy and well-educated family. He was
perhaps the finest poet affiliated with the Western-influenced
Crescent Moon Society School in pre-Revolution China. After a

thorough traditional education in the Chinese classics and a degree from Qinghua University, he studied English literature at Colorado College, Colorado Springs, and painting at the Chicago Art Institute. He then moved to New York. Encouraged by his exposure to Western literature in college, he began writing poetry in the vernacular. While in America he met Carl Sandburg, Amy Lowell, and Harriet Monroe, editor of the distinguished and influential journal *Poetry*, which published many of the American modernist poets. It was John Keats, however, who became his poetic model.

Wen's first book, *The Red Candle*, was published in 1923, while he lived in New York. Disturbed by the racial discrimination he witnessed in American Chinatowns, he moved back to China, hoping to organize an intellectual renewal. While in China he dabbled in politics, helped found the influential Crescent School of poets, which met in his apartment, and became a distinguished scholar, specializing in the study of the *Verses of Chu* but also writing about the *Book of Songs*, Music Bureau poetry, and other topics in classical Chinese literature. He worked at the Beijing Art School and at Wuhan and Qingdao Universities, and in 1932 he became the chair of the Chinese literature department at Qinghua University. After his four-year-old daughter died, he published his second and final volume, *Dead Waters*, in 1928. His poetry is vernacular yet polished and formally rigorous; he makes it "dance in chains," in Han Yu's phrase. He engaged in guerrilla activities in Yunnan against the Nationalist government of the Guomindang, and on July 15, 1946, he was assassinated by hired agents of the Guomindang.

Miracle

I never wanted the red of fire, the black at midnight
of the Peach Blossom Pool, the mournful melody of the *p'i-p'a*,[1]

---

[1] *P'i-p'a*: a musical instrument known as the balloon-guitar.

or the fragrance of roses. I never loved the stern
pride of the leopard, and no white dove ever had

the beauty I craved. I never wanted any of these things,
but their crystallization—a miracle ten thousand

times more rare than them all! But I am famished and harried.
I cannot go without nourishment: even if it is

dregs and chaff, I still have to beg for it. Heaven knows
I do not wish to be like this. I am by no means

so stubborn or stupid. I am simply tired of waiting,
tired of waiting for the miracle to arrive; and

I dare not starve. Ah, who doesn't know of how little worth
is a tree full of singing cicadas, a jug of turbid wine,

or smoky mountain peaks, bright ravines, stars
glittering in the empty sky? It is all so ordinary,

so inexorably dull, and it isn't worth our ecstatic joy,
our crying out the most moving names, or the

longing to cast gold letters and put them in a song.
I also affirm that to let tears come

at the song of an oriole is trivial, ridiculous,
and a waste of time. But who knows? I cannot be otherwise.

I am so famished and harried I take lamb's-quarters
and wild hyssop for fine grain—

                              but there's no harm
in speaking clearly as long as the miracle appears.

Then at once I will cast off the ordinary. I will never
again gaze at a frosted leaf and dream of a spring blossom's

dazzle. I will not waste my strength, peel open
stones, and demand the warmth of white jade.

Give me one miracle, and I will never again whip ugliness,
and compel it to give up the meaning of its

opposite. Actually, I am weary of all this,
and these strained implications are hard to explain.

All I want is one clear word flashing like a Buddhist relic
with fierce light. I want it whole, complete,

shining in full face. I am by no means so stubborn
or stupid; but I cannot see a round fan without

seeing behind it an immortal face. So,
I will wait for as many incarnations as it takes—

since I've made a vow. I don't know how many
incarnations have already passed; but I'll wait

and wait, quietly, for the miracle to arrive.
That day must come! Let lightning strike me,

volcanoes destroy me. Let all hell rise up and crush me!
Am I terrified? No, no wind will blow out

the light in me. I only wish my cast-off body
would turn into ashes. And so what? That, that minutest

fraction of time is a minutest fraction of—
ah, an extraordinary gust, a divine and stellar hush

(sun, moon, and spin of all stars stopped;
time stopped, too)—the most perfectly round peace.

I hear the sound of the door pivoting: and with it
the rustling of a skirt. That is a miracle.

And in the space of a half-open gold door,
you are crowned with a circle of light!

Translated by Arthur Sze

Perhaps

Perhaps you have wept and wept, and can weep no more.
Perhaps. Perhaps you ought to sleep a bit;
then don't let the nighthawk cough, the frogs
croak, or the bats fly.

Don't let the sunlight open the curtain onto your eyes.
Don't let a cool breeze brush your eyebrows.
Ah, no one will be able to startle you awake:
I will open an umbrella of dark pines to shelter your sleep.

Perhaps you hear earthworms digging in the mud,
or listen to the root hairs of small grasses sucking up water.
Perhaps this music you are listening to is lovelier
than the swearing and cursing noises of men.

Then close your eyelids, and shut them tight.
I will let you sleep; I will let you sleep.
I will cover you lightly, lightly with yellow earth.
I will slowly, slowly let the ashes of paper money fly.

Translated by Arthur Sze

The Confession

It's no joke at all, I'm not that sort of poet.
Though I adore the sheen of white quartz,
Though I love green pines, vast seas, the glimmer of sunset on
    a crow's back,
The dusky sky interwoven with the wings of bats,

Though I adore heroes and high mountains,
The flags of nations waving in the wind,
All colors from saffron to the heavy bronze of chrysanthemums,
Remember my food is a pot of old tea.

You should be afraid: there is another person in me:
His imagination is a gnat's and he crawls through muck.

Translated by Ho Yung

The Heart Beats

The lamplight has whitened the walls,
The faithful tables and chairs are as intimate as friends,
There comes from the heaped books the smell of old paper,
My favorite cups look virtuous like virgins,
The baby presses his mouth against his mother's nipples,
From somewhere a snore proclaims the health of my eldest son.
O mysterious calm night, O perfect peace,
O voice of gratitude trembling in my throat!
And then once more the sweet damnable curse returns—
Calm night! No, I refuse to accept your bribe!
Who will fill the narrow space between these walls?
My world is larger and includes other worlds:
These walls cannot be separated from the agony of war.
How can you find a way to stop my heart beating?
Better to let my youth be filled with mud and sand
Than to praise one's own happiness and sufferings!
Better let rats dig deep holes in my skull,
Better let worms feed on the pulp of flesh and blood!
Once, did we live only for a cup of bread and for songs,
For the pleasant sound of the pendulum ticking in a calm night?
How did we hear the groans of our neighbors,
How could we see the shadows of the widows and orphans
        shivering against the wall,
Twitch of death in trenches, madmen biting their beds,

All these tragic scenes running under the mill of life.
Happiness! I shall not receive your bribes!
My world is not enclosed within these narrow walls.
Listen! The cannon shot, the god of Death roaring!
O calm night, how can you stop my heart beating?

Translated by Ho Yung

Dead Water

Here is a ditch of hopelessly dead water.
A cool breeze would not raise the slightest ripple on it.
You might throw in some scraps of copper and rusty tins,
or dump in as well the remains of your meal.

Perhaps the green on copper will turn into emeralds,
or the rust on tin will sprout a few peach blossoms.
Let grease weave a layer of fine silk gauze, and
mold steam out a few red-glowing clouds.

Let the dead water ferment into a ditch of green wine,
floating with pearls of white foam;
but the laughter of small pearls turning into large pearls
is broken by spotted mosquitoes stealing the wine.

Thus a ditch of hopelessly dead water
can yet claim a bit of something bright.
And if the frogs can't endure the utter solitude,
let the dead water burst into song.

Here is a ditch of hopelessly dead water.
Here beauty can never reside.
You might as well let ugliness come and cultivate it,
and see what kind of world comes out.

Translated by Arthur Sze

The End

Dewdrops are sobbing in the hollows of bamboos,
   The green tongues of plantains are licking the windowpanes,
The four walls are receding—
   Alone, I cannot fill this empty room.

I build a fire in my heart
   And wait quietly for the guest from afar.
I stoke it with cobwebs and rat droppings
   And mottled snake scales.

Roosters hurry me when ashes lie in the fireplace.
   A cold wind sneaks up and touches my lips—
So the guest has arrived.
   Closing my eyes, I follow him out.

Translated by Michelle Yeh

LI JINFA

(1900–1976)

Li Jinfa (born Li Shuliang; the pen name "jinfa" means "golden hair") came from Guangdong province and was an artist, a poet, and an essayist. He went to school in Hong Kong and Shanghai and studied sculpture in Paris (he also studied in Dijon and Berlin). He published his three books of poetry between 1919 and 1925 and then returned to China, where he taught in a number of art schools. He became a diplomat in 1932 and served in the Chinese embassies in Iraq and Iran during the war. He moved to the United States in 1951 and lived in New Jersey until his death.

Li Jinfa is known for the difficulty and obscurity of his poetry. As Bonnie S. McDougall and Kam Louie write, "Li Jinfa claims that his poems will encourage the ecstasy of sexual love in his prudish homeland. To this end, he employs a variety of shock tactics: suspension of logical and grammatical relationships, bizarre imagery, and irony. The mode is French symbolism, chiefly Verlaine and Baudelaire; the mood is self-consciously decadent, featuring words denoting weariness, death, and decay. For added exoticism, French and German words and allusions are freely (sometimes perhaps at random) scattered in the text."[1] In "A Record of My Own Inspiration" (1933), Li Jinfa wrote, "When writing poems I never prepared myself to worry if people found them difficult, I simply sought to give vent to the poetic feeling in my heart of hearts. Now, indeed, there are many in the world whose heartstrings have struck a common chord with mine. My style has universal appeal. I just cannot be like others and use poetry to write about revolutionary thought, or stir people to strike out and shed blood. My poetry is a record of my own inspiration, a song sung aloud in intoxication, I cannot hope that everyone will understand it."[2]

Abandoned Woman

My long hair hangs over my eyes
to cut off shameful and wicked quick glances
and the rush of blood and deep sleep of dessicated bones.
Dark night and mosquitoes slowly sneak in
over this corner of a low wall
to screech into my unstained ears
like furious wilderness winds
that throw all nomads into tremulous fear.

I feel a god's spirit trembling in a leaf of grass in an empty valley,
and my grief is imprinted only in the brain of an itinerant wasp
or pours a mountain spring over a high cliff
then vanishes like a red leaf.

---

[1] Bonnie S. McDougall and Kam Louie, *The Literature of China in the Twentieth Century* (New York: Columbia University Press, 1997), p. 60.

[2] Translated by Kirk A. Denton, in Kirk A. Denton, ed., *Modern Chinese Literary Thought: Writings on Literature, 1893–1945* (Stanford: Stanford University Press, 1996), pp. 390–91.

The abandoned woman's secret sorrow burdens her motions,
and the setting sun's fire cannot cremate her malaise of time
into ash flying from a chimney
that dyes the wings of roaming ravens,
and nests with them on a reef in a tsunami,
yet quietly listening to a boatman's song
and to sighs from her stale skirt
as she paces by a tomb
dropping no more hot tears
on the grass
to spangle this world.

LIN HUIYIN

(1904–1955)

Lin Huiyin was born in Fujian province but raised in Beijing. Her father was a powerful governor, and she traveled with him in Europe and the United States. She and her husband, Liang Sicheng, studied together at the University of Pennsylvania, but unlike her husband she was forced to study art instead of architecture because the School of Architecture did not admit women in that era. Nevertheless, she became an important designer and architect, and both she and her husband taught architecture at Qinghua University, where her husband founded the architecture program. They worked together as architectural historians, cataloging and attempting to preserve China's extraordinary heritage of built forms. In China, Lin Huiyin was involved with the Crescent Moon Society. She held literary salons and wrote fiction, drama, and essays in addition to poetry. In the Communist era she and her husband helped to design the national flag, the national emblem, and the Monument to the People's Hero in Tiananmen Square. Her passionate affair with the poet Xu Zhimo has been depicted in a popular Taiwanese television drama, *The April of Humanity.*

Sitting in Quietude

Winter has a message of its own
When the cold is like a flower—
Flowers have their fragrance, winter has its handful of memories.
The shadow of a withered branch, like lean blue smoke,
Paints a stroke across the afternoon window.
In the cold the sunlight grows pale and slanted.
It is just like this.
I sip the tea quietly
As if waiting for a guest to speak.

Translated by Michelle Yeh

DAI WANGSHU

(1905–1950)

Dai Wangshu, also known as Dai Chaocai, is the pen name of Dai Meng'ou. He was born in Hangxian, Zhejiang province, and went to school in Hangzhou. While in high school he and Shi Zhecun founded the Blue Society and published a literary journal called *Friends of the Blue Society*. Starting in 1923 he studied Chinese language and literature at Shanghai University, and then French at Zhendan University. In 1926 he, Shi Zhecun, and Du Heng began publishing the literary journal *Jade Stone*. He joined the Communist Youth Corps in 1925 and the Left-Wing Writers League in 1930 and was arrested for revolutionary activities. When his poem "A Rainy Lane" was published in *Short Story Monthly* in 1928, he won widespread acclaim and earned the nickname "Rainy Lane Poet"; the poem appeared in his first book, *My Memories* (1929). In 1932 Dai Wangshu worked with friends to create The Modern Press, a book and magazine series, and he went to France to study at the University of Lyons and the University of Paris. He published his second book, *Wangshu's Drafts*, in 1933, and then returned to China in 1935 to become editor in chief of *Modern Literature*. After the Sino-Japanese War he moved to Hong Kong and continued to work as an editor. In 1941–1942 he was sent to prison for three months after the Japanese invaded Hong Kong, and it was while he was imprisoned that he wrote "Written on a Prison Wall." He moved back to Shanghai after the war and published his last collection, *The Catastrophic Years*, in 1948. After the 1949 Communist Revolution he worked briefly as a translator of French in the Foreign Language Press before his death in 1950.

A Chopped-off Finger

In an old dusty bookcase
I keep a chopped-off finger soaked in a bottle of alcohol.
Whenever I have nothing better to do than leafing through my
    ancient books,
it summons up a shard of sad memory.

This is a finger from a dead friend,
pale and thin, just like him.
What lingers clearly in my mind
is the moment when he handed me this finger:

"Please preserve this laughable and pitiable token of love for me.
In my splintered life, it just adds to my grief."
His words were slow and calm as a sigh
and with tears in eyes he smiled.

I don't know anything about his "laughable and pitiable love."
I only know that he was arrested from a worker's home.
Then it was cruel torture, then miserable jail,
then sentence of death, the sentence that awaits us all.

I don't know anything about his "laughable and pitiable love."
He never mentioned it to me, even when he was drunk.
I guess it must be very tragic, he hid it,
tried to forget it, like the finger.

On this finger there are ink stains,
red, lovely glowing red
sun-bright on the sliced finger
like his gaze at the cowardice of others that scorched my mind.

This finger gives me a light and sticky sadness
and is a very useful treasure.
Whenever I feel bothered by some trifle, I'll say:
"Well, it's time to take out that glass bottle."

A Rainy Lane

Alone and with an oil-paper umbrella in hand,
I hesitate up and down a long, long
and solitary rainy lane,
hoping to meet
a girl like a lilac
budding with autumn complaints.

She has
the color of lilacs,
the scent of lilacs,
and lilac sorrow,
plaintive in the rain,
plaintive and hesitant;
she walks hesitatingly in this solitary lane,
holding an oil-paper umbrella
like me
and just like me
she silently paces
lost in clear and melancholy grief.

She walks by me close,
close and casting
a sigh-like glance
she floats by
like a dream,
like a sad and hazy dream,

like a floating dream
of lilacs
the girl drifts past;
and in silence walks far, far away
past the ruined fence
at the end of the lane in the rain.

In the sad song of the rain
her color is lost,
her fragrance gone,
and gone is even her
sigh-like glance
and her lilac melancholy.

Alone and with an oil-paper umbrella in hand,
I hesitate down a long, long
and solitary rainy lane,
hoping to see floating past
a girl like a lilac
budding with autumn complaints.

Written on a Prison Wall

If I die here,
Friends, do not be sad,
I shall always exist in your hearts.

One of you died,
In a cell in Japanese-occupied territory,
He harbored deep hatred,
You should always remember.

When you come back,
Dig up his mutilated body from the mud,
Hoist his soul up high
With your victory cheers.

And then place his bones on a mountain peak,
To bask in the sun, and bathe in the wind:
In that dark damp dirt cell,
This was his sole beautiful dream.

Translated by Gregory B. Lee

FENG ZHI

(1905–1993)

Feng Zhi was born Feng Chengzhi in 1905 in Hebei province. He graduated from Beijing University, where he had studied German from 1921 to 1927. He later studied German philosophy and literature in Berlin and Heidelberg and then returned to China to teach at Tongji University. He published two poetry collections, *Songs of Yesterday* (1927) and *Northern Wanderings and Other Poems* (1929), and then didn't publish for over a decade. He began writing again after fleeing Beijing for the south of China, taking refuge in the city of Kunming, Yunnan province, where he worked at Southwest United University. After being driven out of Kunming by the Japanese bombardment, he began to write his famous series of twenty-seven sonnets (published in 1942 as *Sonnets*), which show the influence of Rainer Maria Rilke. He later worked as professor of German language and literature at Lienta and was appointed director of the Foreign Literatures Institute at the Chinese Academy of Social Sciences in 1964.

Sonnet 1

Our hearts are ready to experience
the miracles that take us by surprise:
after millennia with few events,
a sudden comet, or a whirlwind flies.
And it is in those moments in our lives
in passion something like a first embrace,

that all past griefs and happiness contrive
to crystallize a vision in our gaze.
So we adore the tiny insects that
after they copulate once in a life
or after they encounter some deep threat
will terminate their silent luscious lives
—and know that our entire being waits for
a whirlwind or a sudden meteor.

Sonnet 2

Whatever can be shed we jettison
from bodies, let return again to dust
—a way to compose us for age. And thus,
like leaves and the late flowers that one
by one the autumn trees release
off of their forms into the autumn winds
so they can give themselves with naked limbs
to winter, we compose ourselves to lose
in nature, like cicadas abandoning
behind them in the dirt their useless shells.
So we compose ourselves for death, a song
that though shed from the music's form still sings
and leaves a naked music when it's gone,
transformed into a chain of hushed blue hills.

Sonnet 6

I often see in the wild meadows
a village boy or wife who cries
up to the unresponsive sky.
Is it because some evil shadows
them? Or because a husband died?
Or because of a broken toy?
Or sickness in a little boy?
It seems as if they've always cried,
as though their whole life were ensnared

inside a frame and outside of the frame
there is no life, there's no world left.
It seems to me it's been the same
since the world started, and they've wept
for the whole cosmos of despair.

Sonnet 16

We stand together on a mountain's crest
projecting vision far across the steppe
till sight is lost in distance, or else rests
where paths spread on the plain and intersect.
How can the paths and streams not join? Tossed
in sky, can winds and clouds do otherwise?
The cities, mountains, rivers that we've crossed
become a part of us, become our lives.
Our maturation and our grief is near,
is a pine tree on a hill over there,
is a dense mist on a town over here.
We flow inside the waters, blow in air.
We are footpaths that crisscross on the plain
and are the people traveling on them.

Sonnet 21

Listening to the rainstorm and the wind
by lamplight, I am utterly alone,
yet though this cabin is so small I find
between me and the objects in my room
are thousands of miles spreading far away.
The pitcher's brass longs for the mountain's ore
as the ceramic cup craves river clay
and everything whirls like birds in a storm,
dispersed to east and west. So we hold on
in fear our bodies will lift off from us
flying through storm in the deep sky then gone
in rain that pummels all the world to dust.

Nothing is left except this shaking flame
to indicate to me my life remains.

Sonnet 23 (On a Puppy)

For half a month the rain fell constantly
and ever since the moment of your birth
you've known just clamminess and poverty
of light. But now the rain clouds have dispersed,
illuminating sunlight saturates
all the far wall, and so I see your mother
take you in her mouth into the sun's utter
gentleness, utterly immersed and tak-
ing in for the first time the sunlight's heat.
At sunset she will take you back between
her teeth again. You have no memory.
But inside you this incident will dream
and meld into your barking deep at night.
And then all night you will bark forth the light.

Sonnet 24

A thousand years ago this earth
already seemed to sing the way
we would live out our lives today.
Although it was before our birth,
out of the sky of apparitions
and from green grass and the blue cypress
a singing sound seemed to express
our fate and our condition.
How can it be that we expect
these days to hear such singers sing
when we are hunched with heavy grief?
Look over there, a small insect
hovering on its busy wings
is humming songs of endless life.

Sonnet 27

From freely flowing water, undefined,
the water bearer carries a curved jar
and so the water takes on shape and line.
Look, fluttering in autumn wind, the far
flag holds on to the thing that can't be held.
Let distant lights and dark and distant night
and distant plants that grow, decay, and meld
with earth, and thoughts that hunt the infinite,
all be conserved upon this flag. Don't let
us listen uselessly to the night wind
or watch day turn grass gold and make leaves red
in vain. What place is there to hold the mind?
I hope these poems like a wind flag will swell
and hold a bit of that which can't be held.

AI QING

(1910–1996)

Ai Qing is the pen name of Jiang Zhenghan (or Jiang Haicheng), a revolutionary free verse poet born in Jinhua, Zhejiang province. At the age of nineteen he went to France to study painting. Inspired by Western poetry, especially the work of the French symbolists and the Russian poet Vladimir Mayakovsky, he shifted from painting to poetry and began writing free verse. In 1932 he returned to China and after joining the League of Left-Wing Artists in Shanghai was arrested for sedition. While in prison he wrote a famous long poem, *The Dayan River, My Nurse.* He was active in the resistance to the Japanese invasion of China, and published a literary magazine titled *The Battlefield of Literature.* In 1941 he went to Yenan and taught in the Yenan Lu Xun Art Academy. He became a Communist, and though initially accepted in China's post-Revolution society (he was dean of the College of Literature at North China Associated University and

editor of the nationally distributed journal *People's Literature*),
he was purged in the 1957 Anti-Rightist Campaign and sent to
work in state farms in the far provinces for eighteen years. After
Mao's Zedong's death in 1976, Ai Qing was able to return to
writing and in 1979 became vice chairman of the China Writers'
Association. Despite his own experience with official censorship
and persecution, he participated in the government's attacks on
the Misty Poets in the 1980s. In addition to poetry, he published
several books of criticism.

Gambling Men

At the shady bottom of the city wall,
In the dark corner by the houses,
Gamblers squat in the middle of a crowd,
Anxiously awaiting the outcome of a throw.

Filthy, ragged, stupid—yet inflamed—
Their bodies tremble, their heads squirm.
Cheers and curses
Accompany the clink of coins.

Women and children with disheveled hair
Goggle at them;
A hungry child kicks and wails,
But the mother is entranced by her husband's game.

They squat, stand up,
Slap their thighs and cry out in surprise.
Their faces are flushed, their mouths open,
As they try to reverse their fate in one throw.

They lose, then win, win, then lose again;
What stay the same are filth, poverty, and stupidity.
At nightfall they scatter, disappointed,
Returning to their dingy houses one by one.

Translated by Michelle Yeh

BIAN ZHILIN

(1910–)

Bian Zhilin was a poet and a translator of French and English literature into Chinese. He was born in Jiangsu and studied Western literature at Beijing University, graduating in 1933. Under the patronage of Xu Zhimo, Wen Yiduo, and Shen Congwen, he began writing the new, vernacular poetry of his day. His early books, generally considered his best, include *Leaves of Three Autumns* (1933), *Fish Eyes* (1935), and *The Han Garden* (1936), which included work by He Qifang and Li Guangtian; his last book was *Poems of a Decade* (1942). Bian was a schoolteacher for some years and then supported himself as a freelance writer. As Bonnie S. McDougall and Kam Louie write, "Out of intensive study of nineteenth- and twentieth-century English and French literature (and his own much-praised translations), against a general background in classical Chinese poetry and Buddhist and Daoist philosophy, he had perfected a strongly individual style."[1] Like other writers he joined the revolutionaries in Yenan in the late 1930s, but in 1940 he left for Kunming, where he taught literature. He joined the Communist Party in 1956.

> *The following poems by Bian Zhilin*
> *were translated by Michelle Yeh.*

Entering the Dream

Imagine yourself slightly ill
(On an autumn afternoon),
Looking at the gray sky and the sparse tree shadows on the
    windowpanes,
Lying on a pillow left by someone who has traveled far,

---

[1]Bonnie S. McDougall and Kam Louie, *The Literature of China in the Twentieth Century* (New York: Columbia University Press, 1997), p. 75.

And thinking of the blurry lakes and hills, barely recognizable on
    the pillow,
As if they were the elusive trail of an old friend who has vanished
    in the wind,
As if they were things of the past written on faded stationery—
Traces of history visible under a lamp
In a book, yellowed with age, in front of an old man.
Will you not be lost
In the dream?

Fragment

You are standing on a bridge enjoying the view;
Someone's watching you from a balcony.
The moon adorns your window;
You adorn someone else's dream.

Loneliness

Scared of loneliness,
A country boy kept a cricket by his pillow.
When he grew up and worked in town,
He bought a watch with a luminous face.

When little, he was envious of
The grass on a tomb—it was a home for crickets.
Now he has been dead for three hours;
His watch keeps on ticking.

Migratory Birds

How many courtyards, how many squares of blue sky?
Divide them among yourselves, for I am leaving.
Let a belled white pigeon circle three times overhead—
But camel bells are far away. Listen.

I throw a yo-yo to keep you, fly a kite to bind you,
Send a paper eagle, a paper swallow, and a paper rooster
To the sky—to greet the wild geese from the south?
Am I a toy for some child?
I think I'll go to the library to check out *A Study of Migratory Birds.*
Tell me, are you for or against the new law
Forbidding airplanes to fly across the city sky?
My thoughts are like gossamers for little spiders:
They tie me to let me float. I am leaving.
I'll give it some thought at some other place.
How many courtyards, how many squares of blue sky?
How can I go on being an antenna,
Stretching out two arms on the roof in vain,
Never receiving the sound waves I desire?

Train Station

"Pull it out, pull it out"—from the depth of my dream
Another night train comes. This is reality.
Ancients by the river sigh over the tides;
I am standing at the train station like an advertisement.
Boy, listen to the bee fretting inside the window,
Nail a live butterfly to the wall
To decorate my reality here.
The old mattresses that once squeaked,
The small earthquakes that once shook my dreams,
My pounding heartbeats—
Do they now bewilder the train?
When did I ever want to be a station of dreams!

HE QIFANG

(1912–1977)

He Qifang (born He Yongfang) was a poet and an essayist descended from a wealthy family of landowners in Wanxian, Sichuan province. After homeschooling in the classics, he went to Shanghai for a modern education and from 1931 to 1935 studied philosophy at Beijing University. He was deeply influenced by Western literature. As Bonnie S. McDougall and Kam Louie write, "He Qifang's poetry gives an unusually vivid depiction of the author's progress through romanticism, symbolism, neo-romanticism, modernism, and Russian futurism, from dreamer to patriot."[1] In 1938 He Qifang moved to Yenan, where he taught at the Lu Xun Institute of Art and Literature. He joined the Communist Party in Yenan, which was the base of Mao Zedong's Red Army, and after the 1949 Communist Revolution he continued to be an important literary figure in the Writers' Association. He was an editor of the journals *People's Literature* and *Literary Criticism* and the director of the Literary Research Institute of the Chinese Academy of Social Sciences, and he wrote propaganda poetry for the new state. Despite his stalwart Communism, he was persecuted during the Cultural Revolution and sent to the countryside to be "reeducated." He died of stomach cancer.

The following poems by He Qifang
were translated by Michelle Yeh.

Autumn

Shaking down the dew of early morning,
A clinking, lumbering sound drifts beyond the deep ravine.
The scythe, sated with scented rice, is laid down;

---

[1]Bonnie S. McDougall and Kam Louie, *The Literature of China in the Twentieth Century* (New York: Columbia University Press, 1997), p. 77.

Shoulder baskets hold plump melons and fruits from the hedges.
Autumn is resting in a farmer's home.

A round net is cast into the river of cold mist
And collects the shadows of dark cypress leaves, like blue
Hoary frost on the tips of the reeds,
While homeward oars dip and pull.
Autumn is playing in the fishing boat.

The grassy field seems wider when the crickets chirp;
The stream looks clearer when it dries up.
Where did the bamboo flute on the ox's back go,
Its holes overflowing with summery scent and warmth?
Autumn is dreaming in the shepherdess's eyes.

Shrine to the Earth God

Sunlight shines on the broad leaves of castor-oil plants,
Beehives nestle in the earth-god shrine.
Running against my shadow,
I have returned circuitously
And realized the stillness of time.

But on the grass,
Where are those short-armed children who chased after chirping
    crickets?
Where are those joyous cries of my childhood playmates,
Rising to the blue sky at the treetops?
The vast kingdom of childhood
Appears pathetically small
Under my feet, which are dusty with foreign dust.

In the desert, travelers treasure a glass of water;
A sailor resents the white waves beyond his oars.
I used to think I possessed a paradise
And hid it in the darkest corner of my memory.
Since then I have experienced the loneliness of an adult
And grown fonder of the mazes of paths in dreams.

LUO FU

(1928–)

Ma Luofu, known by his pen name Luo Fu, was born in Henyang, in mainland China's Hunan province, and went to Hunan University. He became a military man during the war years of the late 1930s and early 1940s, and in 1949, the year of the Communist Revolution, he moved to Taiwan, where he studied in the English department of Tamkang College. He worked as a Navy broadcast reporter and liaison in Taiwan and in Vietnam, retiring in 1973 at the rank of commander. He was a cofounder of the Epoch Poetry Club and launched the very influential *Epoch Poetry Quarterly*, which published many soldier-poets. He made a large impact with his strange and obscure modernist collection *Death in the Stone Cell* (1964) and has since published many volumes of poetry and criticism.

Song of Everlasting Regret

That rose, like all roses, only bloomed for one morning.

—H. BALZAC

1

From
The sound of water
Emperor Xuan of the Tang dynasty
Extracts the sorrow in a lock of black hair

2

In the genealogy of the Yang clan
She is
An expanse of white flesh
Lying right there on the first page

A rose bush in the mirror
In full flower, caressed by
What is called heaven-born beauty
A
Bubble
Waiting to be scooped up
From the Huaqing Pool
Heavenly music is everywhere
In Li Palace
The aroma of wine wafts in body odors
Lips, after being sucked hard
Can only moan
And the limbs outstretched on the ivory bed
Are mountains
And rivers too
A river sound asleep in another river
Underground rapids
Surge toward
The countryside
Until a white ballad
Breaks out of the soil

3

He raises his burned hand high
And cries out:
I make love
Because
I want to make love
Because
I am the emperor
Because we are used to encounters
Of flesh with blood

4

He begins to read newspapers, eat breakfast, watch her comb her
    hair,
handle official papers in bed

                                                  stamp a seal
                                                  stamp a seal
                                                  stamp a seal
                                                  stamp a seal

From then on
The emperor no longer holds court in the morning

5

He is the emperor
But war
Is a puddle of
Sticky fluid
That cannot be wiped off
Under the brocade coverlets
Slaughter is far away
Distant beacon fires snake upward, the sky is dumbfounded
By heart-stopping hairstyles
Leather drums with flame-red tongues
Lick the earth

6

Rivers and streams
Burn between the thighs
War
May not be abandoned
Campaigns are affairs of state
My lady, women's blood can flow in only one direction
Now the armies refuse to budge
All right, all right, you are the willow catkins
Before Mawei Slope
Let the wind in the square hold you aloft
A pile of expensive fertilizer
Is nourishing
Another rose bush
Or
Another incurable disease
In history

7

Regret probably begins in the middle of fire
He gazes out the window into the distance
His head
Sways with the flight of birds
His eyes change colors as the sun sets
The name that he cries out
Sinks into the echoes
All night long he paces around the room
In front of every window in Weiyang Palace
He stops
Cold pale fingers nip the candlewick
Amid muffled coughs
All the begonias in the Forbidden City
Wilt overnight in
The autumn wind
He ties his beard into knot after knot, unties and ties it again, then
   walks with his hands behind his back, the sound of his footfalls
   footfalls footfalls, a tuberose exploding behind the curtain, then
   he stretches out all ten fingers to grab a copy of the *Annotated
   Classic of Waters*, the water drip-dripping, he cannot understand
   at all why the river sobs instead of bellows when it flows through
   the palm of his hand
He throws on a gown and gets up
He sears his own skin
He is awakened by cold jade
      A thousand candles burn in a thousand rooms
      A bright moon shines on the sleepless
      A woman walks toward him along the wall
      Her face an illusion in the mist

8

Suddenly
He searches in a frenzy for that lock of black hair
And she hands over
A wisp of smoke
It is water and will rise to become a cloud

It is soil and will be trampled into parched moss
The face hiding among the leaves
Is more despairing than the sunset
A chrysanthemum at the corner of her mouth
A dark well in her eyes
A war raging in her body
A storm brewing
Within her palm
She no longer suffers from toothache
She will never again come down with
Tang dynasty measles
Her face dissolved in water is a relative white and an absolute black
She will no longer hold a saucer of salt and cry out with thirst
Her hands, which were used to being held
Now point
Tremblingly
To a cobbled road leading to Changan

9

Time: seventh day of the seventh month
Place: Palace of Longevity
A tall thin man in blue
A faceless woman
Flames still rising
In the white air
A pair of wings
Another pair
Fly into the moonlight outside the palace
Whispers
Receding farther and farther away
Glint bitterly
An echo or two reverberate through the storm

Translated by Michelle Yeh

BEI DAO

(1949–)

Bei Dao is the pen name of Zhao Zhenkai (he took the name, which means "North Island," to hide his identity while publishing an underground magazine). He was born in Beijing, where his father was a cadre (administrator) and his mother a doctor. When he was seventeen years old he joined the Red Guard movement of the Cultural Revolution. He became disillusioned with it and was sent to be reeducated in the countryside, where he was a construction worker, a profession he maintained from 1969 to 1980.

Bei Dao's poetry has long been associated with the Democracy Movement. His early poems were a source of inspiration for the young participants of the April Fifth Democracy Movement (1976) as well as the Beijing Spring of 1979. They were popularized in the famous underground literary magazine *Jintian* (*Today*), which he started with poet Mang Ke. (*Jintian* was shut down by the authorities in 1980 but was launched again in 1990 in Stockholm by Chinese writers in exile.) Bei Dao soon became the leading poet of the 1980s and the most famous representative of Misty (*mengleng*) poetry, a style influenced by Western modernism, symbolism, and surrealism, which came in for fierce criticism by the defenders of the Social Realist poetry that Mao had championed. By the mid-1980s, with the acceptance of Chinese modernism and the thaw in official censorship, Bei Dao gained mainstream recognition. He edited an official magazine, became a member of the Chinese Writers' Association, and worked at the Foreign Languages Press in Beijing, but he did become a target of the government's Anti-Spiritual Pollution Campaign of 1983–1984. During the 1989 Democracy Movement, his poetry was circulated among the student demonstrators, and he signed an open letter asking for the release of political prisoners. At the time of the Tiananmen Square massacre, he was overseas at a writer's conference. He has since elected to remain in exile.

During the Cultural Revolution the Red Guards, in search of "counterrevolutionary" materials, often raided the houses of intellectuals and cadres. Bei Dao participated in these raids. When he was living in the countryside, a cache of books stolen during one of these raids became essential to his education, introducing him to Western literature in translation. Bei Dao's poetics were influenced especially by the transformative imagery of Federico García Lorca; the surrealism of Vicente Aleixandre, Tomas Transtromer, César Vallejo, and Georg Trakl; the pastorals of Antonio Machado; and the sentiment and delicacy of Rainer Maria Rilke. In an interview Bei Dao says that of all the poets who have influenced him, "I like Celan best because I think there is a deep affinity between him and myself in the way he combines the sense of pain with language experiments. He transforms his experience in the concentration camps into a language of pain. That is very similar to what I am trying to do. Many poets separate their experience from the language they use in poetry, but in the case of Celan there is a fusion, a convergence of experience and experimental language."[1]

Bei Dao's work has been widely translated and anthologized, and several collections of his poetry are available in English: *At the Sky's Edge: Poems 1991–1996* (2001), *Unlock* (2000), *Landscape over Zero* (1998), *Forms of Distance* (1994), *Old Snow* (1992), and *The August Sleepwalker* (1988). His short story collection, *Waves*, and his book of essays, *Blue House*, have also appeared in English. He is currently living in the United States and has taught at the University of California, Davis, the University of Michigan, and Beloit College. He is often mentioned as a candidate for the Nobel Prize and has been made an honorary member of the American Academy of Arts and Letters.

---

[1] From Gabi Gleichmann, "An Interview with Bei Dao," *Modern Chinese Literature* 9 (1996), pp. 387–93.

Night: Theme and Variations

Here is where roads become
parallel light beams
a long conversation suddenly broken
Truck drivers' pungent smoke suffuses the air
with rude indistinct curses
Fences replace people in a line
Light seeping out from the cracks of doors
tossed to the roadside with cigarette butts
is tread on by swift feet
A billboard leans on an old man's lost stick
about to walk away
A stone water lily withered
in the fountain pool, a building deliberates collapse
The rising moon suddenly strikes
a bell again and again
the past reverberates within palace walls
The sundial is turning and calibrating deviations
waiting for the emperor's grand morning ceremony
Brocade dresses and ribbons toss up in the breeze
and brush dust from the stone steps
A shadow of a tramp slinks past the wall
colorful neon lights glow for him
but deprive him of sleep all through the night
A stray cat jumps on a bench
watching a trembling mist of floating light
But a mercury lamp rudely opens window curtains
to peer at the privacy of others
disturbing lonely people and their dreams
Behind a small door
a hand quietly draws the catch
as if pulling a gun bolt

*Translated by Tony Barnstone and
Newton Liu*

Ordinary Days

Lock secrets in a drawer
write notes in my favorite book
put a letter in the mailbox and stand silent awhile
gazing after passersby in the wind, worry about nothing
eyes caught by a shop window's neon flash
insert a coin into a pay phone
bum a cigarette from an old man fishing under a bridge
from a river steamer a vast empty foghorn
stare at myself in a dim full-length mirror
in the smoke of a cinema entrance
as window curtains muffle the noisy sea of stars
open some faded photos and letters under the lamplight

Translated by Tony Barnstone and
Newton Liu

Country Night

The sunset and distant mountains
interleaf a crescent moon
moving in the elm woods
an empty bird nest
a small trail encircles the pond
chasing a dog with a dirty coat
then runs into the mud wall at the end of the village
hanging bucket swaying lazily over a well
a bell as silent
as the stone roller in the yard
scattered uneasy wheat stalks
the chewing noise in a horse stall
is redolent with threat
someone's long shadow
slips across the stone doorsteps
firelight from a kitchen range

casts a red glow on a woman's arms
and a chipped earthenware basin

*Translated by Tony Barnstone and
Newton Liu*

A Decade

Over this forgotten land
years entangled with bells on the bridles of horses
rang out until dawn, and on the road harsh panting
under a heavy burden turned into a song
sung by people everywhere.
A woman's necklace lifted into the night sky
to the sound of incantation as if responding to a calling
and the lascivious fluorescent dial struck at random.
Time is honest as a wrought-iron fence;
only the wind sheared by withered branches
can get in or out.
Flowers that blossom only in the eternal prison
of a book become the concubines of truth,
but the lamp that burst yesterday
is so incandescent in a blind man's heart
right to the instant he is shot down
that a picture of the assassin is captured
in his suddenly open eyes.

*Translated by Tony Barnstone and
Newton Liu*

Response

The base make a safe-conduct pass of their own baseness,
while honest men's honor is their epitaph.
Look—the gold-plated sky is brimming
with drifting reflections of the dead.

If the Ice Age is long over
why does everything hang with icicles?
The Cape of Good Hope has been found long ago,
so why do sails still contend in the Dead Sea?

I came to this world with nothing
but paper, rope, and my own shadow
to speak for the condemned
before sentencing:

Listen to me, world,
I—don't—believe!
You've piled a thousand enemies at your feet.
Count me as a thousand and one.

I don't believe the sky is blue.
I don't believe in echoing thunder.
I don't believe dreams are just fantasy,
that there is no revenge after death.

If the ocean must burst through the seawall,
let its bitter water irrigate my heart.
If the continents are destined to pile up,
let us choose the mountain peaks as our hermitage.

Glittering stars and new spinning events
pierce the naked sky,
like pictographs five thousand years old,
like the coming generation's watching eyes.

Translated by Tony Barnstone and
Newton Liu

A Step

The pagoda's shadow on the grass is a pointer
sometimes marking you, sometimes me

we are just a step apart
separation or reunion, this is a repeating
theme: hatred is only one step away
the sky sways on a foundation of fear
a building with windows open in all directions
we live inside
or outside of it: death just one step away
children have learned how to talk to the wall
this city's history is sealed in an old man's
heart: decrepitude is just a step away

Translated by Tony Barnstone and
Newton Liu

Elegy

With thin tears a widow worships an idol
while a pack of newborn hungry wolves waits to be fed
barely alive, they escape the world one by one
my howls echo through the stretching mountains
together we circled the state farm
from which you came, when cooking smoke twined into the sky
and crowns of wild chrysanthemums floated on the wind
thrusting out your slight firm breasts
you came to me in a field
where stone outcrops drown in passionate wheat
now you are that widow and I
am what's been lost, with beauty, life, desire
how we lay together in heavy sweat
how our bed drifted on the morning river

Translated by Tony Barnstone and
Newton Liu

Nightmare

On the unpredictable winds
I painted an eye
the moment frozen then gone
but no one woke up
the nightmare kept right on into the light of day
flooding through streambeds, crawling across cobblestones
increasing in presence and pressure
among branches, along the eaves
the birds' terrified eyes froze
fell out
over cart tracks in the road
a crust of frost formed
no one woke up

Translated by James A. Wilson

Many Years

This is you, this is
driven-mad-by-magic-shadows-whirling you,
first clear then cloudy
I won't go to you again
the bitter cold also deprives me of hope
many years, before the icebergs formed
fish would float to the water's face
then sink away, many years
the reverent wing beats of my heart
bear me gently through the drifting night
lamplight breaks upon steel beams
many years, silent and alone
here there are no clocks in the rooms
when people left they also took
the keys, many years
within thick fog, a whistle blasts
from a fast train over a bridge
season after season

set out from small railway stations among the fields
linger at each tree
the open flowers bear fruit, many years

Translated by James A. Wilson

Sweet Tangerines

Sweet tangerines
flooded with sun, sweet tangerines

let me move through your hearts
bearing burdens of love

sweet tangerines
rinds breaking with delicate rains

let me move through your hearts
worries turned to tears of relief

sweet tangerines
bitter nets keep each fleshy piece

let me move through your hearts
as I wander in the wreckage of dreams

sweet tangerines
flooded with sun, sweet tangerines

Translated by James A. Wilson

A Formal Declaration

Maybe these are the last days
I haven't put aside a will
just a pen, for my mother
I'm hardly a hero

in times with no heroes
I'll just be a man

The calm horizon
divides the ranks of living and dead
I align myself with the sky
no way will I kneel
to state assassins
who lock up the winds of freedom

The star holes of bullets
bleed in the black-bright dawn

Translated by James A. Wilson

Ancient Monastery

With bell sounds gone
the spider webs weave in the cracks of pillars
wrap around the same rings with each turning year
Nothing to remember, stones
empty mist in mountain valleys blends with the echoes
of stones, nothing to remember
when narrow trails wound through this weaving
dragons and weird birds would make their ways
along the temple eaves bearing the silence of bells
Wild grass in a year's time
flourishes indiscriminately,
doesn't care if it bends beneath
a monk's cloth shoe or the wind
Stone relics are worn and pocked, their writings long ruined
as when great flames ravage the center of open fields
If a hand could make out the meaning, then perhaps
catching a glance from the living
the tortoise might stir again in the earth
muddy with dark and holy secrets, crawling to the threshold

Translated by James A. Wilson

Requiem

for the victims of June Fourth

Not the living but the dead
under the doomsday-purple sky
go in groups
Suffering guides forward suffering
at the end of hatred is hatred
the spring has run dry, the conflagration stretches unbroken
the road back is even farther away

Not gods but the children
amid the clashing of helmets
say their prayers
mothers breed light
darkness breeds mothers
the stone rolls, the clock runs backward
the eclipse of the sun has already taken place

Not your bodies but your souls
shall share a common birthday every year
you are all the same age
love has founded for the dead
an everlasting alliance
you embrace each other closely
in the massive register of deaths

Translated by Bonnie S. McDougall
and Chen Maiping

The Morning's Story

A word has abolished another word
a book has issued orders
to burn another book
a morning established by the violence of language
has changed the morning
of people's coughing

Maggots attack the kernel
the kernel comes from dull valleys
from among dull crowds
the government finds its spokesman
cats and mice
have similar expressions

On the road in the sky
the armed forester examines
the sun that rumbles past
over the asphalt lake
he hears the sound of disaster
the untrammeled sound of a great conflagration

Translated by Bonnie S. McDougall
and Chen Maiping

Coming Home at Night

After braving the music of the air-raid alarm
I hang my shadow on the hat stand
take off the dog's eyes
(which I use for escape)
remove my false teeth (these final words)
and close my astute and experienced pocket watch
(that garrisoned heart)

The hours fall in the water one after the other
in my dreams like depth charges
they explode

Translated by Bonnie S. McDougall
and Chen Maiping

Rebel

The shadow that tries to please the light
leads me to pass between
the aspen that has drunk milk
and the fox that has drunk blood
like a treaty passing between
peace and conspiracy

The chair draped with an overcoat sits
in the east, the sun is its head
it opens a cloud and says:
here is the end of history
the gods have abdicated, the temples are locked
you are nothing but
a pictograph that's lost its sound

> *Translated by Bonnie S. McDougall*
> *and Chen Maiping*

Asking the Sky

Tonight a confusion of rain
fresh breezes leaf through a book
dictionaries swell with implication
forcing me into submission

memorizing ancient poems as a child
I couldn't see what they meant
and stood at the abyss of explication
for punishment

bright moon sparse stars
out of those depths a teacher's hands
give directions to the lost
a play of shadow mocking our lives

people slide down the slope of
education on skis
their story
slides beyond national boundaries

after words slide beyond the book
the white page in pure amnesia
I wash my hands clean
and tear it apart, the rain stops

Translated by David Hinton

Untitled

The landscape crossed out with a pen
reappears here

what I am pointing to is not rhetoric
October over the rhetoric
flight seen everywhere
the scout in the black uniform
gets up, takes hold of the world
and microfilms it into a scream

wealth turns into floodwaters
a flash of light expands
into frozen experience
and just as I seem to be a false witness
sitting in the middle of a field
the snow troops remove their disguises
and turn into language

*Translated by Eliot Weinberger and
Iona Man-Cheong*

Delivering Newspapers

Who believes in the mask's weeping?
who believes in the weeping nation?
the nation has lost its memory
memory goes as far as this morning

the newspaper boy sets out in the morning
all over town the sound of a desolate trumpet
is it your bad omen or mine?
vegetables with fragile nerves
peasants plant their hands in the ground

longing for the gold of a good harvest
politicians sprinkle pepper
on their own tongues
and a stand of birches in the midst of a debate:
whether to sacrifice themselves for art or doors
this public morning
created by a paperboy
revolution sweeps past the corner
he's fast asleep

*Translated by Eliot Weinberger and
Iona Man-Cheong*

DUO DUO

(1951–)

Duo Duo is the pen name of Li Shizheng, an important poet of
the Misty school who worked as a journalist for the *Peasant
Daily* in Beijing before leaving China to live in Holland and Lon-
don. It was as a journalist that he witnessed the Tiananmen
Square massacre of June 4, 1989. He had been scheduled to leave
China on the fifth of June for a reading tour, his first poetry tour

in the West. Like many Chinese writers, he chose to stay in the West rather than return to a China once again in the grip of political repression.

Duo Duo's influences include Baudelaire, Robert Desnos, Dylan Thomas, Sylvia Plath, Marina Tsvetaeva, and Federico García Lorca. His poems have an emotional, even nightmarish intensity just below a "misty" surface. Duo Duo began writing poetry privately during the Cultural Revolution, assuming that the political climate would never shift in such a way that he might actually become a published writer. He began to achieve some level of public acceptance in the 1980s, only to find himself a writer in exile, circumstances that make the sense of nightmare underlying his poems seem less surreal than real. His books have appeared in English in the collections *Looking Out from Death* and *The Boy Who Catches Wasps: Selected Poems of Duo Duo*.

Bell Sound

No bell had sounded to awaken memory
but today I heard
it strike nine times
and wondered how many more times.
I heard it while coming out of the stables.
I walked a mile
and again I heard:
> "At what point in the struggle for better conditions
> will you succeed in increasing your servility?"

Just then, I began to envy the horse left behind in the stables.
Just then, the man riding me struck my face.

Translated by John Cayley

Five Years

Five glasses of strong liquor, five candles, five years
Forty-three years old, a huge sweat at midnight
Fifty hands flap toward the tabletop
A flock of birds clenching their fists fly in from yesterday

Five strings of red firecrackers applaud the fifth month, thunder
    rumbles
between five fingers
And four parasitic poisonous mushrooms on four dead horses'
    tongues
in the fourth month
    do not die
Five hours past five o'clock on day five five candies are extinguished
Yet the landscape screaming at dawn does not die
Hair dies but tongues do not die
The temper recovered from the cooked meat does not die
Fifty years of mercury seep into semen and semen does not die
The fetus delivering itself does not die
Five years pass, five years do not die
Within five years, twenty generations of insects die out

Translated by Gregory B. Lee

SHU TING

(1952–)

Shu Ting is the pen name of Gong Peiyu. Associated with the Misty school, she was the leading woman poet in China in the 1980s. A southeast Fujian native, she was sent to the countryside during the Cultural Revolution before she graduated from junior high school. Then she worked in a cement factory and later a textile mill and a lightbulb factory. In 1979 she published her first poem and in 1983 was asked to be a professional writer by the

Writers' Association, Fujian Branch, of which she is now the deputy chairperson. Her collections include *Brigantines* (1982) and *Selected Lyrics of Shu Ting and Gu Cheng* (1985). She has also published several books of prose.

Along with many of the Misty Poets, Shu Ting was attacked in the early 1980s during the Anti-Spiritual Pollution Campaign, and yet she twice won the National Poetry Award, in 1981 and 1983. Deeply romantic in nature, her work can be understood as a reaction to the repression of romance in literature, film, song, and theater during the Great Proletarian Cultural Revolution (1966–1976). Although her poems sometimes don't read as well in English translation as they do in Chinese, they have a crystalline, lyrical strength that often rescues them from their saccharine tendencies and that has made Shu Ting the best-known contemporary Chinese woman poet in the West.

Two or Three Incidents Recollected

> An overturned cup of wine.
> A stone path sailing in moonlight.
> Where the blue grass is flattened,
> an azalea flower abandoned.
>
> The eucalyptus wood swirls.
> Stars above teem into a kaleidoscope.
> On a rusty anchor,
> eyes mirror the dizzy sky.
>
> Holding up a book to shade the candle
> and with a finger in between the lips,
> I sit in an eggshell quiet,
> having a semitransparent dream.

Translated by Chou Ping

Perhaps

—Reply to the Loneliness of a Poet

> Perhaps our hearts
> > will have no reader
> Perhaps we took the wrong road
> > and so we end up lost
>
> Perhaps we light one lantern after another
> > storms blow them out one by one
> Perhaps we burn our life candle against the dark
> > but no fire warms the body
>
> Perhaps once we're out of tears
> > the land will be fertilized
> Perhaps while we praise the sun
> > we are also sung by the sun
>
> Perhaps the heavier the monkey on our shoulders
> > the more we believe
> Perhaps we can only protest others' suffering
> > silent to our own misfortune
> Perhaps
> > because this call is irresistible
> > we have no other choice

*Translated by Tony Barnstone and
Newton Liu*

Missing You

> A colorful hanging chart with no lines.
> A pure algebra problem with no solution.
> A one-string harp, stirring rosaries
> that hang from dripping eaves.

A pair of oars that can never reach
the other side of the ocean.

Waiting silently like a bud.
Gazing at a distance like a setting sun.
Perhaps an ocean is hidden somewhere,
but when it flows out—only two tears.
O in the background of a heart,
in the deep well of a soul.

Translated by Chou Ping

Dream of an Island

I'm at my own latitude
with migrant dreams—

White snow. Ice roads.
A heavy-hanging bell
behind a red palace wall
is tearing the motionless dusk.

O I see a cherry brook
opening its dancing skirt
after a downpour;
I see little pines
put their heads together
to make a speech;
and songs are heard in sandstorms
like a spurting fountain.

Thus, tropical suns are sparkling
under eyelashes with heavy frost;
and blood conducts
reliable spring wind

between frozen palms.
At every crossroad
blessed by street lamps
more than love is silently promised
in the kiss good-bye.

Between sea tide and green shade
I'm having a dream against snowstorms.

Translated by Chou Ping

Mirror

Dark blue night
All at once the old wounds burst open
When simmering the past
The bed's an extremely patient lover
The alarm clock tick tocks tick tocks
Ravages the dream till it is black and blue
Grope along the wall
Grope along the wall for the light cord
Instead by chance catch
A lock of moonbeams
Shimmering silverfish come after the smell, climb up the root
You finally
Soften to a pond

In a slow turn
        You look at yourself
        You look at yourself

The full-length mirror feigns innocence and one-sided love
The ambiguous wallpaper blurs the pattern
And finds itself hard framed
You watch yourself wither one petal after another
        You have no way out no way out

Even if you can leap backward over walls
There are still days you can't leap over blocking you
        From behind

Women have no need of philosophy
Women can shake off moon marks
Like dogs shake off water

Close the heavy curtain
The wet tongue of morning lolls on the windowpane
Go back to the hollow spot in the pillow
Like a film: exposed, unrolled
You put yourself there

The chestnut tree under the window shivers loudly
As if touched by a cold hand

Translated by John Rosenwald and the
Beloit/Fudan Translation Workshop

A Night at the Hotel

The declaration of love, coauthored by lip prints and tears,
Bravely climbs into the mailbox
The mailbox is cold
Long abandoned
Its paper seal, like a bandage, flaps in the wind

The eaves rise and fall softly under the black cat's paws
Large trucks grind sleep till it is hard and thin
The sprinter
In dreams, hears the starter's gun all through the night
The juggler can't catch his eggs
Street lamps explode with a loud shriek
In its coat of yolk the night grows more grotesque

The woman in her nightgown
Yanks the door open, shaking heaven and earth
Like a deer, she runs wildly barefoot across the carpet
A huge moth flits across the wall
Plunges into the crackling fire of a ringing telephone

In the receiver
Silence
Only snow
Goes on singing, far away, on the power lines

*Translated by John Rosenwald and the
Beloit/Fudan Translation Workshop*

YANG LIAN

(1955–)

Yang Lian, one of the original Misty Poets, has been nominated for the Nobel Prize in literature. He was born in Bern, Switzerland, to a family of diplomats posted in the Chinese embassy. His parents returned to China before he was a year old, and he was raised in Beijing. During the Cultural Revolution he was sent to be "reeducated" in the countryside, where he worked as a grave digger and began to write poetry. Yang was a cofounder of *Jintian*, the seminal independent literary magazine associated with the Beijing Spring. In 1983, during the Anti-Spiritual Pollution Campaign, the Chinese government banned his work, criticizing his poem cycle "Nuorilang." Since 1989, the year of the Democracy Movement and the Tiananmen Square massacre, two of his books have been banned on the Chinese mainland. He took on New Zealand citizenship and has also lived in exile in Australia, Germany, and the United States. He has worked at the University of Auckland and has been a writer in residence in Berlin and Taipei City and at the University of Sydney and the Yaddo Foundation. He currently lives in London and is married to Yo Yo, a novelist. Collections of his poetry in English include *Yi*, *In Symmetry with Death*, *Masks and Crocodile*, *Where the Sea Stands Still*, *Notes of a Blissful Ghost*, and *The Dead in Exile*.

An Ancient Children's Tale

(From the Poem Cycle "Bell on the Frozen Lake")

How should I savor these bright memories,
their glowing gold, shining jade, their tender radiance like
silk that washed over me at birth?
All around me were industrious hands, flourishing peonies,
          and elegant upturned eaves.
Banners, inscriptions, and the names of nobility were everywhere,
and so many temple halls where bright bells sang into my ears.
Then my shadow slipped over the fields and mountains, rivers
          and springtime
as all around my ancestors' cottages I sowed
towns and villages like stars of jade and gemstones.
Flames from the fire painted my face red; plowshares and pots
clattered out their bright music and poetry
that wove into the sky during festivals.
How should I savor these bright memories?
When I was young I gazed down at the world,
watching purple grapes, like the night, drift in from the west
and spill over in a busy street. Every drop of juice became a star
set into the bronze mirror where my glowing face looked back.
My heart blossomed like the earth or the ocean at daybreak
as camel bells and sails painted like frescoes embarked
from where I was to faraway lands to clink the gold coin
          of the sun.

When I was born
I would laugh even at
the glazed and opulent palaces, at the bloody red
  walls, and at the people rapt in luxurious dreams

for centuries in their incense-filled chambers.
I sang my pure song to them with passion,
but never stopped to think
why pearls and beads of sweat drain to the same place,
these rich tombs filled with emptiness,
or why in a trembling evening
a village girl should wander down to the river,
her eyes so clear and bright with grief.

In the end, smoking powder and fire erupted in the courtyard;
between endless mountains and the plain, horse hooves
came out of the north, and there was murder and wailing
and whirling flags and banners encircling me like magic clouds,
like the patched clothes of refugees.
I saw the torrential Yellow River
by moonlight unfolding into a silver white elegy
keening for history and silence.
Where are the familiar streets, people, and sounds?
And where are the seven-leaved tree and new grass,
the river's song beneath a bridge
        of my dreams?
There is only the blood of an old man selling flowers
        clotting my soul,
only the burned houses, the rubble and ruins
gradually sinking into shifting sands
and turning into dreams, into a wasteland.

Translated by Tony Barnstone and
Newton Liu

An Elegy for Poetry

The decrepit century's bony brow protrudes
and its wounded shoulders shiver.
Snow buries the ruins—below this whiteness an undertow
of uneasiness, through the deep shadows of trees it drifts,

and a stray voice is broadcast across time.
There is no way
through this land that death has made an enigma.

The decrepit century deceives its children,
leaving illegible calligraphy and snow
on the stones everywhere to augment the ornamental decay.
My hands cling to a sheaf of my poems.
When my unnamed moment arrives, call me!
But the wind's small skiff scuds off bearing history
and on my heels like a shadow
an ending follows.

Now I understand it all.
To sob out loud refutes nothing when the fingers of young girls
and the shy myrtle are drowned in purple thornbrush.
From the eyes meteors streak into the endless sea
but I know that in the end all souls will rise again,
soaked with the fresh breath of the sea,
with eternal smiles, with voices that refuse humiliation,
and climb into blue heaven.
There I can read out my poems.
I will believe every icicle is a sun,
that because of me an eerie light will permeate these ruins
and I'll hear music from this wasteland of stones.
I'll suckle from swollen buds like breasts
and have renewed dignity and a holy love.
I'll bare my heart in these clean white snowfields
as I do in the clean white sky
and as a poet
challenge this decrepit century.

As a poet
when I want the rose to bloom, it will blossom;
freedom will come back carrying a small shell
where you can hear echoes of a howling storm.
Daybreak will return, the key of dawn will unlock
the wailing forests, and ripe fruits will shoot out flame.

I, too, will return, exhume my suffering again,
and begin to plow this land drifted in snow.

*Translated by Tony Barnstone and
Newton Liu*

To a Nine-Year-Old Girl Killed in the Massacre

They say that you tripped on a piece of skipping elastic
And you jumped out of the house of white chalk
On a day of terrifyingly loud rain
Nine bullet holes in your body exude a sweetness
They say that you lost the moon while you were playing
Green grass on the grave   Are new teeth

Sprouting where there is no need for grief
You did not die   They say
You still sit at the small wooden desk

Looks crash noisily against the blackboard
The school bell suddenly rings
A burst of nothingness   Your death is killed

They say   Now   You are a woman and a mother
And each year there is a birthday without you
just as when you were alive

Translated by Mabel Lee

HA JIN

(1956–)

Ha Jin was born in Liaoning. The son of an army officer, he entered the People's Army early in the Cultural Revolution at a time when the schools were closed. He worked as a telegraph operator for some time, then went back to school, earning a BA and an MA. After coming to the United States and taking his Ph.D. in English and American literature at Brandeis University, he taught at Emory University before becoming a professor of English at Boston University. He has published three books of poetry—*Between Silences*, *Facing Shadows*, and *Wreckage*—three short story collections, and four novels, including *Waiting*, for which he won the National Book Award and the PEN/Faulkner Award.

Like so many of his contemporaries, Ha Jin elected to remain in exile from China after the Tiananmen Square massacre: "After June 1989 I realized that I could not return to China in the near future if I wanted to be a writer who has the freedom to write." He is in the unusual position of being a Chinese poet and fiction writer who works in English and lives in America. As he writes in a letter: "Without question, I am a Chinese writer, not an American-Chinese poet, though I write in English. If this sounds absurd, the absurdity is historical rather than personal . . . since I can hardly publish anything in Chinese now." The craft of a novelist can be seen in Ha Jin's poems: he often writes in dramatic monologue, recording history from the inside, from the point of view of its imperfect and often unsympathetic protagonists.

Our Words

Although you were the strongest boy in our neighborhood
you could beat none of us. Whenever
we fought with you we would shout:

"Your father was a landlord.
You are a bastard of a blackhearted landlord."
Or we would mimic your father's voice
when he was publicly denounced:
"My name is Li Wanbao. I was a landlord;
before liberation I exploited my hired hands
and the poor peasants. I am guilty
and my guilt deserves ten thousand deaths."
Then you would withdraw your hard fists
and flee home cursing and weeping like a wild cat.

You fought only with your hands,
but we fought with both our hands and our words.
We fought and fought and fought
until we overgrew you and overgrew ourselves,
until you and we were sent to the same village
working together in the fields
sharing tobacco and sorghum spirits at night
and cursing the brigade leader behind his back
when he said: "You, petty bourgeoisie,
must take your 'reeducation' seriously!"

Until none of us had words.

They Come

Sometimes when you're walking in the street,
returning home or leaving to see a friend,
they come. They emerge from behind pillars and trees,
approaching you like a pack of hounds besieging a deer.
You know there's no use to hide or flee,
so you stop and light a cigarette, waiting for them.

Sometimes when you're eating in a restaurant,
your soup served and your dish not ready yet,
they come. A steady hand falls upon your shoulder.

You are familiar with such a hand
and don't need to turn around to meet the face.
The scared diners are sneaking out,
the waitress's chin is trembling when she speaks,
but you sit there, waiting patiently for the bill.
After settling it, you'll walk out with them.

Sometimes when you open your office,
planning to finish an article in three hours,
or read a review, but first make some tea,
they come. They spring out from behind the door,
like ghosts welcoming a child to their lair.
You don't want to enter, seeing cups and paper on the floor.
You're figuring how to send a message home.

Sometimes when you have worked day and night,
dog tired, desiring to have a good sleep
after taking a shower and an extra nightcap,
they come. They change the color of your dream:
you moan for the wounds on your body,
you weep for the fates of others,
only now dare you fight back with your hands.
But a "bang" or an "ouch"
brings you back to silence and sleeplessness again.

See, they come.

Permissions Acknowledgments

A version of the preface previously appeared as "The Poem Behind the Poem: Literary Translation as American Poetry" in *Manoa* 11:2 (1999): 66–75, and in Frank Stewart, ed., *The Poem Behind the Poem: Translating Asian Poetry* (Port Townsend, WA: Copper Canyon Press, 2004). A number of the translations by Tony Barnstone and Chou Ping have previously appeared in the following journals: *The International Quarterly, Nimrod, The Mid-American Review, Chelsea, Blue Unicorn, The Paterson Literary Review, The Kennesaw Review, The Drunken Boat, The Literary Review, The Centennial Review, Paintbrush: A Journal of Poetry and Translation, Shambhala Sun, The Hungry Mind Review, The Threepenny Review, City Lights Review, Quarry West, Occident, Artful Dodge, The Red Rock Review, The Cumberland Poetry Review, Agni, The Tampa Review*, and *The Formalist*. The editors gratefully acknowledge these journals and thank them for permission to reprint the poems.

Grateful acknowledgment is made to the following for permission to reprint previously published material:

Tony Barnstone and Chou Ping: "The Placid Style," "The Potent Style," "The Natural Style," "The Implicit Style," "The Carefree and Wild Style," "The Big-Hearted and Expansive Style," and "The Flowing Style" by Sikong Tu and excerpt from "The Art of Writing" by Lu Ji, from Tony Barnstone and Chou Ping, *The Art of Writing: Teachings of the Chinese Masters* (Boston: Shambhala Publications, Inc., 1996). Reprinted by permission of Tony Barnstone and Chou Ping.

Tony Barnstone and Willis Barnstone: "White Moonrise" from the *Book of Songs*, "To Be a Woman" by Fu Xuan, and "To the Tune of 'Thinking About Nature'" by Ma Zhiyuan, translated by Tony Barnstone and Willis

University Press of New England: "Watching the Hunt," "Walking into the Liang Countryside," "A Young Lady's Spring Thoughts," "For Someone Far Away," "Climbing the City Tower North of the River," "Deep South Mountain," "Living in the Mountain on an Autumn Night," "Drifting on the Lake," "Cooling Off," "Return to Wang River," "Written on a Rainy Autumn Night after Pei Di's Visit," "To Pei Di, While We Are Living Lazily at Wang River," "Birds Sing in the Ravine," "Sketching Things," "Deer Park," "House Hidden in the Bamboo Grove," "Luan Family Rapids," "White Pebble Shoal," "Lakeside Pavilion," "Magnolia Basin," "Things in a Spring Garden," "Answering the Poem Su Left in My Blue Field Mountain Country House, on Visiting and Finding Me Not Home," "About Old Age, in Answer to a Poem by Subprefect Zhang," "To My Cousin Qiu, Military Supply Official," "On Being Demoted and Sent Away to Qizhou," "For Zhang, Exiled in Jingzhou, Once Adviser to the Emperor," "Seeing Off Prefect Ji Mu As He Leaves Office and Goes East of the River," "Winter Night, Writing About My Emotion," "Seeing Zu Off at Qizhou," "A White Turtle Under a Waterfall," "Song of Peach Tree Spring," "Sitting Alone on an Autumn Night," "Green Creek," "Visiting the Mountain Courtyard of the Distinguished Monk Tanxing at Enlightenment Monastery," "Questioning a Dream," "Weeping for Ying Yao," "Suffering from Heat" by Wang Wei, from *Laughing Lost in the Mountains: Poems of Wang Wei*, translations by Tony Barnstone, Willis Barnstone, and Xu Haixin, copyright © 1991 by University Press of New England. Reprinted by permission of University Press of New England.

The Estate of Arthur Waley: "Madly Singing in the Mountains," "After Getting Drunk, Becoming Sober in the Night," "Resignation," "On His Baldness," "Old Age," "Since I Lay Ill," and "A Dream of Mountaineering" by Bai Juyi, translated by Arthur Waley, from *Chinese Poems* (London: Allen & Unwin, 1946), copyright © 1946 by Arthur Waley. Reprinted with the permission of the estate of Arthur Waley c/o The Permissions Company.

Wesleyan University Press: "An Ancient Children's Tale" and "An Elegy for Poetry" by Yang Lian, translated by Tony Barnstone and Newton Liu; "Two or Three Incidents Recollected" by Shu Ting, translated by Chou Ping; "Perhaps" by Shu Ting, translated by Tony Barnstone and Newton

Index of Authors

This index presents the poets' names in Pinyin and Wade-Giles transliteration. Although Pinyin is the commonly used transliteration system today, many sinologists were trained in Wade-Giles, and many English-language readers came to know the poets in Wade-Giles transliteration.

Pinyin Finding List

The poets' names are listed here in Pinyin transliteration, with the Wade-Giles version in parentheses.

Wade-Giles Finding List

The poets' names are listed here in Wade-Giles transliteration, with the Pinyin version in parentheses.

Printed in the United States
by Baker & Taylor Publisher Services